Public Health in International Investment Law and Arbitration

Is a State free to adopt measures to protect the public health of its citizens? If so, what are the limits, if any, to such regulatory powers? This book addresses these questions by focusing on the clash between the regulatory autonomy of the state and international investment governance. As a wide variety of state regulations allegedly aimed at protecting public health may interfere with foreign investments, a tension exists between the public health policies of the host state and investment treaty provisions. Under most investment treaties, States have waived their sovereign immunity, and have agreed to give arbitrators a comprehensive jurisdiction over what are essentially regulatory disputes. Some scholars and practitioners have expressed concern regarding the magnitude of decision-making power allocated to investment treaty tribunals.

This book contributes to the current understanding of international investment law and arbitration, addressing the fundamental question of whether public health has, and/or should have, any relevance in contemporary international investment law and policy. With a focus on the 'clash of cultures' between international investment law and public health, the author critically analyses the emerging case law of investment treaty arbitration and considers the theoretical interplay between public health and investor rights in international investment law. The book also explores the interplay between investment law and public health in practice, focusing on specific sectors such as pharmaceutical patents, tobacco regulation and environmental health. It then goes on to analyze the available means for promoting consideration of public health in international investment law and suggests new methods and approaches to better reconcile public health and investor rights.

Dr. Valentina Vadi is a Marie Curie Postdoctoral Fellow at Maastricht University, the Netherlands. She holds degrees in law from the University of Siena, the European University Institute and the University of Oxford. She has lectured in international investment law in several countries and has published extensively in this area.

Routledge Research in International Economic Law

Public Health in International Investment Law and Arbitration

Valentina Vadi

LONDON AND NEW YORK

First published 2013
by Routledge
2 Park Square, Milton Park, Abingdon, Oxon OX14 4RN

Simultaneously published in the USA and Canada
by Routledge
711 Third Avenue, New York, NY 10017

Routledge is an imprint of the Taylor & Francis Group, an informa business

British Library Cataloguing in Publication Data
A catalogue record for this book is available from the British Library

Library of Congress Cataloging in Publication Data
Vadi, Valentina.
    Public health in international investment law and arbitration /
    Valentina Vadi.
        p. cm.
    Includes bibliographical references.
    ISBN 978-0-415-50749-3 (hardback) —
    ISBN 978-0-203-10674-7 (e-book)   1. Public health laws.
    2. Investments, Foreign (International law)   3. Dispute resolution
    (Law)   4. Arbitration and award.   I. Title.
    K3570.V33 2012
    344.03'21—dc23   2012002517

ISBN 978-0-415-50749-3 (hbk)
ISBN 978-0-203-10674-7 (ebk)

Typeset in Garamond No.3®
by RefineCatch Limited, Bungay, Suffolk

Printed and bound in the United States of America by Edwards Brothers Malloy

Contents

Table of treaties

Table of cases

Investment Arbitration

This Table contains an alphabetical listing of all arbitral awards cited in the text. The awards are cited to a print source, where this was available at the time of this writing. Unreported awards and notices of intent are cited by giving a docket number, where one has been used. The majority of such awards can be accessed electronically on one or more of the following websites: <http://www.worldbank.org/icsid> (the official ICSID website); <http://www.state.gov> (the official site of the Government of the United States); <http://ita.law.uvic.ca> and, in the case of claims under NAFTA, <http://www.naftaclaims.com>.

International

Regional

National

Foreword

This book is the result of an in-depth re-elaboration of a doctoral thesis successfully completed and defended by the author at the European University Institute of Florence in 2009. It is also the ultimate product of a decade-long process of intense elaboration of Valentina Vadi's ideas on the role of international law in accommodating the public and the private interest in the context of the phenomenal expansion of international economic law over the past twenty years. I say this because I had the opportunity of supervising the author's first steps in this field at the time she wrote her law degree thesis at the University of Siena on the interaction between the law of TRIPS/WTO and access to essential medicines. The thesis was approved with honours and helped the author win a fellowship to attend the Master of Law programme at the University of Oxford, where she was able to further explore the interplay between trade liberalisation and the protection of public health in her M. Juris thesis. After that experience Valentina Vadi joined the European University Institute as a PhD candidate with a solid academic background and with a growing record of academic publications that paved the way to the successful completion of her doctoral thesis.

With this book Valentina Vadi moves away from trade law and places the issue of public health within the field of international investment law and arbitration. One could hardly think of a more timely choice. International investment law and arbitration have undergone an impressive development in the past ten years, with thousands of bilateral investment agreements in force, regional agreements such as NAFTA, CAFTA, ASEAN covering the promotion and protection of foreign investments, and with the European Union entering the field of foreign investments by way of expansion of its commercial policy competence after the entry into force of the Lisbon Treaty. An important aspect of this development has been the opening of international dispute settlement to private investors who can now directly access investment arbitration without the need to resort to the traditional method of diplomatic protection and interstate dispute settlement. The hundreds of cases adjudicated by investment arbitration, under ICSID (International Centre for the Settlement of Investment Disputes), Chapter 11 of NAFTA, (North American Free Trade Agreement), and UNCITRAL, bear witness to the vitality of this branch of international law and its importance for economic development world-wide. At the same time the rapid growth of the law and practice of foreign investment has raised the question of how to harmonise the enhanced protection of the private rights of the investor with the pursuit of the public interest by the host state. Strains have emerged in recent practice, particularly with regard to attempt by investors to use arbitration as a form of judicial review of regulatory measures enacted by the host state in order to advance public goods such as health, environmental quality and social justice.

This book brings an innovative approach to the role played by international law in accommodating norms on the protection of foreign investments with the law safeguarding public health. It rejects the idea that the law governing foreign investments, largely developed through a web of treaties, constitute a self-concluded system impervious to the influence of other norms of international law, including norms protecting the value of public health. The author recognizes that the present system of investment protection by bilateral or regional treaties falls short of striking an ideal balance between the protection of the economic interests of the investor and the safeguarding of the public interests of the host state. However, with regard to public health, she concludes that even in the absence of specific legal tools to protect this important human and social value through investment arbitration, international law provides suitable methods and techniques to bring considerations of public health in the interpretation and implementation of international investment law. This conclusion is reached through a painstaking investigation of the practice in three different areas: that of regulation of pharmaceutical patents and its relation with access to medicines essential to the safeguarding of public health; that of tobacco regulation and its possible impact on the rights of investors; and that of environmental health as a possible justification for the host state interference with the economic interests of the investor.

Far from casting doubts on the importance and legitimacy of investment arbitration as a driver of socio-economic development, this book contributes to the 'greening' of international investment law and to its conceptualisation as an important branch of public international law capable of integrating the legitimate aim of safeguarding public health within the system of international protection of investors' rights.

Francesco Francioni
Chair of International Law and Human Rights
and Co-Director, Academy of European Law
European University Institute
February 2012

Preface

This book is the outcome of an intense intellectual and personal journey. Having been fascinated by the clash of paradigms between overlapping legal regimes, I started a PhD programme on this theme at the European University Institute in 2005. The completed doctoral thesis constituted a first rough draft of this book. It was only in the past two years, however, that I was able to finalize the manuscript for the book. Upon completion and defence of my PhD in 2009, I was appointed Lecturer in international law at Maastricht University in the Netherlands. The lectureship at Maastricht University, which involved lecturing in international law and international economic law at both graduate and postgraduate levels, gave me the possibility to rethink all my previous research conducted during the pursuit of my PhD, and provided me with the opportunity to rewrite and finalize such research, in the light of the most recent developments. New developments in state practice and in the arbitral jurisprudence have made this topic timelier than ever. I have endeavoured to state the law accurately as of 1 January 2012. May the reader forgive the possible imperfections of the book and enjoy the outcome of the journey.

V.V.
Maastricht, the Netherlands, 15 January 2012

Acknowledgements

In writing this book, I have benefited greatly from the guidance and inspiration of many people. First, I would like to thank Professor Francesco Francioni, for his generous and inspiring guidance throughout the years. His courses on international public law at the University of Siena and at the European University Institute have inspired generations of students who have had the opportunity to benefit from his knowledge. Second, I would also like to thank Professor Pierre-Marie Dupuy. His seminar on the law of foreign investments inspired me to move the focus of my research from international trade law to international investment law. At Oxford, Professor Vaughan Lowe's seminar on international dispute settlement was enlightening. Third, I wish to thank Professor Ernst-Ulrich Petersmann for his encouragement and support. The distinguished and outstanding work of this scholar has provided me with much food for thought. I can only hope that I have made the best of the discussions which I have had with such brilliant minds.

Parts of this book were also presented at conferences and seminars held in Cambridge, Catania, Florence, Geneva, Keele, London, Montreal, and Rome. I greatly benefited from the comments received on these occasions. In particular, I would like to thank Bruno De Witte, Antonietta Di Blase, Judy Carter, Andrea Giardina, Owen McIntyre, Federico Lenzerini, Bronwen Morgan, Peter Muchlinski, Amanda Perry Kessaris, Sol Picciotto, Giuliano Scarselli, Dalindyebo Shabalala, Michael Spence, Peter Van den Bossche, Gus Van Harten, and Laura Westra. I particularly thank Ana Filipa Vrdoljak for her inspiring work, encouragement and support. Finally, I thank Katherine Carpenter and Stephen Gutierrez of Routledge for helping steer this book through the publication process.

On a personal note, I would like to thank all my friends who have supported me during these six years: a list to include them all would be too long. A special thanks goes to Gianluca for his love and support. My greatest debt is to my family and above all my grandparents, Lora and Giovanni (Nino), and parents, Lidiana and Carlo, who have encouraged and supported me in every possible way.

V.V.
Maastricht, the Netherlands, 15 January 2012

List of abbreviations

AJCL	American Journal of Comparative Law
AJIL	American Journal of International Law
ASEAN	Association of Southeast Asian Nations
AUSFTA	Australia–United States Free Trade Agreement
BIICL	British Institute of International and Comparative Law
BIT	Bilateral Investment Treaty
BMJ	British Medical Journal
Bull. WHO	Bulletin of the World Health Organization
BYIL	British Yearbook of International Law
CAFTA	Central American Free Trade Agreement
CARIFORUM	Caribbean Forum
CHR	United Nations Commission on Human Rights
CMLR	Common Market Law Review
DSB	Dispute Settlement Body
DSU	Dispute Settlement Understanding
EC	European Communities
ECHR	European Convention of Human Rights
ECommHR	European Commission of Human Rights
ECtHR	European Court of Human Rights
ECJ	European Court of Justice
EFTA	European Free Trade Association
EHRR	European Human Rights Reports
EIA	Environmental Impact Assessment
EJIL	European Journal of International Law
EJLS	European Journal of Legal Studies
FCN	Friendship, Commerce and Navigation
FCTC	Framework Convention on Tobacco Control
FDI	Foreign Direct Investment
FET	Fair and Equitable Treatment
FTA	Free Trade Agreement
GA	General Assembly
GAL	Global Administrative Law

GAOR	Official Records of the General Assembly
GATS	General Agreement on Trade in Services
GATT	General Agreement on Tariffs and Trade
GYIL	German Yearbook of International Law
Harvard ILJ	Harvard International Law Journal
Harvard LR	Harvard Law Review
IAR	Investment Arbitration Reporter
IBRD	International Bank for Reconstruction and Development
ICC	International Chamber of Commerce
ICCPR	International Covenant on Civil and Political Rights
ICESCR	International Covenant on Economic, Social and Cultural Rights
ICJ	International Court of Justice
ICLQ	International and Comparative Law Quarterly
ICSID	International Centre for Settlement of Investment Disputes
ICSID Convention	Convention on the Settlement of Investment Disputes between States and Nationals of Other States
ICSID Review-FILJ	ICSID Review Foreign Investment Law Journal
IIA	International Investment Agreement
IISD	International Institute for Sustainable Development
ILC	International Law Commission
ILJ	International Law Journal
ILM	International Law Material
ILR	International Law Review
IMF	International Monetary Fund
IP	Intellectual property
ITN	Investment Treaty News
ITO	International Trade Organization
IYIL	Italian Yearbook of International Law
JIEL	Journal of International Economic Law
JIL	Journal of International Law
JWIP	Journal of World Intellectual Property
JWIT	Journal of World Investment and Trade
JWT	Journal of World Trade
KB	King's Bench Law Reports
LDC	least developed country
MAI	Multilateral Agreement on Investment
MDG	Millennium Development Goals
MEAs	Multilateral Environmental Agreements
MIT	Massachusetts Institute of Technology
MFN	Most-Favoured-Nation
MSA	Master Settlement Agreement

NAAEC	North American Agreement on Environmental Cooperation
NAFTA	North American Free Trade Agreement
NGO	Non-Governmental Organization
NT	National Treatment
NYU	New York University
OECD	Organization for Economic Cooperation and Development
PCA	Permanent Court of Arbitration
PCIJ	Permanent Court of International Justice
PMA	Pharmaceutical Manufacturers Association
Rec des Cours	Recueil des Cours de l'Académie de Droit International
Rev	Review
RIAA	Reports of International Arbitral Awards
SCC	Stockholm Chamber of Commerce
TDM	Transnational Dispute Management
TRIMS	Trade Related Investment Measures
TRIPS	Trade Related Intellectual Property Rights
UC Davis L Rev	University of California Davis Law Review
UDHR	Universal Declaration of Human Rights
UK	United Kingdom
UN	United Nations
UNCITRAL	United Nations Commission on International Trade Law
UNCTAD	United Nations Conference on Trade and Development
UNESCO	United Nations Educational, Scientific and Cultural Organization
UNTS	United Nations Treaty Series
US	United States
VCLT	Vienna Convention on the Law of Treaties
WHO	World Health Organization
WIPO	World Intellectual Property Organization
WIR	World Investment Report
WTO	World Trade Organization
YIEL	Yearbook of International Environmental Law
YIL	Yearbook of International Law

Introduction

Salus populi suprema est lex

Cicero, *De Legibus*, III, 3, 8

This book addresses the fundamental question as to whether public health has, and/or should have, any relevance in contemporary international investment law and policy. While public health is a core element of state sovereignty, economic globalization has posed tremendous challenges to public health policy.[1] The increase in global trade and foreign direct investment (FDI) has determined the creation of legally binding and highly effective regimes that demand states to promote and facilitate trade and FDI. An *international economic culture* has emerged that emphasizes productivity and development at the expense of the common weal.[2] When countries pursue economic growth, their policy makers may have an incentive to lower health standards to promote FDI. By the same token, foreign investors may be attracted by lower standards in existing regulations to externalize the health-related costs which are associated to their business. More importantly, economic globalization has also entailed a restriction of state sovereignty to regulate public matters.

As a wide variety of state regulations allegedly aimed to protect public health may interfere with foreign investments, a tension exists between the public health policies of the host state and investment treaty provisions. The law of foreign investment is one of the most complex areas of international law and has now gained pre-eminence in international law. Although public health concerns are rarely mentioned in bilateral investment treaties (BITs), a number of recent arbitrations have shown the increased interaction between economic integration and public health.

An example may well illustrate the issues at stake. After Uruguay adopted anti-smoking legislation requiring *inter alia* that 80 per cent of every cigarette

---

1 See L.O. Gostin and A.L. Taylor, 'Global Health Law: A Definition and Grand Challenges', *Public Health Ethics* 1, 2008, 53–63.
2 R.D. Lamm, 'The Culture of Growth and the Culture of Limits', *The Social Contract TSC Journal* 9, 1999.

package show graphic images of the consequences of smoking,[3] a few tobacco manufacturers initiated proceedings against Uruguay[4] before an ICSID tribunal. While the claimants 'do not challenge the Uruguayan Government's sovereign right to promote and protect public health', they claim that the government 'cannot abuse the right and invoke it as a pretext for disregarding the Claimant's legal rights' under the Switzerland–Uruguay BIT and international law.[5] The claimants state that the images that illustrate the adverse health effects of smoking 'undermine and indeed destroy the good will associated with . . . trademarks and not to promote . . . health policies.'[6] Should the rights of investors prevail over public health?

A number of questions arise in this context. *First*, is it legitimate for the state to adopt interventionist approaches to public health issues? What are the limits, if any, to state intervention in public health matters? *Second*, if the state intervenes to protect public health, how do we set the boundaries between legitimate regulation (that cannot be compensated) and (that can be compensated) violation of the investment treaty provisions? To what extent may investment treaty obligations collide with states' obligations to protect public health? *Third*, how have arbitrators dealt with these crucial policy issues? *Fourth*, while foreign investors have been recognized as 'international corporate citizens' and have been afforded direct access to investment treaty arbitration,[7] the procedural rights of the investment-affected communities have remained almost unchanged.[8] Is investor-state arbitration a suitable forum to protect public interests?

This book aims to provide a fresh approach to these questions, offering an in-depth analysis of the almost unexplored linkage between international investment law and public health. To date, there is no comprehensive study to cover the interplay between public health and FDI in international

---

3 Presidential Decree 287/009 dated 15 June 2009.
4 *FTR Holding S.A. (Switzerland), Philip Morris Products S.A. (Switzerland) and Abal Hermanos S.A. (Uruguay) v. Oriental Republic of Uruguay* (ICSID Case No. ARB/10/7). On 26 March 2010, the Secretary-General of the ICSID registered a request for the institution of arbitration proceedings filed by FTR Holding S.A., Philip Morris Products S.A. and Abal Hermanos S.A. against Uruguay under the ICSID Convention and 1988 Switzerland-Uruguay BIT.
5 *Philip Morris Products v. Uruguay*, Request for Arbitration, 19 February 2010, ¶ 7, available at http://ita.law.uvic.ca/documents/PMI-UruguayNoA.pdf .
6 Ibidem, ¶ 4.
7 The foreign investor has evolved from an object of international law to a confident participant in the legal process. See R. Higgins, 'Conceptual Thinking About the Individual in International Law', *New York Law School L. Rev.*, 24, 1978–1979, 11. Muchlinski defines multinational corporations as 'international corporate citizens'. See P. Muchlinski, 'Global Bukovina Examined: Viewing the Multinational Enterprise as a Transnational Law Making Community', in G. Teubner (ed.), *Global Law Without a State*, Dartmouth: Aldershot, 1997, p. 79.
8 See N. Gal-Or, 'The Investor and Civil Society as Twin Global Citizens: Proposing a New Interpretation in the Legitimacy Debate', *Suffolk Transnational Law Review* 32, 2008–2009, 284.

law.[9] Given the broad policy implications that foreign investments have in host countries and the recent boom of investment arbitrations including elements of public health, scrutiny is needed. The purpose of this study is to fill this gap in academic literature, bringing new ground of inquiry to the fore, to the benefit of academic debate and policy makers.

At the same time the book presents some lines of continuity with the available literature that can be placed in five broad categories: 1) literature on international investment law;[10] 2) literature on international investment law and other values;[11] 3) literature on multinational corporations and the law;[12] 4) literature on the interplay between international trade and public health policies;[13] and 5) public health scholarship.[14]

The book complements the existing literature in several ways. *First*, if investment law scholars have analyzed some of the relevant cases, they have approached them from a mere investment law standpoint, leaving aside public health arguments or merely citing them in passing. In sum, light has been shed on more conventional economic law topics, such as the definition of regulatory expropriation, and so on and so forth. This book adopts a multidisciplinary approach in that it also looks at the existing public health literature and the international law instruments governing public health.

---

9 For almost a decade, the unique existing contribution which explored the linkage between international investment law and public health has been a seminal article written by Samrat Ganguly. See S. Ganguly, 'The Investor-State Dispute Mechanism (ISDM) and a Sovereign's Power to Protect Public Health', *Columbia Journal of Transnational Law* 38, 1999–2000, p. 113.

10 The existing literature is too vast to be mentioned here; suffice it to say that international investment law has become a topical issue and the literature on this matter is booming. See e.g. C. Binder, U. Kriebaum, A. Reinisch and S. Wittich (eds), *International Investment Law for the 21st Century*, Oxford: Oxford University Press, 2009.

11 See e.g. P.-M. Dupuy, F. Francioni and E.-U. Petersmann (eds), *Human Rights in International Investment Law and Arbitration*, Oxford: Oxford University Press, 2009; S. Subedi, *International Investment Law: Reconciling Policy and Principle*, Oxford: Hart Publishing, 2008.

12 See e.g. P. Muchlinski, *Multinational Enterprises and the Law*, 2nd edn., Oxford: Oxford University Press, 2007, at pp. 507–37.

13 See e.g. B. McGrady, *Trade and Public Health: The WTO, Tobacco, Alcohol and Diet*, Cambridge: Cambridge University Press, 2012; L. Gruszczynski, *Regulating Health and Environmental Risk Under WTO Law – A Critical Analysis of the SPS Agreement*, Oxford: Oxford University Press, 2010; J. Scott, *The WTO Agreement on Sanitary and Phytosanitary Measures – A Commentary*, Oxford: Oxford University Press, 2007; World Health Organization and World Trade Organization Secretariat, *WTO Agreements and Public Health*, Geneva: WHO, 2002; M. Prabhu and K. Garforth, 'International Public Health and Trade Law', in M. Gehring and M.-C. Cordonnier Segger (eds), *Sustainable Development in World Trade Law*, The Hague: Kluwer Law International, 2005, pp. 549–73; M.G. Bloche, 'Introduction: Health and the WTO', *JIEL* 5, 2002, pp. 821–3; S. Charnovitz, 'Environment and Health Under WTO Dispute Settlement', *International Lawyer* 32, 1998, p. 901; D. Fidler, 'Trade and Health: The Global Spread of Diseases and International Trade', *GYIL* 40, 1997, pp. 309–54.

14 See, for instance, L.O. Gostin, *Public Health Law: Power, Duty, Restraint*, 2nd edn., Berkeley: University of California Press, 2008.

Second, with regard to the existing literature on international investment law and other values, the book deepens the discussion by focusing on the linkage between international investment law and public health. While some research has touched upon environmental protection and international investment law,[15] public health is a more inclusive concept which includes more than the protection of environmental goods.

Third, while there is a growing amount of literature on the impact that multinational corporations have on human rights, the interplay between public health and investor rights has never been studied from a perspective internal to international investment law and arbitration. *Fourth*, in a systemic perspective, this study complements the literature on 'trade and health' by offering an updated and systematic analysis of the parallel linkage between 'investment & health'.

Fifth, the book complements the existing books and information resources on public health governance in a two-fold manner. On the one hand, it complements the existing literature on the role of science in international law. While authors have explored the role of science in international law rule-making and adjudication,[16] its role in investment treaty law and arbitration has been almost neglected despite the salience of the latter field.[17] On the other, the book contributes to mapping the interplay between intellectual property regulation, public health and international investment law by offering an extensive overview and critical assessment of the investor-state arbitrations that have involved intellectual property rights and public health elements. While much of the existing academic debate has focused on public health, intellectual property and free trade,[18] the book examines the parallel connection among public health, intellectual property and FDI which is gaining prominence in current analysis due to the recent emergence of relevant investment arbitrations. Some authors have explored the interplay between intellectual property, public health and international investment law in earlier contributions; however, this has been done in a piecemeal fashion.[19] Finally, the comprehensive analysis offered by the book may be of help to both practitioners and scholars alike, who are interested in the legitimacy of

---

15 See e.g. K. Tienhaara, *The Expropriation of Environmental Governance*, Cambridge: Cambridge University Press, 2009.

16 See, for instance, J. Peel, *Science and Risk Regulation in International Law*, Cambridge: Cambridge University Press, 2010; C. Forster, *Science and the Precautionary Principle in International Courts and Tribunals*, Cambridge: Cambridge University Press, 2011.

17 For a pioneering contribution, see M. Orellana, 'Science, Risk and Uncertainty: Public Health Measures and Investment Disciplines', in P. Kahn and T. Wälde (eds), *New Aspects of International Investment Law*, Leiden/Boston: Martinus Nijhoff and Hague Academy of International Law, 2007, pp. 671–789, at p. 675.

18 See, e.g., H. Yamane, *Interpreting TRIPS: Globalization of Intellectual Property Rights and Access to Medicines*, Oxford: Hart Publishing, 2011.

19 See, e.g., V. Vadi, 'Trademark Protection, Public Health and International Investment Law: Strains and Paradoxes', *EJIL* 2009, pp. 773–803.

international investment law and arbitration and debate on the need of a
'globalization with a human face'.[20]

Chapter plan

The book proceeds as follows. The first part of the study explores the theoretical
interplay between public health and investor rights in international investment
law. The first chapter briefly explores the rationale behind the protection
of foreign investment and the elements of investment rules that will be of
particular importance when considering their impact on the protection of
public health. After defining foreign direct investment, the main characteristics
of investment treaties will be scrutinized, with particular focus on the
provisions on expropriation and investment treaty arbitration. The second
chapter will analyse the conceptual and theoretical framework under which
public health is protected at the international law level. The third chapter will
then scrutinize the 'conflict areas' between investment treaty provisions and
public health regulation.

The second part of this study explores the interplay between investment law
and public health in practice, focusing on specific sectors such as pharmaceutical
patents, tobacco regulation and environmental health. In particular, the fourth
chapter will scrutinize pharmaceutical patent regulation in investment treaties
in relation to access to medicines. The fifth chapter will address some important
issues related to tobacco regulation in investment treaties. The sixth chapter
will examine the interplay between environmental health and international
investment law. A rich collection of arbitrations provides evidence that the
regime established according to investment treaties does not strike an appropriate balance between the different interests concerned, and that
international investment law has not yet developed any machinery for the
protection of public health through investment dispute settlement.

The third part of this study analyzes the available means for promoting
consideration of public health in international investment law and suggests
methods and approaches. The seventh chapter suggests the use of available
mechanisms to better reconcile public health and investor rights. *De lege lata*,
investment treaties should not be considered as self-contained regimes, but as
an important component part of public international law. The conclusions will
then sum up the key findings of the study.

Methodological framework

Because of the interdisciplinary character of the book, methods and insights
of different disciplines and traditional fields of study are taken into account.

---

20 See J. Stiglitz, *Globalization and Its Discontents*, New York: WW Norton & Co., 2002; but
see J. Bhagwati, *In Defense of Globalization*, Oxford: Oxford University Press, 2004.

In particular, reference will be made to public health studies elaborated under the aegis of the World Health Organization (WHO), and public health literature. The analysis has mainly a legal character and rests on sound theoretical and empirical methodological grounds. The project rests on a firm theoretical standpoint, elaborated by Hart.[21] The author adopts a 'moderate external point of view'[22] that combines 'explanation' (which implies the distance of the scientist, commitment to objectivity and focus on causality) with 'comprehension' (understanding the inner logic of the object of study) and provides the rational structure on which the scientific nature of her approach is based. Although neither radical nor particularly new, this approach has produced authoritative and stimulating results, as it does not follow a mere positivist stance but considers the legal norms as the results of balance of interests. This is very appropriate to the study of international law which is the outcome of intense political processes and negotiations.

While the interrelationship between public health and investor rights may be studied from a variety of different perspectives and institutional settings, this book adopts an 'internal' approach with respect to international investment law and arbitration. The choice of this approach is not meant to imply that the institutional setting of international investment law is to be preferred to other approaches to reconcile the interests at stake.[23] Instead, looking at the linkage between public health and FDI from an inside view of international investment law allows a reflection on the emerging case law of investment treaty arbitration. Although investment treaty arbitration may not constitute the most ideal forum in which disputes with public health elements can be settled, a rich case law has emerged in recent years. Therefore, an analysis and critical assessment of this emerging field of study is necessary.

The experimental aspect of the work is based on the adoption of a double track. On the one hand, the study will focus on the impact of investors' rights on the three different but related categories of public health law: 1) access to essential medicines; 2) tobacco control; and 3) environmental health. Specific chapters of the book will be dedicated to the analysis of the interplay between international investment law and each of these aspects of public health policies. The way in which the work is organized facilitates the reader who can immediately spot the thematic area of interest. On the other hand, within each of these tracks, the analysis will proceed adopting investment law categories; and the relevant case studies will be analyzed according to the traditional elements of investment law. This will permit a rigorous discussion of the case law with regard to each specific theme; more general analysis and critical

21 H.L.A. Hart, *The Concept of Law*, Oxford: Clarendon Press, 1961.
22 Ibidem, pp. 86–8. See also F. Ost and M. Van de Kerchove, *De la pyramide au réseau, Pour une théorie dialectique du droit*, Bruxelles: Publication des facultés universitaires St-Louis, 2002, p. 458.
23 On the contrary, it is acknowledged that other fora, like the International Court of Justice and regional human rights courts, represent useful alternatives.

assessment follows in the seventh chapter. By adopting a double track, the methodological differences between the legal systems regulating foreign investments and public health are acknowledged. In order to make the analysis relevant to public health law and investment law, the language will deliberately be kept technical, but efforts will be undertaken to avoid assumptions and to achieve clarity and cohesion. As a result, this study will be of relevance for a wide audience, including but not limited to: international scholars, investment law arbitrators and practitioners, and state officials, as well as public health experts and other interested audiences.

Part I

Foreign direct investments and public health

Defining and connecting the two fields

Introductory note

Traditionally, international investment law and international public health law have been considered two separate branches of public international law. However, these two disciplines have increasingly intersected, and this is confirmed by an emerging jurisprudence. This book scrutinizes the interplay between public health and investor rights in international investment law and arbitration, coping with an existing lacuna in contemporary legal studies.

In a preliminary fashion, since foreign direct investment is deemed to promote economic development, which is of fundamental importance to the achievement of the fullest attainable standard of health, it is clear that in abstract terms the linkage between foreign direct investment and public health may endorse positive outcomes. However, this is not always the case. When countries pursue economic growth, their policy makers may have an incentive to lower health standards to attract foreign investors. In this manner, foreign companies can externalize the health-related costs which are associated to their business and achieve more profits. This regulatory *race to the bottom*, however, has a negative impact on policy goals such as public health and environmental protection.[1] In addition, the mere possibility of a dispute with a powerful investor can exert a chilling effect on governments' decisions to regulate in the public interest.[2]

Part I of this book provides the legal framework and proceeds as follows. The first chapter defines foreign direct investment and briefly explores the main features of contemporary international investment law and policy.

---

1 N. Rudra, *Globalization and the Race to the Bottom – Who Really Gets Hurt?* Cambridge: Cambridge University Press, 2008. *Contra*, see J. Bhagwati, *In Defense of Globalization*, Oxford: Oxford University Press, 2004, pp. 122–95.

2 For instance, commentators have reported that in 2002 a group of mainly foreign-owned mining companies threatened to commence international arbitration against the government of Indonesia in response to its ban on open-pit mining in protected forests. Six months later, the Ministry of Forestry agreed to change the forest designation from *protected* to *production* forests. *See* S. Gross, 'Inordinate Chill: BITs, Non-NAFTA MITs and Host-State Regulatory Freedom – An Indonesian Case Study', *Michigan JIL* 24, 2002–2003, p. 894.

References to international and regional human rights law, international trade law and intellectual property law will often be made by way of analogy. The elements of investment rules that may affect the protection and promotion of public health are set out. The second chapter explores the legal sources which discipline public health in international law. The third chapter concludes the first part of the book exploring the interaction between public health and international investment law at the theoretical level. Particular reference will be made to the contemporary conceptualization of investment law as a species of global administrative law. Also, the third chapter paves the way to the second part of the book which investigates the interaction between public health and international investment law in practice.

1   International investment law

Introduction

The law of foreign investment is one of the most complex areas of international law.[1] Traditionally, international investment law has constituted an important part of public international law mainly referring to the concepts of state responsibility and diplomatic protection and being articulated in amity, commerce and navigation treaties. As there is still no single comprehensive global treaty, investor rights are mainly defined by a plethora of bilateral investment treaties (BITs)[2] and investment rules included in Free Trade Agreements (FTAs).[3]

After defining foreign direct investment and exploring the normative framework which disciplines it, this chapter sets out the elements of investment rules that will be of particular importance when considering their impact on the protection and promotion of public health.

Foreign direct investment: definition and function

Foreign Direct Investment (hereinafter FDI) can be defined as 'the transfer of tangible or intangible assets from one country into another for the purpose of

1 For a historical overview, see A. Lowenfeld, *International Economic Law*, Oxford: Oxford University Press, 2002, pp. 391–415; M. Sornarajah, *The International Law on Foreign Investment*, 2nd edn., Cambridge: Cambridge University Press, 2004, pp. 18–30; N. Rubins and S. Kinsella, *International Investment, Political Risk and Dispute Resolution*, Oxford: Oxford University Press, 2005, pp. 153–74.
2 On the recent flourishing of bilateral and regional investment treaties, see for instance, J. Salacuse, 'The Treatification of International Investment Law', in J. Norton and P. Rogers (eds), *Law, Culture, and Economic Development – Liber Amicorum for Professor Roberto McLean*, London: BIICL, 2007, pp. 241–52; S.M. Schwebel, 'The Reshaping of the International Law of Foreign Investment by Concordant Bilateral Investment Treaties', in S. Charnovitz, D.P. Steger and P. van den Bossche (eds), *Law in the Service of Human Dignity – Essays in Honour of Florentino Feliciano*, Cambridge: Cambridge University Press, 2005, pp. 241–5; J. Salacuse and N. Sullivan, 'Do BITs Really Work? An Evaluation of Bilateral Investment Treaties and Their Grand Bargain', *Harvard ILJ* 46, 2005, pp. 67–115.
3 Investment chapters of free trade agreements often have very similar or even identical contents with those of BITs. See C. Lo, 'A Comparison of BIT and the Investment Chapter of Free Trade Agreements from Policy Perspective', *Asian Journal of WTO & Int' Health Law* 3, 2008, p. 165.

12   *Public health in international investment law and arbitration*

their use in that country to generate wealth under the total or partial control of the owner of the assets'.[4] The majority of economists and policy-makers in both developing and developed countries see FDI as an engine for promoting economic growth and development.[5]

As contained in investment treaties, investment is an all-encompassing concept, including almost any kind of business activity. All assets of an enterprise, such as movable and immovable property, contractual rights, intellectual property rights, concessions, licenses, and similar rights are included. Given the broad scope of the concept, some investment provisions include both a general clause and an illustrative list of covered investments, as well as a negative list of areas specifically excluded from the scope of the agreements.[6] For instance, in the US draft Model BIT,[7] in relation to the notion of what constitutes an investment, an interpretative note indicates that in order to qualify as an investment, certain characteristics must be present, such as the commitment of capital or other resources, the expectation of gain or other profit or the assumption of risk. These characteristics would exclude from the definition trade operations and financial transactions as such. However, the case law presents a trend to consider some of these features as sufficient to indicate an investment.[8]

As investment treaties are 'the most important instruments for the protection of foreign direct investment',[9] there is a general expectation that the conclusion of such treaties will encourage FDI.[10] Therefore, investment treaties are being strategically pushed by both developed and

---

4 Sornarajah, *The International Law on Foreign Investment*, p. 7.
5 J. Bhagwati, 'Why Multinationals Help Reduce Poverty', *World Economy* 30, 2007, pp. 211–28; V.N. Balasubramanyam, M. Salisu and D. Sapsford, 'Foreign Direct Investment and Growth: New Hypotheses and Evidence', *J Int'l Trade and Economic Development* 8, 1999, pp. 27–40. See also UNCTAD, *WIR 1999 – Foreign Direct Investment and the Challenge of Development*, Geneva: 1999, and UNCTAD, *WIR 2003 – FDI Policies for Development: National and International Perspectives*, Geneva: UN, 2003.
6 See e.g. NAFTA, Article 1101.2.
7 In February 2004 the US State Department released a draft text of its BIT template (the US draft Model BIT). The text is available at http://www.state/gove/documents/organizations/29030.doc .
8 See, for instance, *S.D. Myers v. Government of Canada*, Partial Award, 13 November 2000, ¶ 232.
9 UNCTAD, *Bilateral Investment Treaties: 1959–1999*, Geneva: UNCTAD, 2000, p. 1.
10 Earlier work did not provide support for such a positive impact. See M. Hallward-Driemeier, 'Do Bilateral Investment Treaties Attract Foreign Direct Investment? Only a Bit . . . And They Could Bite', Policy Research Working Paper No 3121, Washington: World Bank, 2003. However, recent research suggests that the empirically identified impact is positive. See A. Bénassy-Quéré, M. Coupet and T. Mayer, 'Institutional Determinants of Foreign Direct Investment', *World Economy* 30, 2007, pp. 764–82; P. Egger and V. Merlo, 'The Impact of Bilateral Investment Treaties on FDI Dynamics', *World Economy* 30, 2007, pp. 1536–49; J. Tobin and S. Rose-Ackerman, 'Foreign Direct Investment and the Business Environment in Developing Countries: The Impact of Bilateral Investment Treaties', Yale Law and Economics Research Paper No. 293 (2005).

developing countries albeit for different reasons. On the one hand, host countries – generally developing and least developed countries – assume broad obligations for the protection of foreign investors in order to attract foreign investments. On the other hand, developed countries have adhered to these dealings to protect their nationals' economic interests and possibly obtain favourable standards.

Recently, however, the traditional distinction between capital importers and capital exporters has become blurred as emerging economies – like India and China – have become capital exporters. In this sense, it is interesting to highlight that investment treaties have increasingly been signed not only among industrialized countries on the one side and developing countries on the other side, but also among less developed countries (LDCs) and emerging economies. As the primary objective of would-be investors is to obtain the effective guarantee that the host state will not act opportunistically once the investment has been made, investment treaties seem to be appropriate solutions to this problem. Therefore, such treaties have come to play a major role in the growing competition to attract FDI and to provide conditions regarded necessary to make countries attractive for foreign investment.

Multilateral failures and bilateral successes

Efforts to constitute a set of global rules to protect investor rights and to settle potential disputes between host countries and investors have been pursued by industrialized countries for a long time.[11] A first attempt to create a unified global investment law was made at the Bretton Woods conference in 1944. The conference, which stemmed from the consensus among the major international actors on the importance of establishing international economic institutions to foster peace and economic growth, determined the inception of the charters of the International Monetary Fund (IMF)[12] and the International Bank for Reconstruction and Development (IBRD).[13] Although the participants at the conference contemplated the necessity of an International Trade Organization (ITO), the Havana Charter which included rules on investment never came into force.[14]

Although the World Trade Organization in some ways has become 'the missing leg' of the Bretton Woods 'stool',[15] the moves to adopt multilateral

---

11 See e.g. R. Dattu, 'A Journey From Havana to Paris: The Fifty Year Quest for the Elusive Multilateral Agreement on Investment', *Fordham ILJ* 24, 2000–2001, pp. 275–316.
12 Articles of Agreement of the International Monetary Fund, adopted on 22 July 1944 and entered into force 27 December 1945, 2 UNTS 40.
13 Articles of Agreement of the International Bank for Reconstruction and Development as amended in 1965, 606 UNTS 294.
14 Havana Charter for an International Trade Organization, Final Act of the United Nations Conference on Trade and Employment, held at Havana, Cuba from 21 November 1947 to 24 March 1948, UN Document E/Conf. 2/78.
15 See J. Jackson, *The World Trading System*, Cambridge, MA: MIT Press, 2002, p. 32.

investment rules initiated at the Doha Ministerial Conference in 2001 had to be abandoned at the Ministerial Conference in Cancun in 2003, due to the growing opposition from developing countries and strong criticism from the NGO community.[16] Similarly, the Organization for Economic Cooperation and Development (hereinafter OECD)[17] attempted to establish a Multilateral Agreement on Investment (MAI),[18] but this effort collapsed because of the opposition from civil society.[19]

However, authors have submitted that there are global rules on foreign investment.[20] On the one hand, many instruments under the World Trade Organization aegis directly deal with areas of foreign investment.[21] On the other hand, the provisions of the Havana Charter, although never ratified, served as an inspiration to many national and regional investment provisions.[22] Notwithstanding the persistent failures at the multilateral level, successful negotiations on investment protection have been undertaken at the bilateral and regional levels. In recent years, there has been steady growth of BITs for

16 Despite significant efforts by developed countries to push forward the development of a new investment treaty, there is a strong resistance by developing countries to initiate negotiations on this subject. See J. Kurtz, 'A General Investment Agreement in the WTO? Lessons from Chapter 11 of NAFTA and the OECD Multilateral Agreement on Investment', *University of Pennsylvania JIEL* 23, 2003, pp. 713–89. See also P. Sauvé, 'Multilateral Rules on Investment: Is Forward Movement Possible? *JIEL* 9, 2006, pp. 325–55 and P. Mavroidis, 'All Clear on the Investment Front: A Plea for a Restatement', in J. Alvarez and K.P. Sauvant (eds), *The Evolving International Investment Regime – Expectations, Realities and Options*, Oxford: Oxford University Press, 2011).

17 The Organization for Economic Cooperation and Development is a forum of thirty industrialized countries aimed at 'help[ing] governments achieve sustainable economic growth and employment and raising standards of living in member countries so as to contribute to the development of the world economy.' See *The OECD*, Paris: OECD, 2008, p. 5.

18 OECD Multilateral Agreement on Investment, Consolidated Text and Commentary, Draft DAFFE/MAI/NM(97)2.

19 The shortcomings of the MAI were evident. It was a one-sided instrument, unilaterally prepared by OECD Countries to ensure higher standards of protection and legal security for foreign investors. It did not adequately take into account the developmental needs of the host states, omitting crucial environmental and social issues. See S. Picciotto, 'Linkages in International Investment Regulation: The Antinomies of the Draft Multilateral Agreement on Investment', *University of Pennsylvania JIEL* 19, 1998, pp. 731–68.

20 S.W. Schill, *The Multilateralization of International Investment Law*, Cambridge: Cambridge University Press, 2009; R. Leal Arcas, 'Towards the Multilateralization of International Investment Law', *JWIT* 10, 2009, pp. 865–919.

21 While the Agreement on Trade Related Aspects of Intellectual Property Rights (TRIPS Agreement) covers intellectual property, which is deemed to be a form of investment, the General Agreement on Trade in Services (GATS) deals with the service sector and covers the provision of services through a commercial presence in another country. Also, the Agreement on Trade Related Investment Measures (TRIMS) deals with performance requirements associated with foreign investment.

22 See Havana Charter, Article 12.

the protection of foreign investment,[23] and a growing number of wider economic agreements establishing FTAs have incorporated BIT-style provisions into an investment chapter. All these treaties are designed to clarify what standards of protection will apply to investments from one country into another and to provide a stable environment for investments. Because of the similarities among these different investment treaties, it has been argued that BITs – along with various other regional agreements – are incrementally building a *de facto* global investment regime.[24]

Contents of investment treaties

While investment treaties differ in their details, their scope and content have been standardized over the years, as negotiations have been characterized by an ongoing sharing and borrowing of concepts.[25] Moreover, the inclusion of the Most Favoured Nation clause in most BITs drives convergence in treaty interpretation. Therefore, some authors have underlined the development of a *common lexicon* of investment treaty law.[26]

Typically, investment treaty provisions deal with the scope and definition of foreign investment, non-discrimination (both national treatment and most-favoured-nation treatment), minimum standards and fair and equitable treatment. Other common provisions in investment treaties concern the repatriation of profits and other investment-related funds. A small number of investment treaties also include provisions prohibiting certain forms of performance requirements.[27] Investment treaties generally include protection against expropriation in the form of guarantees of compensation in the event of nationalization, expropriation, or indirect expropriation, and clarify what level of compensation will be owed in such cases.

The concept of expropriation is broadly construed in investment treaties which do not only protect foreign assets from the direct and full taking of property but also from *de facto* or *indirect* expropriation. While direct and overt

23 More than three thousand bilateral investment treaties (BITs) govern foreign investments and provide foreign investors direct access to international arbitration. *E.g.* A. Aust, *Handbook of International Law*, 2nd edn., Cambridge: Cambridge University Press, 2010, p. 345.
24 Lowenfeld argues that the BIT movement has moved beyond *lex specialis* to the level of customary law. See A. Lowenfeld, 'Investment Agreements and International Law', *Columbia Journal of Transnational Law* 42, 2003–2004, pp. 123–30.
25 C. McLachlan, 'The Principle of Systemic Integration and Article 31(3)(c) of the Vienna Convention', *ICLQ* 54, 2005, p. 284.
26 C. McLachlan, L. Shore and M. Weiniger, *International Investment Arbitration*, Oxford: Oxford University Press, 2007, p. 6.
27 Performance requirements are provisions that impose certain obligations on investors to act in ways considered beneficial for the host economy. The most common requirements relate to local content, joint ventures, technology transfer and employment of nationals. Usually these provisions may appear in contracts between foreign investors and the host state as a means to ensure that FDI in the host state will contribute to domestic development.

expropriations have become rare – after the nationalization move that marked the 60s and 70s[28] – indirect expropriation constitutes the typical form in which expropriations take place nowadays. Treaty provisions lack a precise definition of indirect expropriation and their language encompasses a potentially wide variety of state activity that may interfere with investor property.[29] States tend to achieve the same result (of expropriation) by indirect means (hence indirect or disguised or *de facto* expropriation), interfering in the use of property or with the enjoyment of its benefits even where the property is not seized and the legal title of the property is not affected.[30] For instance, the host state may target a foreign investor by imposing very high taxes or regulatory requirements which may make the foreign investment economically unviable.

Of critical importance is the distinction between simple regulatory measures and those which amount to indirect expropriation. The boundaries however are blurred and the jurisprudence and legal opinion is divided on this matter. In observing the growing tide of arbitral jurisprudence, two streams have emerged concerning expropriation: the *sole-effects* doctrine and the *police powers* doctrine.[31] While the first concentrates on the effects of the state measure on the foreign property, and thus favours the investor's perspective, the second focuses on the alleged goal of the state measure. If one adopts the *sole effects doctrine*, which focuses on the negative impact of regulation on the foreign investment, compensation has to be paid whenever the foreign investment is economically affected by a given regulation. If one adopts the *police powers* doctrine, general regulation adopted *bona fide* and in a non-discriminatory manner to protect public health, cannot be compensated. Both doctrines have generated significant jurisprudence.[32]

Some elements may indicate that the measure at stake constitutes an indirect expropriation. If a state adopts a general regulation which *de facto* targets a foreign investor or only applies to foreign investments, such discrimination may constitute evidence that there is indirect expropriation that can be compensated. Furthermore, if there is a significant interference or economic damage to the foreign investor, this may constitute evidence of expropriation.

28 For instance, during the 1960s and 1970s many developing countries asserted the sovereign right of governments to nationalize property without paying full compensation. This contentious political environment and the continual failure to agree upon multilateral standards impelled developed countries to pursue bilateral investment treaties. See A. Akinsanya, 'International Protection of Foreign Direct Investments in the Third World', *ICLQ* 36, 1987, pp. 58–75.

29 L.Y. Fortier and S.L. Drymer, 'Indirect Expropriation in the Law of International Investment: I Know When I See It, or *Caveat Investor*', *ICSID Review-FILJ* 19, 2004, pp. 293–327.

30 OECD, 'Indirect Expropriation and the Right to Regulate in International Investment Law', Working Paper on International Investment No 4, 2004, pp. 3–4.

31 M. Brunetti, 'Introduction', *International Law Forum de Droit International* 5, 2003, p. 151.

32 The relevant investment arbitrations will be analysed in more detail in Chapters 4–6.

For instance, in *Biloune v. Ghana*, Ghanaian governmental authorities had stopped a project, imposed demolition, arrested, detained and deported Mr Biloune. The arbitral tribunal found that the sum of these actions constituted 'constructive or indirect expropriation'.[33] In *Metalclad*, an arbitral tribunal found that refusal of a construction permit by the municipality amounted to expropriation.[34]

If, however, the general regulation aimed to protect public health affects both citizens and foreign companies, has a legitimate objective and does not involve the acquisition or transfer of property from the investor to the state, then it may be deemed a legitimate exercise of the police powers of the state. An example of such a legitimate exercise of the police powers of the state is the prohibition of advertisement distracting car drivers in highways. If scientific evidence were to prove that car drivers are distracted by advertisement on highways, then a prohibition of such advertisements would likely be deemed not to constitute indirect expropriation. Some authors consider the police powers doctrine as a justification of state conduct that would otherwise lead to compensation. More correctly, others see it as the legitimate exercise of state sovereignty and the state's right or duty to protect the environment, public health, etc.[35]

The settlement of disputes between foreign investors and states

While international investment law is a well established area of public international law, investment treaty arbitration is a recent phenomenon.[36] Under this mechanism, foreign investors may bring claims against the host state before international arbitral tribunals, which may be *ad hoc* or administered under the aegis of different institutions, such as the Permanent Court of Arbitration (PCA), the International Chamber of Commerce (ICC), the International Centre for the Settlement of Investment Disputes (ICSID)[37] etc. Investor-state arbitration has become a standard feature in international investment treaties since the 1980's, and such mechanism has been used increasingly.[38] When the ICSID was established in 1966 it was hardly foreseen

---

33 *Biloune, et al. v. Ghana*, 95 I.L.R.183, pp. 207–10 (1993).

34 *Metalclad Corporation v. United Mexican States*, Award, 30 August 2000, ¶ 107.

35 This theme will be analysed more in detail in Chapters 4–6.

36 *See* A. Newcombe and L. Paradell, *Law and Practice of Investment Treaties – Standards of Treatment*, Austin/Boston: Kluwer Law International, 2009, p. 45.

37 Convention on the Settlement of Investment Disputes Between States and Nationals of Other States, arts. 1–3, 18 March 1965, 575 U.N.T.S. 159 [hereinafter ICSID Convention].

38 From 1995 to 2004 the ICSID registered four times as many claims as in the previous 30 years and the growth rate appears to be increasing in the last seven years. The ICSID renaissance is probably due to economic globalization and the proliferation of investment treaties. There seems to be a parallel growth in other fora, but data is not available because of the confidentiality requirements. Also, some disputes may be unknown because settled

that it would in due course become one of the most active arbitral centres, which as of June 2011, had registered 351 cases.[39] No one could predict that investment treaty arbitration would move 'from a matter of peripheral academic interest to a matter of vital international concern'.[40] Most contemporary investment treaties include investor-state arbitration for the settlement of disputes which may arise between the foreign investor and the host state.[41]

This development has transformed the landscape of modern investment protection,[42] as customary international law did not confer such a right to individuals.[43] Similarly, Friendship, Commerce and Navigation (FCN) treaties and investment treaties that pre-dated the establishment of the ICSID, only provided for state to state disputes.[44] According to the traditional paradigm of states as the only subjects of international law and the only ones having the capacity to raise international claims against other states in legal proceedings, customary law and FCN treaties used to leave the dispute settlement of investment-related disputes to the exercise of diplomatic protection of the state of origin of the given corporation.[45] However, diplomatic protection constitutes a prerogative and not a duty for states which may exercise it at their will.[46] When violations of treaty or customary law obligations are limited

before registration. See D. Sedlak, 'ICSID's Resurgence in International Investment Arbitration: Can the Momentum Hold?', *Penn St Int'l L Rev* 23, 2004, p. 147.

39 See ICSID Secretariat, *The ICSID Caseload – Statistics* (2011), available at http://icsid.worldbank.org/ICSID/FrontServlet?requestType=ICSIDDocRH&actionVal=CaseLoadStatistics (accessed 2 January 2012).

40 S.D. Franck, 'Development and Outcomes of Investment Treaty Arbitration', *Harv. Int'l L.J.* 50, 2009, p. 435.

41 *See* Sedlak, 'ICSID's Resurgence', p. 147.

42 C. McLachlan, L. Shore and M. Weiniger, *International Investment Arbitration: Substantive Principles*, p. 5.

43 *See* J. Collier and V. Lowe, *The Settlement of Disputes in International Law: Institutions and Procedures*, Oxford: Oxford University Press, 1999, pp. 1–10; P. Muchlinski, 'The Diplomatic Protection of Foreign Investors: A Tale of Judicial Caution', in C. Binder, U. Kriebaum, A. Reinisch and S. Wittich (eds), *International Investment Law for the 21st Century – Essays in Honour of Christoph Schreuer*, Oxford: Oxford University Press, 2009, p. 341.

44 H. Walker, Jr., 'Modern Treaties of Friendship, Commerce, and Navigation', *Minn. L. Rev.* 42, 1957, 805.

45 '. . . Diplomatic protection consists of the invocation by a State, through diplomatic action or other means of peaceful settlement, of the responsibility of another State for an injury caused by an internationally wrongful act of that State to a natural or legal person that is a national of the former State, with a view to the implementation of such responsibility'. ILC Draft Articles on Diplomatic Protection, Article 1. *See* ILC Draft Articles on Diplomatic Protection (2006), Official Records of the General Assembly, Sixty first Session, Supplement No. 10 (A/61/10).

46 Diplomatic protection is generally deemed to be a right of the state: '[. . .] in taking up the case of one of its nationals, by resorting to diplomatic action or international judicial proceedings on his behalf, a State is in reality asserting its own right, the right to ensure in the person of its nationals respect for the rules of international law'. PCIJ, *Penevezys-Saldutiskis Railway Case*, *Estonia v. Lithuania*, Preliminary Objections, PCIJ Ser A/B (1939) No. 76.

in scope and discriminate against a foreign investor only, its national state will be reluctant to initiate an international dispute because of political and *de minimis* considerations. Furthermore, even if the state were to bring an international claim for its own injury, it would be under no obligation to pay any reparations received to the national actually injured.

In contrast with this traditional paradigm, modern investment treaties do not require the intervention of the home state in the furtherance of the dispute. Foreign investors no longer depend on the discretion of their home states in the context of diplomatic protection, in deciding whether or not a claim should be raised against another state;[47] and recourse to diplomatic protection has become 'residual'.[48] In practice, this means that foreign investors have access to arbitration against the host state if there is a BIT between the home state and the host state. In the absence of such a legal instrument, foreign investors have access only to the traditional dispute settlement mechanisms, including the host state national courts, human rights courts and, if diplomatic protection is exercised, inter-state dispute settlement mechanisms.

Suggestively described as 'arbitration without privity',[49] the internationalization of investment disputes has been conceived as an important valve for adequately recognizing and protecting the assets of foreign investors from expropriation, nationalization or other forms of regulation by the host state, by guaranteeing a neutral forum. Through arbitration clauses the host state signatory to the treaty agrees in advance to arbitrate disputes over the treaty meaning and application at the investor's initiative. Such clauses are to some degree necessary to render meaningful the substantive investment treaty provisions. By themselves, treaty-based provisions are meaningless if they are not accompanied by an effective dispute settlement mechanism. As the late Professor Thomas Wälde once held, 'The effectiveness of substantive rights is . . . linked to the availability of an effective enforcement . . . Right and procedural remedy, are, in practical and effective terms, one.'[50] The

---

47 M. Sornarajah, *The Settlement of Foreign Investment Disputes*, The Hague: Kluwer Law International, 2000, pp. 61–84; K.-H. Böckstiegel, 'Arbitration of Foreign Investment Disputes – An Introduction', in A.J. Van Den Berg (ed.), *New Horizons in International Commercial Arbitration and Beyond*, The Hague: Kluwer Law International, 2005, pp. 125–31.

48 While in the seventies, the ICJ in the *Barcelona Traction* case found it 'surprising' that the evolution of international investment law had not gone further in the light of the expansion of economic activities in the preceding half century, in the more recent *Diallo* case, the Court has recognized the residual nature of the exercise of diplomatic protection and recourse to the Court in case of investment disputes. *Barcelona Traction, Light and Power Company, Limited (Belg. v. Spain)*, 1970 I.C.J. 3, at ¶ 89 (Feb 5); *Case Concerning Ahmadou Sadio Diallo (Guinea v. Dem. Rep. Congo)*, (Preliminary Objections), at ¶¶ 88–91 (Judgment of 24 May 2007), available at http://www.icj-cij.org/docket/files/103/13856.pdf.

49 J. Paulsson, 'Arbitration Without Privity', *ICSID rev-FILJ* 10, 1995, p. 256.

50 T. Wälde, 'The Umbrella Clause in Investment Arbitration: A Comment on Original Intentions and Recent Cases', *JWIT* 6, 2005, p. 185. See also K.-H. Böckstiegel, 'Enterprise v. State: the New David and Goliath?', *Arbitration International* 23, 2007, pp. 93–104 (noting that the traditional David–Goliath relationship between private investors and

rationale for internationalizing investor-state disputes lies in the assumed independence and impartiality of international arbitral tribunals, while national dispute settlement procedures are often perceived as biased or inadequate.[51]

Importantly, the paradigm shift is significant under two further respects. *First*, in investor-state arbitration there is a transfer of adjudicative authority from national courts to arbitral tribunals. In this sense, it has been argued that access to investor-state arbitration shares many characteristics of the direct right of action before human rights courts.[52] However, arbitral tribunals do not only constitute an additional forum with respect to state courts, but also an alternative to the same. Thus, not only can foreign investors seek another decision after an eventual recourse to the national courts, but they are not required to exhaust local remedies prior to pursuing an international legal claim. This is in stark counterpoint to international human rights treaties which oblige the claimants to recur to local courts in the first instance. Even where contracts between an enterprise and a state expressly limit recourse to local dispute settlement options, claimants can directly surmount national jurisdictions and bring investment claims to arbitral tribunals in situations where a BIT has been concluded by the investor's home state and the host state.[53]

Second, under most investment treaties, states have waived their sovereign immunity, and have agreed to give arbitrators a comprehensive jurisdiction over what are essentially regulatory disputes. Indeed, investment treaty arbitration encompasses the full panoply of the state's regulatory relations with foreign investors. As a result, it can be said that investment treaty arbitration basically replaces judicial organs with private adjudicators in matters of public law.[54] Clearly, adjudication over a state's *acta jure imperii* implies a significant departure from the conventional use of international arbitration in the commercial sphere.[55] Indeed, many of the recent arbitral

states has been replaced, at least procedurally, by a level playing field and that in some circumstances, private claimants, such as large multinational companies, may well have more resources available than some small states who are respondents).

51 See, for instance, Newcombe and Paradell, *Law and Practice of Investment Treaties*, p. 24. For a critical discussion, see, however, G. Van Harten, 'Five Justifications for Investment Treaties: A Critical Discussion', *Trade Law and Development* 2, 2010, pp. 19–58.

52 See G. Burdeau, 'Nouvelles perspectives pour l'arbitrage dans le contentieux economique intéressant l'Etat', *Revue de l'Arbitrage* 1, 1995, p. 16.

53 Several ICSID cases have upheld jurisdiction to hear treaty claims, notwithstanding the fact that the foreign investor was party to a contract which specified that contract claims would be the exclusive province of a given domestic court. See, for instance, *Compañia de Aguas del Aconquija SA and Vivendi Universal v Argentine Republic* (ICSID Case No. ARB/97/3) Annulment Decision of 3 July 2002, 41 ILM 1135 (2002).

54 See G. Van Harten, 'The Public-Private Distinction in the International Arbitration of Individual Claims Against the State', *ICLQ* 56, 2007, pp. 371–94.

55 Traditionally, public international law has distinguished the conduct of a state between *acta jure imperii* and *acta jure gestionis*, with regard to its public or private nature.

awards have concerned the determination of the appropriate boundary between two conflicting values: the legitimate sphere for state regulation in the pursuit of public goods on the one hand, and the protection or private property from state interference on the other.

Main characteristics of investor–state arbitration

The arbitral process in investment arbitration presents characteristics similar to those in a typical international commercial arbitration.[56] The composition of the tribunal is determined by the parties who generally choose law scholars or professionals. While 'arbitrators . . . are expected to be both independent of the party appointing them and impartial . . . it is usually conceded that without violating in any way this theoretical obligation of independence, the arbitrator may quite acceptably share the nationality, or political or economic philosophy, or "legal culture" of the party who has nominated him – and may therefore be assumed from the very beginning to be "sympathetic" to that party's contentions or favourably disposed to its positions . . .'[57] Arbitrators have clear incentives to adopt a high level standard of conduct because of reputation;[58] the arbitrator has an obligation to disclose eventual conflicts of interest; and the parties can challenge him or her if a conflict of interest is deemed to have arisen.

Confidentiality is one of the main features of the proceedings as generally hearings are held *in camera* and the documents submitted by the parties remain confidential in principle. Final awards may not be published, depending on the will of the parties. Even the names of the parties, and much less the details of the dispute, may not be disclosed.[59] While confidentiality well suits commercial disputes, the same may be problematic in investor-state arbitration, because investment arbitrations can deal with public policy matters. The lack of transparency may hamper efforts to track investment treaty disputes, to monitor their frequency, and their settlement, and to assess the relative policy implications involved. Importantly, as a judge once put it, 'it is of fundamental importance that justice should not only be done, but should manifestly and undoubtedly be seen to be done'.[60]

See Z. Douglas, 'The Hybrid Foundations of Investment Treaty Arbitration', *BYIL* 74, 2003, pp. 221–2.

56 N. Blackaby, 'Investment Arbitration and Commercial Arbitration (or the Tale of the Dolphin and the Shark)', in J. Lew and L. Mistelis, *Pervasive Problems in International Arbitration*, Kluwer Law International, 2006, pp. 217–33.

57 A.S. Rau, 'Integrity in Private Judging', *South Texas L R* 38, 1997, p. 507.

58 See A. Lowenfeld, 'The Party-Appointed Arbitrator in International Controversies: Some Reflections', *Texas ILJ* 30, 1995, pp. 59–72.

59 For instance, Article 46 of the 2007 Arbitration Rules of the Arbitration Institute of the Stockholm Chamber of Commerce (SCC Institute) provides that unless otherwise agreed by the parties, the SCC Institute and the Arbitral Tribunal shall maintain the confidentiality of the arbitration and the award. The new arbitration rules entered into force on 1 January 2007. The text is available at http://www.sccinstitute.com .

60 Lord Hewart in *R. v. Sussex Justices* [1924] 1 KB 256 at 260.

In recent years, efforts to make investment arbitration more transparent have been undertaken in different fora. In response to calls from civil society groups, the three parties to the NAFTA – Canada, the US and Mexico – have pledged to disclose all NAFTA arbitrations and to open future arbitration hearings to the public.[61] Similarly, the ICSID Rules provide for the public disclosure of the dispute proceedings under their auspices.[62] Increasingly, investment arbitration tribunals have allowed public interest groups to present *amicus curiae* briefs or to have access to the arbitral process.[63] ICSID Rules have undergone amendments, and now also grant ICSID Tribunals discretion to allow interested third parties to make written submissions in arbitral proceedings.[64] These important moves, however, involve the conduct of the proceedings of a limited number of investment disputes. Indeed, the vast majority of existing treaties do not mandate such transparency, which means that most of the proceedings are resolved behind closed doors.

Finally and perhaps more importantly, awards rendered against host states are, in theory, readily enforceable against host state property worldwide, due to the widespread adoption of the New York and Washington Conventions.[65] The decisions have only limited avenues for revision and cannot be amended by the domestic legal system or a supreme court.[66] Arbitration under the ICSID Rules is wholly exempted from the supervision of local courts, with awards subject only to an internal annulment process.[67] If arbitration is sited in a country other than the host state, then there may be

---

61 NAFTA Free Trade Commission, *Statement of the Free Trade Commission on Non-Disputing Party Participation*, 7 October 2003, 16 W.T.A.M. (2004).
62 See ICSID Regulation 22: '(1) The Secretary-General shall appropriately publish information about the operation of the Centre, including the registration of all requests for conciliation or arbitration and in due course an indication of the date and method of the termination of each proceeding . . .' The Administrative and Financial Regulations of ICSID are available at http://icsid.worldbank.org/ICSID/ICSID/RulesMain.jsp.
63 On the issue of *amicus curiae* briefs in investor-state arbitration, see e.g. A. Kawharu, 'Participation of Non-Governmental Organizations in Investment Arbitration as Amici Curiae', in M. Waibel et al., *The Backlash against Investment Arbitration: Perceptions and Reality*, Netherlands: Kluwer Law International, 2010, pp. 275–95.
64 ICSID Arbitration Rule 37. ICSID Arbitration Rules are available at http://icsid.worldbank.org/ICSID/ICSID/RulesMain.jsp.
65 New York Convention on the Recognition and Enforcement of Foreign Arbitral Awards, 10 June 1958, 330 UNTS 38.
66 New York Convention, Article V.
67 ICSID Convention Article 52. The ICSID annulment process provides for a very limited review. ICSID annulment committees only have the ability to annul awards and send them back to the tribunal or to a new tribunal for a new decision, but cannot replace the decision with their own. The grounds for annulment are very narrow and concern due process issues: the tribunal was not properly constituted, it manifestly exceeded its powers, there was corruption on the part of a member, there was a fundamental serious departure from a procedural rule, or the award did not state the reasons on which it was based.

no capacity whatsoever for the host government to challenge the award in its own legal system.[68]

An issue arises as to whether public health can be protected within a framework aimed primarily at protecting private interests. While arbitration structurally constitutes a private model of adjudication, investment treaty arbitration can be viewed as public law adjudication.[69] Arbitral awards ultimately shape the relationship between state, on the one hand, and private individuals on the other.[70] Arbitrators determine matters such as the legality of governmental activity, the degree to which individuals should be protected from regulation, and the appropriate role of the state.[71]

Final remarks

Having defined the legal framework of our enquiry, that is, international investment law, this study now proceeds to define the proper subject matter of such enquiry, that is, the relationship between investor rights and public health in international investment law. Before moving to the theoretical interplay between these two different values, it will be necessary to investigate the contemporary conceptualization of health in public international law.

68 L.E. Peterson, *Bilateral Investment Treaties and Development Policy Making*, Winnipeg: IISD, 2004, p. 22.
69 Van Harten, 'The Public-Private Distinction in the International Arbitration of Individual Claims Against the State', p. 372; Douglas, 'The Hybrid Foundations of Investment Treaty Arbitration', pp. 221–37.
70 G. Van Harten, *Investment Treaty Arbitration and Public Law*, Oxford: Oxford University Press, 2007, p. 70; B. Choudhuri, 'Recapturing Public Power: Is Investment Arbitration's Engagement of the Public Interest Contributing to Democratic Deficit?', *Vanderbilt Journal of Transnational Law* 41, 2008, pp. 775–1042.
71 M. Sornarajah, 'The Clash of Globalizations and the International Law on Foreign Investment', *Canadian Foreign Policy* 12, 2003, p. 17.

2 Public health in contemporary international law and policy

Introduction

Traditionally, there is a historic chasm between international law and health concerns, as health issues have been considered as technical problems to be solved, rather than social and political ones.[1] Although some elements of public health have been regulated transnationally in the past, only in the past century has public health law become a growing component of public international law; similarly some of its elements have increasingly intersected and fused with other areas of international law.[2] As this study investigates the linkage between international investment law and public health regulation, one of its conceptual pillars is the reconceptualization of public health in contemporary international law.

The argument will proceed in three parts. First, this chapter will analyze the reasons behind the historical neglect and the contemporary renaissance of the conceptualization of public health in international law. Second, after briefly exploring the more general concept of health, public health will be defined, and the role of the government – its power and obligation to adopt mandatory measures to eliminate a threat to public health – in relation to international investment law and policy will be investigated. Reference to the individual right to health will be made to clarify key concepts, in consideration of the fact that public health and the individual right to health are complementary,[3] and that the evolution of international health law has been

---

1 See M. Prabhu, 'International Health and Sustainable Development Law', in M.-C. Cordonier-Segger and A. Khalfan, *Sustainable Development Law – Principles, Practices and Prospects*, Oxford: Oxford University Press, 2004, p. 323.
2 For instance, the health discourse has been increasingly linked to international trade. See e.g. L. Gruszczynski, *Regulating Health and Environmental Risks Under WTO Law*, Oxford: Oxford University Press, 2010.
3 A scholarly approach deems it artificial to create a barrier between *public* and *private* health. The argument is that 'matters of private health are of concern to public health in some way or another' and vice versa. G. Van Der Schyff, *Limitation of Rights – A Study of the European Convention and the South African Bill of Rights*, Nijmegen: Wolf Legal Publishers, 2005, ¶ 154.

very much tied to the protection and promotion of human rights.[4] Third, the international law framework which governs public health will be scrutinized and critically assessed.

A historical overview

Law and health issues have interacted for a long time.[5] As 'law can be an essential tool for creating conditions to enable people to lead healthier and safer lives',[6] regulation of health-related matters has roots in antiquity. From the beginnings of human civilization, public authorities have often taken measures to prevent the spread of diseases. Quarantine, the compulsory isolation to contain the spread of disease, represents one of the most ancient regulations concerning public health.[7] For instance, the 643 *Edict of Rothari* devoted a chapter to the treatment of lepers and provided for the *Separatio Leprosorum*, a practice which would keep the ill separate from the community in order to limit the spread of the disease.[8] During the 14th century Black Death in Europe, as a measure of disease prevention related to the plague, ships and people had to spend forty days in isolation prior to entering Venetian ports.[9] Public health measures in the modern sense were systematically adopted in the mid-19th century in several countries (England, continental Europe, and the USA) as part of both social reform movements and the growth of biological and medical knowledge.[10] These national measures could affect international trade.[11] For instance, vessels could be ordered to be burned with their cargoes, the owners receiving a mere indemnity.

However, these national measures were fragmented; only in the 19th century did major European states conclude that the international spread of infectious diseases could no longer be handled as a matter only of national governance: the nature of the problem – diseases spreading across borders through international trade and travel – demanded international cooperation.

---

4 A.L. Taylor and D.W. Bettcher, 'International Law and Public Health', *Bull. WHO* 80, 2002, p. 823.

5 P. Frati, 'Quarantine, Trade and Health Policies in Ragusa-Dubrovnik until the Age of Armmenius Baglivi', *Medicina nei secoli* 12, 2000, pp. 103–27.

6 L.O. Gostin, *Public Health Law: Power, Duty, Restraint*, Berkeley: University of California Press, 2008, p. 4.

7 The word quarantine comes from the 14th century Venetian 'quarentena' which indicated forty days of isolation. See Frati, 'Quarantine, Trade and Health Policies'.

8 See T.S. Miller and R. Smith-Savage, 'Medieval Leprosy Reconsidered', *International Social Science Review* 81, 2006, pp. 16–28.

9 See Frati, 'Quarantine, Trade and Health Policies'.

10 J.P. Koplan et al., 'Towards a Common Definition of Global Health', *The Lancet* 373, 6 June 2009, p. 1993.

11 D.P. Fidler, 'From International Sanitary Conventions to Global Health Security: The New International Health Regulations', *Chinese JIL* 4, 2005, p. 329.

Thus, several international conferences were held with a view to uniform action in preventing the spread of cholera and other diseases.[12]

Despite these early international sanitary conventions, public health was marginalized for an extensive period of time in both international law and policy.[13] Even after World War II, only limited scholarly analysis has been done until recent years.[14] There are several reasons behind this neglect. *First*, traditionally public health was considered as a matter of medical practice or of the exclusive domestic domain of policy makers. International lawyers traditionally limited their scope of enquiry to more traditional subdisciplines. *Second*, even after the conceptualization of the right to health after World War II, this right was undertheorized due to political reasons.[15] Given the political divide between the Eastern and Western blocs determined by the Cold War, the right to health as well as other economic, social and cultural rights were deemed to be politicized as reflecting a socialist perspective. The traditional distinction between civil and political rights and economic, social and cultural rights was also based on the assumption that while the first category of rights was susceptible to immediate realization, the second was deemed to be only of gradual implementation. The dichotomy was formalized by the division of the so-called International Bill of Rights into two Covenants adopted in 1966.[16]

Since the fall of the Berlin Wall, however, a trend towards the reconciliation of the opposing views has gradually emerged. Economic, social and cultural rights on the one hand, and civil and political rights on the other, have been understood in their unity and complementarity. Not only is there no fundamental difference between the ethical basis of the first and second set of rights, but 'both are related to each other and both may be viewed as prerequisites for one another'.[17] Suddenly, the door was opened for a recon-ceptualization of the right to health and its contents. Nowadays, more than one hundred national constitutions explicitly protect the right to health.[18]

---

12 Ibidem, p. 327.
13 Ibidem, p. 332. See generally A. Obijiofor, *Global Health Governance: International Law and Public Health in a Divided World*, Toronto: University of Toronto Press Inc., 2005; D. Fidler, 'International Law and Global Public Health', *Kan. L. Rev.* 48, 1999, p. 1.
14 Most notably, in 1978 The Hague Academy of International Law organized a workshop on the 'Right to Health as a Human Right'. See R.-J. Dupuy (ed.), *The Right to Health as a Human Right*, Aalphen aan den Rijn, the Netherlands: Sijthoff & Noordhoff, 1979. However, as Toebes highlights, 'from the aggregate of studies that were conducted for this workshop, it can be deduced that there was great confusion over the content and meaning of the right to health'. B. Toebes, *The Right to Health as a Human Right in International Law*, Amsterdam: Intersentia, 1999, pp. 4–5.
15 See P. Hunt, *Reclaiming Social Rights*, Dartmouth: Aldershot, 1996, p. 8.
16 On the 1966 Covenants, see section below.
17 See K. Raes, 'The Philosophical Basis of Social, Economic and Cultural Rights', in P. Van der Auweraert et al. (eds), *Social, Economic and Cultural Rights: An Appraisal of Current European and International Developments*, Antwerp: Maklu, 2002, p. 44.
18 See E. Kinney and B. Clark, 'Provisions for Health and Health Care in the Constitutions of the Countries of the World', *Cornell Int L J* 37, 2004, pp. 285–355.

More importantly, this renaissance is also visible in international law instruments.

Defining health

Health can be conceptualized both as a right of the individual and as a duty of the state. Rather than separating the individual right to health from public health,[19] this study follows the holistic conceptualization which conceives health in a comprehensive fashion.[20] This broader discourse maintains the premise that all human rights are rights of individuals and not group rights, but allows a better understanding of health as a unitary phenomenon. As Professor René-Jean Dupuy once put it, there is a sort of *dialectics* between the individual and the society with regard to health,[21] as the notion of health presents inherent ambiguities. While the right to health is connected to the great tradition of individual rights, 'there are nevertheless two phases in the right to health: on the one hand, it is to be wished that the state does not interfere with the individual's right to health; on the other hand, it is necessary to have a . . . collective policy which impl[ies] the intervention of the state power.'[22] Health thus presents both individual and collective dimensions, and is linked with human rights frames of discussion.[23]

A major issue in conceptualizing health is whether it represents a negative or positive concept, or whether health should be considered as more than simply the absence of disease.[24] A complete definition of health cannot be derived by Article 12 of the International Covenant on Economic, Social and Cultural Rights (hereinafter ICESCR),[25] which affirms 'the right of everyone to the enjoyment of the highest attainable standard of physical and mental

---

19 Some authors adopt a rigid distinction between the right to health and public health. For instance, Toebes deems the right to health to be individual rather than public in character. According to Toebes 'As a human right [the right to health] seeks primarily to provide individuals with a right to a number of health services and freedoms rather than to provide a tool for the State to take certain measures necessary for public health'. Toebes, *The Right to Health as a Human Right in International Law*, pp. 274–5. However, when the author describes 'what exactly individuals are entitled to on the basis of a right to health and what the ensuing obligations are on the part of States', she implicitly acknowledges the duality of health as an individual right and a state obligation. Ibidem, p. 25.

20 Van Der Schyff, *Limitation of Rights*, ¶ 154.

21 Dupuy, *The Right to Health as a Human Right*, pp. 126–7.

22 J.-M. Dufour, 'Summing up', in Dupuy, *The Right to Health as a Human Right*, p. 142.

23 In this sense, see D.P. Fidler, 'A Globalized Theory of Public Health Law', *Journal of Law, Medicine & Ethics* 30, 2002, pp. 150–61.

24 A. Chapman, 'Core Obligations Related to the Right to Health', in A. Chapman and S. Russell (eds), *Core Obligations: Building a Framework for Economic, Social and Cultural Rights*, Antwerp: Intersentia, 2002, ¶ 5.1.

25 The International Covenant on Economic, Social and Cultural Rights UNGA resolution 2200 (XXI) 16 December 1966, entered into force on 3 January 1976 (999 UNTS 171) [hereinafter ICESCR].

health'.[26] This formulation neither expressly defines health nor conceives it as the mere absence of illness.[27] However, arguing *a contrario*, the lack of reference to an absolute standard of health seems to suggest a more complex legal concept. What is clear from this formulation is that because of human dignity, everyone has the right to achieve the highest attainable standard of health. The ill and the weakest are not excluded; this provision requires adequate care and support for them in order to help them achieve their highest attainable standard of health and well-being.[28] Accordingly, health is not an absolute concept but a relative one which depends both on the individual conditions and a state's available resources. Subsequent legal instruments have also clarified that health is an inclusive right extending not only to health care but also to the underlying determinants of health, such as access to safe and potable water and adequate sanitation, supply of safe food, disease prevention, and environmental health.[29] States cannot guarantee good health, but they have the obligation both to protect and to possibly enhance public health.[30]

From an individual perspective, health – intended as the entitlement to the enjoyment of the highest attainable standard of health – is linked to other human rights.[31] Health is a tool for human well-being and provides capabilities – a series of capacities and opportunities which empower individuals.[32] In this sense, like other social rights, the right to health is linked to human dignity and complement civil and political rights.[33] This interconnectedness and indivisibility of all human rights – be they civil, political, economic, social or cultural – has been repeatedly stressed in the human rights discourse.[34] The right

---

26 ICESCR, Article 12.
27 By contrast, the preamble to the World Health Organization (WHO) Constitution offers perhaps the most comprehensive definition of health, conceptualizing it as 'a state of complete physical, mental and social well-being and not merely the absence of disease or infirmity'. The Constitution was adopted by the International Health Conference on 22 July 1946 and entered into force on 7 April 1948. 14 UNTS 221.
28 ICESCR, Article 12.2.d.
29 ICESCR, Article 12.2 and General Comment No 14, ¶ 11.
30 B. Toebes, 'The Right to Health', in A. Eide, C. Krause and A. Rosas (eds), *Economic Social and Cultural Rights*, 2nd edn,, The Hague: Martinus Nijhoff, 2001, p. 169.
31 In the words of the Supreme Court of Costa Rica 'of what use are all other rights and guarantees, the institutions and programs, the advantages and benefits of our system of liberties, if even one person cannot count on having the rights to health and life guaranteed?' *William García Alvarez v. Caja Costarricense de Seguro Social*, Exp. 5778-V-97, No 5934–97 (Sala Constitucional de la Corte Suprema de Justicia de Costa Rica), 23 September 1997.
32 A. Sen, *Commodities and Capabilities*, Oxford: Oxford University Press, 1985; M. Nussbaum, *Women and Human Development: The Capabilities Approach*, Cambridge: Cambridge University Press, 2000).
33 See E. Wiles, 'Aspirational Principles or Enforceable Rights? The Future for Socio-Economic Rights in National Law', *American University ILR* 22, 2006–2007, p. 48.
34 For instance, the Proclamation of Teheran in 1968 states that 'since human rights and fundamental freedoms are indivisible, the full realization of civil and political rights without the enjoyment of economic, social and cultural rights is impossible'. International Conference on Human Rights, Proclamation of Teheran, 13 May 1968, available at http://www.un.org.

to health serves as a paradigmatic example of the fact that there is no clear cut division between the two categories of rights.

From a state's perspective, public health is a salient public value and lies at the heart of state sovereignty not only because of practical reasons – national authorities are better placed to appreciate the local society's needs – but also because public health is functional to the very existence of the state: population is recognized to be one of the constituting elements of statehood.[35] Therefore, protecting public health is a primary duty of states which arises from constitutional and statutory law, as well as from the fundamental 'social contract' upon which most governments rest.[36]

Paradigm cases of public health intervention by the state are the prevention of infectious diseases, anti-smoking regulation, adequate sanitation and the prevention of environmental pollution. While public health involves a recognition of the multidimensional nature of the determinants of health, questions arise with regard to the possible evolution of the scope of public health measures and the limits of the same. As scientific knowledge develops, new areas of state intervention may become necessary. For instance, the increase of childhood obesity and the concomitant increase in type II diabetes among children is a health problem that has only recently emerged.

A typical taxonomy of the legal tools available to governments to advance the public's health include: taxation;[37] circulation of relevant information;[38] direct regulation;[39] and indirect regulation through the tort system.[40] However, views differ as to what compulsory measures are necessary to safeguard the public's health and, therefore, regulations differ from one country to another. For instance, the prohibition of vending machines in schools to prevent child

Similarly, the 1993 Vienna Declaration states that 'all human rights are universal, indivisible and interdependent and interrelated', United Nations World Conference on Human Rights, Vienna Declaration and Programme of Action, 25 June 1993, UNGA doc. A/CONF 157/23, available at http://www.un.org, at 5.

35 B. Conforti, *Diritto internazionale*, Napoli: Editoriale Scientifica, 1997, p. 12.

36 As Professor Gostin points out, 'the word *public* in public health has two overlapping meanings – one that refers to the entity that takes primary responsibility for the public's health, and another that indicates who has a legitimate expectation of receiving the benefits'. See Gostin, *Public Health Law: Power, Duty, Restraint*, p. 6.

37 'Tax relief can be offered for health-producing activities such as medical services . . . At the same time, tax burdens can be placed on the sale of hazardous products, such as cigarettes, alcoholic beverages, and firearms.' Ibidem, p. 31.

38 For instance, government can require businesses to label their products to include health warnings and can regulate advertising for potentially harmful products, such as cigarettes. Ibidem, p. 32.

39 Governments can directly regulate individuals, professionals, and businesses to protect the health and safety of workers, consumers, environmental goods and the population at large.

40 As Gostin points out, 'Civil litigation can redress many different kinds of public health harms: environmental damage (e.g., air pollution or groundwater contamination), exposure to toxic substances (e.g., pesticides, radiation, or chemicals), hazardous products (e.g., tobacco or firearms), and defective consumer products (e.g., children's toys, recreational equipment, or household goods).' Ibidem, pp. 29–36.

obesity is a controversial issue: while a French law has banned vending machines from schools, in Latvia, the Netherlands, Norway and the United Kingdom an attempt is being made to provide fruit free of charge in schools, or to make it easily accessible.[41] One may also envisage the conversion of vending machines in healthy vending machines. On the other hand, Denmark has introduced what is believed to be the world's first fat tax.[42]

Crucially, what best serves the common weal may not always be in the interests of all its members, 'making public health highly political'.[43] In some circumstances, the protection and preservation of public health is not possible without constraining a wide range of private activities. In the example of the French law prohibiting vending machines in schools to prevent child obesity, it is evident that the business of machine vendors will be constrained, if not eliminated *tout court*. During the spread of the mad cow disease, in an effort to protect public health, Italian public authorities prohibited the commerce of T-bone steaks (bistecca alla fiorentina) which is a traditional food in Tuscany, irrespective of the protests of restaurateurs and cattlemen.[44] While the industry may have economic incentives to produce goods without consideration of public health concerns and often asserts that economic principles militate against state interference, public health has historically constrained the rights of individuals and businesses so as to prevent nuisance. Furthermore, the reconciliation of diverging opinions about the desirability of governmental action in a given situation 'is an issue for political resolution'.[45]

What are the boundaries to the state police powers to regulate public health matters? As primary responsibility for public health policy and enforcement is vested in the states,[46] the risk is that relevant governmental authorities abuse their coercive authority and unnecessarily infringe upon individual freedoms and investor rights.[47] Furthermore, some authors have cautioned that 'in principle, . . . public health could be limitless as almost all human activities (and many inactivities) may affect health'.[48]

---

41 World Health Organization, *Nutrition, Physical Activity and the Prevention of Obesity: Policy Developments in the WHO European Region*, Copenhagen: WHO Regional Office for Europe, 2007, p. 4.
42 'Denmark Introduces the World's First Food Fat Tax', *BBC News*, 1 October 2011.
43 Gostin, *Public Health Law: Power, Duty, Restraint*, p. 6.
44 M. Vincenzi, 'L'emergenza mucca pazza, oggi muore la fiorentina', *La Repubblica*, 31 March 2001.
45 Gostin, *Public Health Law: Power, Duty, Restraint*, p. 10.
46 Ibidem, chapters 1–2.
47 As Rothstein puts it, 'Unless the scope of permissible governmental action is carefully circumscribed, there is a threat to civil liberties by governmental confiscation of property, restraint on the movement of individuals, mandating of medical examinations and similar measures'. M. Rothstein, 'Rethinking the Nature of Public Health', *J.L. Med. & Ethics* 30, 2002, p. 147.
48 M. Verweij and A. Dawson, 'The Meaning of Public in Public Health', in A. Dawson and M. Verweij (eds), *Ethics, Prevention and Public Health*, Oxford: Oxford University Press, 2009, p. 17.

However, the legal powers and duties of the state to protect public health are not absolute, but there are 'limitations on the power of the state to constrain the autonomy, privacy, liberty, proprietary, or other legally protected interests of individuals for the common good'.[49] These limits have both a procedural and substantive dimension. On the one hand, public health powers must be exercised consistently with due process of law. For instance, Rothstein stresses the need for transparency and legality of public health measures.[50] On the other hand, the coercive measures that a state can adopt in the exercise of its police powers to protect public health need to be balanced with respect for other international law obligations including individual rights. The police powers of the state, i.e. its inherent prerogative to protect the public's health, safety, and welfare may clash with individual rights to privacy, liberty, property, and other legally protected interests. Rothstein suggests that the use of such authority is only justified if three conditions are met: first, where the health of the population is threatened; second, where the government has powers or expertise to meet that threat; and, third, where the action of government is efficient or proportionate.[51] Accordingly, 'placing limits on public health activities narrows the government's coercive powers, sets bounds on when such measures may be used, allocates responsibilities, sets priorities and steers government away from inappropriate undertakings'.[52]

The interplay between the police powers of the state to protect public health and private interests is of particular relevance in investment treaty arbitration, as recent arbitrations have dealt with the question of whether state regulation allegedly aimed to protect public health could amount to a violation of relevant BIT provisions. Achieving a fair balance between the economic rights of foreign investors and the powers and duties of the state to defend and advance the public's health poses an enduring problem for international investment law.

The international legal framework

With globalization transforming international relations, the state's legal duty to protect the health of its population has evolved. At the international level, several international law instruments have recognized the states' duty to protect public health and have set a number of standards clarifying the content of this duty. International cooperation in public health matters is a fluid process which ranges from non-binding instruments, such as recommendations, guidelines, resolutions and declarations to binding ones

---

49 Gostin *Public Health Law: Power, Duty, Restraint*, chapter 1.
50 M. Rothstein, 'The Limits of Public Health: A Response', *Public Health Ethics* 2, 2009, pp. 84–8.
51 Rothstein, 'Rethinking the Nature of Public Health'.
52 Ibidem, p. 147.

such as treaties.[53] Because of the difficulties of securing widespread consent to new binding rules, whether by treaty or by customs, states often recur to *soft law* instruments to give a discipline to public health matters.[54] For instance, the World Health Organization (WHO)[55] has traditionally adopted a series of non-binding instruments on public health matters. As these standards are commonly respected by states, some authors have highlighted that the boundaries between law and non-law are blurred.[56] Furthermore, repetition and *opinio juris* may determine the consolidation of such standards in customary law. More recently, the WHO has adopted a series of international instruments of binding character.[57]

In parallel, the right to health is expressly included in a large number of treaties and other instruments of international relevance. While reference to health appears in Article 55 of the UN Charter,[58] the right to health was first formulated in the WHO Constitution.[59] Furthermore, Article 25 of the Universal Declaration of Human Rights (hereinafter UDHR)[60] affirms: 'Everyone has the right to a standard of living adequate for the health of himself and of his family, including food, clothing, housing, medical care and necessary social services.'[61] Although the UDHR does not have binding character, it has been the source of inspiration for the United Nations in

53 A. Taylor and D.W. Bettcher, 'International Law and Public Health', *Bull. WHO* 80, 2002, p. 12.

54 On soft law, see more generally, C.M. Chinkin, 'The Challenge of Soft Law: Development and Change in International Law', *ICLQ* 38, 1989, p. 850; A. Boyle, 'Some Reflections on the Relationship of Treaties and Soft Law', *ICLQ* 48, 1999, pp. 901–13.

55 The World Health Organization was established in 1948 as a specialized agency of the United Nations and was designed to promote and protect the health of all peoples. The WHO membership includes 193 countries and two associate members. *See* Member Country list, available at http://www.who.int/countries/en/. *See also* WHO, *Working for Health – An Introduction to the World Health Organization*, Geneva: WHO, 2007.

56 D. Shelton, 'Law, Non-law and the Problem of "Soft Law"', in D. Shelton (ed.), *Commitment and Compliance: The Role of Non-Binding Norms in the International System*, Oxford: Oxford University Press, 2000, p. 10.

57 See below Chapter 5.

58 Article 55 of the UN Charter states: 'with a view to the creation of conditions of stability and well-being which are necessary for peaceful and friendly relations among nations [. . .] the United Nations shall promote: [. . .] solutions of international economic, social, *health and related problems* [. . .]' [emphasis added]. Charter of the United Nations signed on 26 June 1945 in San Francisco and entered into force on 24 October 1946, 1 UNTS XVI.

59 WHO Constitution, Preamble. For a commentary, see I. Bilmore, 'The "Right to Health" According to the WHO', in T. Wagner and L. Carbone (eds), *Fifty Years After the Declaration – The United Nations' Record on Human Rights*, Lanham: University Press of America, 2001, pp. 25–31.

60 Universal Declaration of Human Rights (doc. UNGA Res. 217 A (III)), adopted on 10 December 1948.

61 UDHR, Article 25.

making advances in standard settings as contained in the existing international human rights instruments.[62]

As mentioned, the most comprehensive provision on the right to health in international law is provided by the International Covenant on Economic, Social and Cultural Rights which recognizes 'the right of everyone to the enjoyment of the highest attainable standard of physical and mental health'.[63] The ICESCR further enumerates, by way of illustration, a number of steps taken by states parties to achieve the full realization of this right, including 'those necessary for [. . .] the prevention, treatment and control of epidemic, endemic, occupational and other diseases'.[64] The Covenant is legally binding for the states which have ratified it,[65] and provides an international mechanism to control the application of its provisions, under which the parties must send periodic reports to the UN Committee on Economic, Social and Cultural Rights on the measures adopted. This Committee has further established the content of the right to health in its *General Comment No. 14* on the *Right to the Highest Attainable Standard of Health*[66] which constitutes an 'authoritative interpretation of the right to health'.[67] The *General Comment* expressly links the right to health to human dignity[68] and interprets it as an inclusive right extending not only to the right to timely and appropriate health care, but also to 'a wide range of socio-economic factors that promote conditions in which people can lead a healthy life', thus extending to 'the underlying determinants of health, such as food and nutrition, housing, access to safe and potable water and adequate sanitation, safe and healthy working conditions, and a healthy environment'.[69]

---

62 The right to health is recognized, *inter alia*, in Article 5 (e) (iv) of the International Convention for the Elimination of All Forms of Discrimination (adopted by UNGA 21 Dec 1965, UN GAOR Res 2106 A (XX) entered into force 4 January 1969) and in Article 24 of the Convention on the Rights of The Child (20 November 1989 GA Res 44/25 UN GAOR, 44th Sess., Supp. No 49, at 167, UN Doc A/44/49) (1989).

63 ICESCR, Article 12.1.

64 ICESCR, Article 12.2(c).

65 See P. Alston, 'U.S. Ratification of the Covenant on Economic, Social and Cultural Rights: The Need for an Entirely New Strategy', *AJIL* 84, 1990, pp. 365–93. *See also* C.A. Bradley, 'Unratified Treaties, Domestic Politics, and the US Constitution', *Harvard ILJ* 48, 2007, pp. 307–37.

66 UN Committee on Economic, Social and Cultural Rights, *General Comment No. 14*. The General Comment was adopted at the Committee's twenty-second session, 25 April–12 May 2000 (E/C.12/2000/4). General comments are authoritative interpretations of aspects related to specific treaty provisions that are intended to assist states in complying with their obligations. While General Comments are not legally binding, they are influential in shaping the opinion of states. *See* G. Abline, 'Les observations générales, une technique d'élargissement des droits de l'homme', *Revue trimestrielle des droits de l'homme* 74, 2008, pp. 449–79.

67 Toebes, *The Right to Health as a Human Right in International Law*, p. 173.

68 'Every human being is entitled to the enjoyment of the highest attainable standard of health conducing to living a life in dignity.' *General Comment No. 14*, at ¶ 39.

69 *General Comment No. 14*, p. 4.

The question of whether or not elements of public health or the right to health belong to customary law remains open. On the one hand, some authors have interpreted the right to life, which has achieved customary law status,[70] as embracing the right to health.[71] If such an extensive interpretation were adopted, the elements of the right to health which overlap with the elements of the right to life would be part of customary law. Therefore, a narrow core of the right to health would have taken on the status of customary law.[72] A further question is whether some norms relating to public health belong to *jus cogens*.[73] *Jus cogens* refers to intransgressible or peremptory norms of general international law from which no derogation is possible.[74] Peremptory norms 'do not exist to satisfy the needs of the individual states but the higher interest of the whole international community'.[75] The problem of identifying these norms has always been a vivid one in the international legal literature, and the Vienna Convention has by no means ended the scholarly debate.[76] There is no consensus on which norms are part of *jus cogens*, nor on how a norm reaches that status.[77] Rather, the concept of *jus cogens* arises out of case law and can evolve through time.[78] This is why it is important to analyze the recent *opinio juris*

---

70 C. Tomuschat, *Human Rights: Between Idealism and Realism*, Oxford: Oxford University Press, 2003, p. 35.

71 *General Comment No. 6*, Right to Life, adopted 30 April 1982.

72 P. Alston, 'Ships Passing in the Night: The Current State of the Human Rights and Development Debate Seen Through the Lens of the Millennium Development Goals', *Human Rights Quarterly* 27, 2005, p. 773.

73 There is considerable literature on *jus cogens* in international law. See, *inter alia*, A. Verdross, 'Forbidden Treaties in International Law', *AJIL* 31, 1937, pp. 571–7; H. Rolin, 'Vers un ordre public rèellement international', in *Hommage d'une génération de juristes au Président Basdevant*, Paris: Pedone, 1960, pp. 441–62; G. Schwarzenberger, 'International *Jus Cogens?*', *Tex L Rev* 43, 1964–1965, pp. 455–78; G. Schwarzenberger, 'The Problem of International Public Policy', *Current Legal Problems* 18, 1965, pp. 191–214; A. Verdross, 'Jus Dispositivum and Jus Cogens in International Law', *AJIL* 60, 1966, pp. 55–63; N. Ronzitti, 'Trattati contrari a norme imperative del diritto internazionale', in *Studi in onore di Giuseppe Sperduti*, Milan: Giuffrè, 1984, pp. 209–272; M.R. Saulle, 'Jus Cogens and Human Rights' in *Le droit international à l'heure de sa codification*, Milan: Giuffrè, 1987, pp. 385–96; M.W. Janis, 'The Nature of Jus Cogens', *Connecticut JIL* 3, 1987–1988, pp. 359–63; A. Orakhelashvili, *Peremptory Norms in International Law*, Oxford: Oxford University Press, 2006; A. Bianchi, 'Human Rights and the Magic of Jus Cogens', *EJIL* 19, 2008, pp. 491–508.

74 See Vienna Convention on the Law of Treaties, Article 64. Vienna Convention on the Law of Treaties (VCLT), done at Vienna on 23 May 1969, entered into force on 27 January 1980, UNTS vol 1155 p 331.

75 Verdross, 'Jus Dispositivum and Jus Cogens', p. 58.

76 J. Sztucki, *Jus Cogens and the Vienna Convention on the Law of Treaties*, Vienna/New York: Springer, 1974, p. 4.

77 It is generally accepted that peremptory norms include, *inter alia*, the prohibition of genocide, maritime piracy, apartheid, slavery and torture. I. Brownlie, *Principles of Public International Law*, 5th edn, Oxford: Oxford University Press, 1998, p. 517.

78 This dynamism is acknowledged by the Vienna Convention on the Law of Treaties which admits that new peremptory norms may emerge, causing the voidness or termination of any

and state practice in order to verify whether some elements of the right to health have achieved peremptory character.[79] Indeed, an argument can be made that as long as public health norms embody elementary considerations of humanity, they need to be respected.[80]

Certain national courts and regional bodies have adopted an extensive interpretation of some components of the right to health, acknowledging their non-derogable character.[81] For instance, injurious biological experiments, particularly when committed on a wide scale 'can be considered to be prohibited in peremptory terms', in light of 'elementary considerations of humanity'.[82] This line of jurisprudential reasoning traces its roots to the Nuremberg trials, and has developed through the past decades.[83] In a notable Declaration, Judge Bedjaoui affirmed that 'most of the principles of humanitarian law and, in any event, the [. . .] principl[e] [. . .] which prohibits the use of arms causing unnecessary suffering form[s] part of *jus cogens*'.[84]

Critics have argued that this line of argument goes too far, as it mixes up different human rights, suppressing any meaningful distinction between the right to health and the right to life and making the right to life a catch-all clause.[85] However, the interdependence and permeability of human rights is not a new concept.[86] Putting emphasis on rights as separate categories is not only conceptually wrong, but also risks undermining the protection of the essential minimum of each right. While authors may disagree on the essence or archetypical understanding of the right, it cannot be denied that every norm aims to fulfil certain objectives. Therefore, if the objectives or nuclei of the right to health and the right to life partially overlap, the moral and legal persuasiveness of the right to life may contribute to the protection of the right to health. In the context of this book, such a categorization is of fundamental

---

treaty which is in conflict with that norm (Article 64) and that newly arisen peremptory norms can modify previous norms having the same character (Article 53).

79 The analysis will be done with regard to the specific elements of public health which are scrutinized in Chapters 4, 5, and 6.

80 See the dissenting opinion of Judge Weeramantry, ICJ Advisory Opinion on the *Legality of the Threat or Use of Nuclear Weapons* of 8 July 1996.

81 For an overview of this jurisprudential trend, see K. Young, 'The Minimum Core of Economic and Social Rights: A Concept in Search of Content', *Yale JIL* 33, 2008, p. 129.

82 L. Hannikainen, *Peremptory Norms (Jus Cogens) in International Law*, Helsinki: Lakimiesliiton Kustannus, 1988, pp. 509–13.

83 See J. Cavallaro and E. Schaffer, 'Less As More: Rethinking Supranational Litigation of Economic and Social Rights in the Americas', *Hastings L J* 56, 2004, p. 217.

84 See the Declaration of Judge Bedjaoui, ICJ Advisory Opinion on the *Legality of the Threat or Use of Nuclear Weapons* of 8 July 1996, ICJ Reports 1996, 226, ¶ 21.

85 See T. Melish, 'Rethinking the "Less as More" Thesis: Supranational Litigation of the Economic, Social and Cultural Rights in the Americas', *NYU JIL & Policy* 39, 2006, p. 326.

86 C. Scott, 'The Interdependence and Permeability of Human Rights Norms: Towards a Partial Fusion of the International Covenants on Human Rights', *Osgoode Hall L J* 46, 1989, p. 771.

importance, because in no case may an investment law obligation be allowed to conflict with a *jus cogens* norm.[87] Although it is not possible to adopt a definitive position on the issue as the debate has not yet been settled, it is worth exploring the scope and extent of the right to health, because any discourse on the character of such right presupposes and touches upon the scope and content of the same.

The scope and the content of state obligations

Although this book focuses on the interplay between public health policies and investor rights in investor-state arbitration, and thus leaves the possible interaction between the human right to health and investor rights before other fora to further studies, in order to clarify the content of state obligations concerning health, it may be useful to scrutinize the analytical framework elaborated by human rights scholars in relation to economic, social and cultural rights. Human rights scholars have elaborated a tripartite scheme to illustrate the content of economic, social and cultural rights, making a distinction between obligations to respect, obligations to protect and obligations to fulfil. As one author clarifies, 'whereas obligations to respect are in essence negative obligations to refrain from action, obligations to protect and fulfil are positive obligations to protect individuals from certain acts by third parties, or to provide or facilitate a certain service.'[88] Therefore, the trilogy allows interpreters to overcome the traditional conceptualization of the right to health as a positive right that requires state intervention to be realized. While some aspects of the right to health require positive actions, such as vaccinations, others require a more nuanced approach. For instance, the right to health includes the right to be free from non-consensual medical experimentation.[89]

Specifically, the obligation to *respect* the right to health requires the state to refrain from actions, policies or laws that contravene the right. For instance, the *General Comment No 14* directs states to refrain from unlawfully polluting air, water and soil.[90] The obligation to *protect* requires the state to adopt legislation or to take other measures to ensure that third parties do not violate the right to health. For instance, the *General Comment No 19* directs states to ensure equal access to health care and health-related services provided by third parties.[91] The obligation to *fulfil* requires states to give recognition to the right to health in the legal system and to adopt health policies for realizing the right to health. For instance, states are required to adopt measures against

87 VCLT, Article 53.
88 Toebes, *The Right to Health as a Human Right in International Law*, p. 179.
89 *General Comment No 14*, ¶ 8.
90 *General Comment No 14*, ¶ 34.
91 Committee on Economic, Social and Cultural Rights, *General Comment No 19, The Right to Social Security*, 4 February 2008, E/C.12/GC/19, ¶¶ 13–14.

environmental health hazards and to formulate and implement policies aimed at reducing and eliminating pollution of air, soil and water.

In addition, scholars and UN bodies have delineated a core content in the right to health which would consist of certain elements that states must guarantee under any circumstance, irrespective of their available resources.[92] Although the core content cannot be determined in the abstract, the *General Comment No 14* sets out key elements such as essential primary health care, minimum essential and nutritious food, sanitation, safe and potable water and essential medicines.[93] Another core obligation would be the adoption and implementation of a national public health strategy and plan of action to address the health concerns of the whole population.[94] The concept of minimum core contributes to make the right to health less theoretical and more concrete, establishing a 'floor below which health conditions and services should not be permitted to fall'.[95]

With regard to the legal nature of such minimum core, the Committee has asserted that 'the minimum core gives rise to national responsibilities for all states'.[96] An argument may be made that the objective character and the 'cogency' of the minimum core would make it part of *jus cogens*. Again, authors are divided on the issue, and even the relevant jurisprudence is not conclusive.[97] The core elements of the right to health will probably be further delineated by the adjudication of complaints against states under the Covenant.[98] Although some authors deem that a new international complaints mechanism does not necessarily help to bridge the gap between human rights commitments and concrete action,[99] others consider that the adoption of the Protocol

---

92 See *General Comment No. 14*, ¶ 47: 'A State Party cannot under any circumstance whatsoever, justify its non compliance with . . . core obligations . . . which are . . . non derogable'.

93 See *General Comment No 14*, ¶ 43.

94 Ibidem.

95 Chapman, 'Core Obligations Related to the Right to Health', at ¶ 5.3.

96 Committee on Economic, Social and Cultural Rights, Substantive Issues Arising in the Implementation of the International Covenant on Economic, Social and Cultural Rights: Poverty and the International Covenant on Economic, Social and Cultural Rights, ¶ 16, UN. Doc. No. E/C.12/2001/10, May 2001.

97 For a discussion of the different conceptualizations of the minimum core, see Young, 'The Minimum Core of Economic and Social Rights', p. 113.

98 On 10 December 2008, the UN General Assembly unanimously adopted the Optional Protocol to the ICESCR. According to the Optional Protocol, individuals will be allowed to submit communications to the Committee after exhaustion of local remedies. The Committee will then bring the communication to the attention of the state party concerned, which will submit written statements within six months to clarify the matter or the measures, if any, that may have been provided. If the attempt to settle the dispute did not succeed, the procedure would require the Committee to examine the communication and to transmit its views and recommendations to the state. In parallel, the Optional Protocol provides for inter-state communications and enquiry procedures where states expressly consent to them.

99 See, for instance, M. Dennis and D. Stewart, 'Justiciability of Economic, Social and Cultural Rights: Should There Be an International Complaints Mechanism to Adjudicate the Rights to Food, Water, Housing and Health?', *AJIL* 98, 2004, p. 515.

represents 'a milestone in the history of human rights'.[100] Admittedly, it gives 'an important impetus for renewed and focused attention to economic, social and cultural rights',[101] contributing to their re-conceptualization from mere good faith obligations to justiciable rights. A verifiable assessment based on rigorous analysis will be needed at a later stage of implementation.

The linkage between public health and development

The achievement of economic growth and social welfare is a general precondition to the achievement of the highest attainable standard of health. In turn, health is fundamental to poverty reduction, human development and economic growth.[102] Studies have shown that illness can be both a cause and consequence of poverty as poor people are more susceptible to illness.[103] As the Declaration of Alma Ata[104] remarkably stated more than thirty years ago: 'Economic and social development [. . .] is of basic importance to the fullest attainment of health for all and to the reduction of the gap between the health status of the developing and developed countries. The promotion and protection of the health of the people is essential to sustained economic and social development and contributes to a better quality of life and to world peace.'[105]

The adoption of the UN Millennium Declaration[106] has brought new attention to the complex relationship between health and development, listing among the Millennium Development Goals (MDGs) elements of public health. Health is at the heart of the MDGs, a set of specific targets and commitments including development, poverty eradication and respect for all internationally recognized human rights.[107] Indeed, three of the eight MDGs relate to health, namely reducing child mortality, improving maternal health

---

100 See Statement by Ms L. Arbour, High Commissioner for Human Rights to the Open-ended Working Group on an Optional Protocol to the International Covenant on Economic, Social and Cultural Rights, 31 March 2008 available at http://www.unhchr.ch/huricane/huricane.nsf/view01/56935B5FB6A5B376C12574250039EAE0?opendocument.

101 Ibidem.

102 On the interdependence between development and health, see for instance M. Belanger, 'Droit international de la santé et developpement', in A. Pellet and J.-M. Sorel (eds), *Le droit international du developpement social et culturel*, Paris: L'Hermès, 1997, p. 118.

103 See, for instance, GA Res. 58/173 adopted on 10 March 2004 (UN Doc A/RES/58/173) p 2 ff.

104 The Declaration of Alma Ata was adopted by the International Conference on Primary Health Care, Alma Ata, presently Kazakhstan, on 12 September 1978, available at http://www.who.int/hpr/NPH/docs/declaration_almaata.pdf.

105 Declaration of Alma Ata, at point III.

106 United Nations Millennium Declaration, GA Resolution A/RES/55/2, 18 September 2000.

107 For a listing of the goals, see: http://www.un.org/millenniumgoals. The World Health Organization is promoting and monitoring the implementation of the MDGs. See WHO, *Health and the Millennium Development Goals*, Geneva: WHO, 2005.

and combating the spread of communicable diseases.[108] Also, the contribution of health to the achievement of all the other goals has been acknowledged, particularly in relation to those goals concerning education, the eradication of extreme poverty and hunger, and environmental sustainability. Therefore, health is central to global agenda promoting development and needs to be prioritized within overall development and economic policies. Because the MDGs are concrete, they are seen to provide quantifiable benchmarks against which to judge success.[109]

The interplay between economic development and public health may also be seen through the lens of *sustainable development*.[110] Literally, *sustainable* means that it 'meets the needs of the present generation without compromising the ability of future generations to meet their own needs'.[111] According to a restrictive interpretation, sustainable development would be an environmental law concept requiring the optimal use of the world's resources to protect and preserve the environment.[112] However, in recent times, the principle of sustainable development, restated not only in multilateral environmental agreements but also in international economic law instruments,[113] has been broadened to include a social dimension. Accordingly, a sustainable approach to development would be one which takes into account economic, social and environmental factors, and does not exhaust finite resources. The emphasis is put on human needs rather than wants, and on inter- and intra-generational equity. For instance, in the *Shrimp Turtle* case, the WTO Appellate Body acknowledged that '[the concept of sustainable development] has been generally accepted as integrating economic and social development and environmental protection'.[114]

Although the concept of sustainable development has gradually been codified in international law instruments, there is no consensus on its legal status. Authors highlight that 'normative uncertainty coupled with the absence of justiciable standards for review, strongly suggest that there is as yet

---

108 MDGs No. 4, 5 and 6.
109 The MDGs provide quantifiable targets to be reached within a certain time frame – by 2015.
110 See F. Francioni, 'Sviluppo sostenibile e principi di diritto internazionale dell'ambiente', in P. Fois (ed), *Il Principio dello sviluppo sostenibile nel diritto internazionale ed europeo dell'ambiente*, Napoli: Editoriale Scientifica, 2007, pp. 41–62.
111 Report of the World Commission on Environment and Development, *Our Common Future (Brundtland Report)* 4 August 1987, UN GA Res A/42/427 (1987).
112 See, *inter alia*, 1992 *Rio Declaration on Environment and Development*, Principle 4, Report of the United Nations Conference on Environment and Development, UN Doc A/CONF. 151/6/Rev.1; *Agenda 21*, Report of the UNCED, I (1992) UN Doc. A/CONF.151/26/Rev. 1, (1992) 31 ILM 874, ¶ 39.1; *Stockholm Declaration on the Human Environment*, Principle 13 UN Doc A/C 48/14 (1972) 11 ILM 1461 (1972).
113 See for instance, the preamble to the Agreement Establishing the World Trade Organization, 15 April 1994, 33 ILM (1994).
114 WTO Panel Report, *United States-Import Prohibition of Certain Shrimp and Shrimp Products* (20 September 1999), WT/DS58/R, ¶ 129.

no international legal obligation that development must be sustainable [. . .]'.[115] Instead, sustainable development would be an emerging soft law concept,[116] whose elements may gradually achieve binding character and inspire international courts and tribunals.[117]

While the concept of sustainable development is inherently vague, it proposes a *method*[118] or integrated approach to the different objectives of development, public health and environmental protection. In this sense, it helps bridging the gap between different sets of international law norms. Judge Weeramantry noted that environmental objectives and developmental ones may collide, and stated that 'the law necessarily contains within itself the principle of reconciliation. That principle is the principle of sustainable development'.[119] Sustainable development thus constitutes a useful 'element of the process of judicial reasoning'[120] which may help adjudicators reconcile the different interests and values reflected in legal norms. Furthermore, it may contribute to the coherence of the legal system and enhance its ultimate legitimacy entailing a holistic approach to the settlement of disputes.[121]

The conceptualization of sustainable development as the principle of reconciliation between economic development and cultural, environmental and social concerns, including public health, is confirmed by the text of recent investment treaties. Some investment treaties recognize not only the importance of a favourable investment climate, but also the importance of other policy goals, such as environmental protection, health promotion and sustainable development. In this sense, the NAFTA preamble mentions the goal of sustainable development.[122] Similarly, the recent Canadian Model BIT expressly lists sustainable development among the objectives of the treaty.[123] Sustainable development is also mentioned by some recent Economic

---

115 A. Boyle and D. Freestone, 'Introduction', in A. Boyle and D. Freestone (eds), *International Law and Sustainable Development – Past Achievements and Future Challenges*, Oxford: Oxford University Press, 1999, p. 16.

116 Soft law norms are non binding and include guidelines, resolutions, declarations and recommendations that are made by the parties to an international agreement in the course of its implementation. Although soft law is not binding it may be persuasive in the way that it influences the conduct of states. See Shelton, 'Law, Non-Law and the Problem of "Soft Law"', pp. 4–10.

117 P. Sands, 'International Law in the Field of Sustainable Development', *BYIL* 65, 1994, p. 303.

118 Francioni, 'Sviluppo sostenibile', p. 43.

119 ICJ *Gabcikovo-Nagymaros Dam*, Judgment 25 September 1997, ICJ Reports 1997. Judge Weeramantry Separate Opinion.

120 V. Lowe, 'Sustainable Development and Unsustainable Arguments', in A. Boyle and D. Freestone (eds), *International Law and Sustainable Development: Past Achievements and Future Challenges*, Oxford: Oxford University Press, 1999, p. 31.

121 Ibidem p. 32.

122 North American Free Trade Agreement, adopted 17 December 1992 and entered into force 1 January 1994, (1993) 32 ILM 289.

123 2004 Canadian Model BIT.

Partnership Agreements concluded by the EC.[124] The codification of the principle in investment treaties requires the consideration of such principle in the context of investment treaty disputes.

Conclusions

This chapter has analyzed the conceptual and legal framework which governs health at the international level. Health has both an individual and collective dimension. While health has been described as having an individual character in the sense that it constitutes an individual right and aspiration, public health represents the other side of the same coin, as it expresses peoples' aspirations as reflected by the international community. Both aspects of the health discourse have been increasingly codified in international law.

On the one hand, it is generally acknowledged that states have the right/ duty to protect public health.[125] From a constitutional law perspective, such a competence is intrinsic in the social pact between the state and its citizens. From an international law perspective, the population of a state represents one of the founding elements of statehood. While most public health laws and regulation have deep historical roots and strong public support, much controversy involves the legitimate scope, or 'reach', of public health law. On the other hand, adopting a human rights framework allows policy makers to better define and articulate the content of health policies. Representing an essential condition for the enjoyment of other human rights, the right to health is expressly recognized in a series of international law instruments.[126] Some authors even argue that the right to health already belongs to customary international law.[127] If this were the case, even states who are parties but have not ratified the ICESCR would have to respect the number of its provisions which have achieved customary law status.

A peculiar articulation of the claim that the right to health is objectively binding upon states, is the argument that the *minimum core* of the right to health would then have achieved the character of *jus cogens*. *Jus cogens* guards the most fundamental and highly-valued interests of the international community but is an elusive concept. Notwithstanding some recent jurisprudential trends and opinions which point to the possibility that some elements of public health hold *jus cogens* status, there is no consensus on this

---

124 *See* Article 3.1 of the Economic Partnership Agreement Between the CARIFORUM States, of the One Part, and the European Community and Its Member States of the other Part, available at http://ec.europa.eu/trade/issues/bilateral/regions/acp/pr220208_en.htm.

125 *General Comment No. 14*, ¶ 1.

126 See e.g. E.D. Kinney, 'The International Human Right to Health: What Does this Mean for Our Nation and the World?', *Indiana Law Review* 34, 2001, p. 1457.

127 See F. Abbott, 'WTO TRIPS Agreement and Its Implications for Access to Medicines in Developing Countries', Study Paper for the British Commission on Intellectual Property Rights, Geneva, 2002, pp. 56–7.

point. Some courts and international human rights bodies have adopted an extensive interpretation of some components of the right to health, acknowledging their non-derogable character. For instance, injurious biological experiments, particularly when committed on a wide scale, have been considered to be prohibited in peremptory terms.[128] Other courts have adopted a more conservative approach on the grounds that mixing up different human rights would suppress any meaningful distinction between the right to health and the right to life.[129] However, putting emphasis on rights as separate categories is not only conceptually wrong, but it also risks undermining the protection of the essential minimum content of each right. It cannot be denied that every norm aims at fulfilling certain goals and objectives. Therefore, as previously stated, if the objectives or nuclei of the right to health and the right to life partially overlap, the moral and legal persuasiveness of the right to life may contribute to the protection of the right to health. Such a categorization is of fundamental importance, because in no case may an investment law obligation be allowed to conflict with a *jus cogens* norm.[130]

Even if such an extensive interpretation of the right to health was not adopted, the gradual and progressive nature of the right to health should not necessarily lead interpreters and adjudicators to deem such right to be a mere moral obligation. If the state fails to adopt appropriate policies, it may be found internationally responsible under the ICESCR.[131] The adoption of the Optional Protocol signals an international consensus on the binding nature of the obligations provided by the ICESCR. The fact that the content of the right to health may evolve through time and may contain non-derogable elements indicates that interpreters and adjudicators need to take these developments into account when balancing the different interests concerned.

Finally, this chapter has highlighted the linkage between development goals and public health and stressed the need to address health and development concerns in an integrated manner. While the linkage between development and public health may endorse positive synergies, their relationship remains fundamentally ambiguous, as in certain circumstances economic activities may endanger public health. The challenge is thus to find the optimal equilibrium between development and public health. In this context, the concept of sustainable development might play the important role of the 'interstitial norm', reconciling conflicts between norms of international law and filling in the gaps in the law.[132]

---

128 See, *inter alia*, *Rabi Abdullahi v. Pfizer, Inc.* (2nd Cir. 30 Jan. 2009).
129 See Melish, 'Rethinking the "Less as More" Thesis', p. 326.
130 VCLT, Article 53.
131 *See* H.M. Haugen, 'Patents Rights and Human Rights: Exploring their Relationship', *JWIP* 10, 2007, pp. 97–124.
132 See V. Lowe, 'The Politics of Law Making: Are the Method and Character of Norm Creation Changing?', in M. Byers (ed), *The Role of Law in International Politics: Essays in International Relations and International Law*, Oxford: Oxford University Press, 2000, pp. 214–15.

3 The interplay between public health and foreign direct investments

Introduction

This chapter scrutinizes the interplay between public health and foreign direct investment (FDI) at a theoretical level, looking at the impact that investment rules may have upon public health policies. As FDI is deemed to generally promote economic development, the linkage between foreign investment and public health may endorse positive outcomes. An increased prosperity and economic growth constitute essential elements in furthering broader societal interests.

However, this is not necessarily the case. Not only do investment treaties reshape state sovereignty, having an impact on the foreign policy of the host state, but they also influence and determine aspects of its internal judicial and legislative functions. Assuming that states were to adopt measures allegedly aimed at protecting public health, issues could arise with regard to the violation of the investment treaties to which the state is a party. The foreign investor whose assets are negatively affected by such a regulatory measure might recur to investment treaty arbitration to obtain restitution or compensation. Is any state measure justified by the fact that it allegedly aims to protect public health? What are the limits, if any, of public health regulations? Would a state be free to establish a *health dictatorship*? In order to answer these questions, some preliminary considerations may be made.

From a legal perspective, the notion of health in public international law includes both the public interest and individual entitlements. In general terms, states are free to set a high level of health protection as long as they respect *jus cogens* and international law obligations such as those related to human rights. States may pursue public policy objectives in a number of complementary approaches through the formulation of general health policies and/or the adoption of specific legal measures. However, the mere public health goal of a regulatory measure does not exempt it from scrutiny. The jurisprudence of international courts and tribunals is replete with cases of disguised discrimination, whereby foreign suppliers are indirectly discriminated against by alleged environmental and/or public health regulations.[1]

A hypothetical example may clarify the issues at stake. If the United Kingdom put a tax on 'fat' products including chocolate in order to tackle increasing levels of obesity and related illnesses,[2] would such a decision be compatible with the state obligations under investment treaties? What if such a tax mainly affected Swiss producers of chocolate and the affected companies recurred to investor-state arbitration? As Gostin puts it, 'public health gains credibility from its adherence to science, and . . . if [it] conceives of itself too expansively, it will be accused of overreaching and invading a sphere reserved for politics, not science'.[3]

While states are free to establish the level of health protection they deem appropriate, they are nonetheless bound to respect relevant international law obligations. If conflicts arise between a foreign investor and the host state, several *fora* are available to adjudicate such conflicts: national courts, regional courts, human rights bodies, the International Court of Justice (ICJ) and arbitral tribunals. This book explores and critically assesses these conflicts of values within investment treaty arbitration. The choice to limit the scope of analysis to investor-state arbitration is due to the peculiar characteristics of such mechanism and its extraordinary success in the past decades. The selection of this forum does not imply any *a priori* judgment on the preferability of a dispute settlement mechanism vis-à-vis another. Rather, such selection is due to the rich case law and the fact that the linkage between public health and investor rights is relatively unexplored from this particular perspective, notwithstanding the growing case law.

This chapter will proceed as follows. First, it will explore how international investment law impacts state sovereignty. Second, it will scrutinize the regulatory autonomy of the state vis-à-vis its obligations under international investment law; questions of compatibility of investment treaty provisions

---

1 See, for instance, the *Danish Bottles* case, ECJ, *Commission (Supported by the United Kingdom) v. Kingdom of Denmark*, judgment of 20 September 1988. Denmark introduced a system under which all containers for beer and soft drinks should be re-usable and approved by an administrative organ. Non-approved containers could be used for quantities not exceeding 3,000 hectolitres a year per producer. Denmark argued that such a regulation was justified by environmental concerns. However, the ECJ deemed the regulation to be disproportionate to the pursued objective. In the same way, in another case, the ECJ found that the British ban on the importation of pasteurized milk and cream on the grounds of health protection was disproportionate; a system of certificates and control would have produced the same results. *Commission v. United Kingdom*, ECR [1988].

2 While the former Prime Minister Tony Blair ultimately dismissed the plan, as too paternalistic (see 'Fat Taxes Could Save Thousands', *BBC News*, 11 July 2007) the debate is still ongoing. See 'UK Could Introduce "Fat Tax", Says David Cameron', *Guardian*, 4 October 2011.

3 L.O. Gostin, *Public Health Law: Power, Duty, Restraint*, Berkeley: University of California Press, 2000, p. 41. But see D.S. Goldberg, 'Against the Very Idea of the Politicization of Public Health Policy', *American J of Public Health* 102, 2012, pp. 44–9.

with other non-investment treaty obligations of the host state will be addressed as well. Third, the available dispute settlement mechanisms will be scrutinized. Fourth, this chapter briefly examines the interplay between public law and investment treaty arbitration, summarizing and anticipating key themes that will be more specifically dealt with in the context of Chapters 4, 5 and 6. Finally, the conceptualization of international investment law as a form of global administrative law is critically assessed.

Globalization, state sovereignty and neo-medievalism in international law

Globalization has modified how power is distributed among states and the degree to which states rule their communities, changing both the horizontal and the vertical dimension of sovereignty.[4] While according to the state-centred paradigm reflecting the Westphalian order, states were seen as the prime creators and the main subjects of international law, the post-Westphalian order has been characterized by the paradigm shift from government to global governance.[5] There has been a 'transition of the arena in which the political process is carried out, and a shift in the role of actors'.[6] Regulation of matters that once constituted an exclusive realm of national law, has now become the increasing concern of international law.[7] As stated by the Permanent Court of International Justice (PCIJ), 'The question of whether a certain matter is or is not within the jurisdiction of a state is an essentially relative question; it depends upon the developments of international relations.'[8] While some authors have thus argued that the concept of sovereignty has lost its relevance in the current international system,[9] others have adopted a more nuanced approach.[10] Concretely, in the decentralized system of international law, different normative orders overlap, supplement and complete each other. Thus, several authorities have overlapping and competing competencies.

This complex regime of legal pluralism has been compared to the medieval order where 'each ruler ha[d] to share authority and multiple

---

4 I. Wallerstein, 'States? Sovereignty?', in D.A. Smith, D.J. Solinger, and S.C. Topik (eds), *States and Sovereignty in the Global Economy*, London: Routledge, 1999, p. 23.

5 R. Pierik, 'Globalization and Global Governance: A Conceptual Analysis', in W. Heere (ed.), *From Government to Governance*, The Hague: TMC Asser Press, 2004, p. 458.

6 Ibidem, p. 460.

7 O. Schachter, 'The Decline of the Nation-State and Its Implications for International Law', *Columbia Journal of Transnational Law* 36, 1998, p. 7; A. and A.H. Chayes, *The New Sovereignty*, Cambridge, MA: Harvard University Press, 1995, p. 1.

8 *Nationality Decrees Issued in Tunis and Morocco* (1923) PCIJ Adv Op (Series B) No 4, 27.

9 L. Henkin, *International Law: Politics and Values*, Dordrecht: Martinus Nijhoff Publishers, 1995, p. 10.

10 R. Jennings, 'Sovereignty and International Law', in G. Kreijen *et al.* (eds), *State, Sovereignty and International Governance*, Oxford: Oxford University Press, 2002, p. 35.

loyalty'.[11] Such neo-medieval analogy is a 'heuristic device', to properly describe 'a world which is neither anarchic nor organised around a centre, but is ruled by interdependent forms of universalism'.[12] Stretching the suggestive metaphor a bit further, it may be held that public health law and economic globalization are two contemporary forms of universalism that coexist in international relations. In conclusion, modern sovereignty seems to be a residual concept. As Reisman highlights 'Sovereignty in its modern sense is simply the demand of each territorial community [. . .] to be permitted to govern itself without interference by the entire [international] community'.[13]

The ratification of treaties necessarily involves the surrender of a part of sovereignty, as states limit their authority in exchange for certain benefits.[14] In this regard, however, investment treaties are more intrusive than trade agreements as foreign investment takes place within the borders of a state. As one author highlights, 'although States are the loci of power and authority in classic international law, international investment law transfers some of this power and authority to other decision-makers, including investors and arbitral tribunals [. . .]'.[15] Authors have studied this transfer of power from three distinct but related perspectives.

First, authors have highlighted that investment treaties may impose asymmetric burdens.[16] When an industrialized country and a developing one sign a BIT, 'although both states promise to provide certain protections for investors, in practice it is the developing country that is entering into a significant commitment, because much more investment flows from north to south than from south to north'.[17] Furthermore, BITs currently do not provide

---

11 H. Bull, *The Anarchical Society: A Study of Order in World Politics*, London: Macmillan, 1977, p. 254.
12 J. Friedrichs, 'The Neomedieval Renaissance: Global Governance and International Law in the New Middle Ages', in I. Dekker (ed.), *Governance and International Legal Theory*, Utrecht: Martinus Nijhoff, 2004, p. 19; J. Friedrichs, 'The Meaning of New Medievalism', *European Journal of International Relations* 7, 2001, pp. 475–502; J. Friedrichs, 'What's New About the New Middle Ages', *Leiden JIL* 16, 2003, pp. 649–53.
13 W.M. Reisman, 'Why Regime Change is (Almost Always) a Bad Idea', *AJIL* 98, 2004, p. 516.
14 See generally W. Shan, P. Simons and D. Singh (eds), *Redefining Sovereignty in International Economic Law*, Oxford: Hart Publishing, 2008.
15 T.-H. Cheng, 'Power, Authority and International Investment Law', *American University L Rev* 20, 2004–2005, p. 467.
16 According to Guzman, developing countries sign BITs because they 'face a prisoner's dilemma in which it is optimal for them, as a group, to reject the Hull Rule, but in which each individual LDC is better off "defecting" from the group by signing a BIT that gives it an advantage over other LDCs in the competition to attract foreign investment'. See A. Guzman, 'Explaining the Popularity of Bilateral Investment Treaties: Why LDCs Sign Treaties that Hurt Them', *Vanderbilt Journal of Transnational Law* 38, 1997, p. 667.
17 See A. Guzman, *How International Law Works*, Oxford: Oxford University Press, 2008, p. 159.

more beneficial standards for developing countries, and arbitral tribunals 'generally do not consider the context of a country's individual capabilities or needs in judging the country's compliance with investment obligations'.[18] Developing countries sign investment treaties to attract foreign investment. However, one may wonder whether some form of differential treatment should be introduced in the text of BITs, or whether arbitrators should take context into account when adjudicating these disputes.

Second, as the signature of investment agreements is the faculty of the executive power of the contracting states, the question arises as to whether national constituencies have been duly taken into account.[19] The procedure may lack parliamentarian control and long-term consequences and restrictions on policy spaces may not be adequately scrutinized by policy makers.[20] In many instances, the treaties appear to have been drafted with insufficient forethought by the executive branch, and without useful safeguards, exceptions and limitations.[21]

Third, in analyzing the content of investment treaties, what appears to be perhaps their most relevant feature is that, on the one hand, countries seek to make the regulatory framework for FDI more transparent, stable, and predictable and thus, more attractive to foreign investors. On the other, such treaties may limit the policy space or the autonomy of policy makers in drafting and adopting national laws since they have gradually become regulating instruments. As one author puts it, 'While [investment] treaties may be a useful bulwark against egregious interference or expropriation of foreign-owned property, they may condition more subtle measures taken by governments [. . .] in the realm of regulation, taxation, legislation and judicial decision making'.[22] In addition, investment treaties provide foreign investors with direct access to the investor-state dispute settlement mechanism, which constitutes an alternative to the national courts of the host state. With regard to investment disputes, the national courts of the host states have only concurrent jurisdiction over disputes arising in a given territory.[23]

---

18 E.A. Alexander, 'Taking Account of Reality: Adopting Contextual Standards for Developing Countries in International Investment Law', *Vanderbilt JIL* 48, 2007–2008, p. 823.

19 See B. Ackerman and D. Golove, *Is NAFTA Constitutional?* Cambridge, MA: Harvard University Press, 1995).

20 This is a constitutional problem that each state addresses differently. Suffice it to say that a more accurate scrutiny would require better drafting and entail more guarantees. See J. Verhoeven, *Droit International Public*, Bruxelles: Larcier 2000, pp. 387–9.

21 Some treaties do provide for a public health exception. See below, Chapters 4–7.

22 L.E. Peterson, *The Global Governance of Foreign Direct Investment: Madly Off in All Directions*, Geneva: Friedrich Ebert Stiftung Publisher, 2005, p. 4.

23 The so-called fork-in-the-road provisions in BITs require foreign investors to choose either a domestic or an investment arbitration when a dispute arises. Such clauses are specifically intended to prevent multiple flora for one set of facts. UNCTAD, *Investor-State Disputes Arising From Investment Treaties: A Review*, New York and Geneva: UN, 2005, p. 20.

The regulatory powers of the host state

Tensions can arise between investment treaty guarantees and the need for governments to perform their regulatory functions. Under international law, the right to regulate arises out of a state's control over its own territory and represents a basic attribute of sovereignty under international law.[24] Traditionally, the sovereign powers of the state include the authority to adopt legislation, impose taxes, enforce judgments and to adopt those policies that it holds to be essential to promoting the basic needs of its citizens, such as public health. In certain cases, states own not only a right to regulate, but also a duty to do so, because of mandatory international and/or regional obligations. In these cases, regulation has the function of ensuring the safeguard of internationally or regionally recognized values.[25]

State measures – *prima facie* a lawful exercise of powers of governments – may affect foreign interests. First, the exercise of public authority by the state, such as the passage of legislation or the issuance of judicial decisions, may be tainted with protectionism. Governments may attempt to use domestic regulation to defect from their investment-related commitments or to discriminate against the foreign investor.[26] Second, even in cases in which regulation is legitimate and taintless, questions could arise with regard to the impact such measure has on the foreign property involved. In a seminal study on the matter, Rosalyn Higgins refined the question as the determination of who is to pay the economic cost of attending to the public interest involved in the measure in question. The pendulum swings between the society as a whole, represented by the state, and the foreign investor.[27] If the state never had to provide compensation to an investor who would be deprived of its property as a result of the exercise by the state of its regulatory power, the opportunity for abuse of such a rule would be evident.[28] Vice-versa, if the government always had to compensate investors deprived of their property as a result of the exercise by the state of its regulatory power, this would paralyze the regulatory activity of the state.

The problem is that there is not a clear divide between regulation that cannot be compensated and violation of investment treaty provisions that can

---

24 M. Sornarajah, 'Right to Regulate and Safeguards', in UNCTAD, *The Development Dimension of FDI: Policy and Rule Making Perspectives*, New York and Geneva: UN, 2003, p. 205.

25 In these cases, international institutions that have 'rendered the erosion of sovereignty more legible, actually serve as a means to reassert sovereignty'. K. Raustiala, 'Rethinking the Sovereignty Debate in International Economic Law', *JIEL* 6, 2003, p. 841.

26 J. Trachtman, 'FDI and the Right to Regulate: Lessons from Trade Law', in UNCTAD, *The Development Dimension of FDI*, p. 189.

27 R. Higgins, 'The Taking of Property by the State: Recent Developments in International Law', *Rec des Cours* 176, 1982, pp. 276–7.

28 C. Lévesque, 'Distinguishing Expropriation and Regulation under NAFTA Chapter 11: Making Explicit the Link to Property', in K. Kennedy (ed.), *The First Decade of NAFTA: The Future of Free Trade in North America*, New York: Transnational Publishers, 2004, p. 297.

be compensated. From the investor's perspective, however, the diminution of value of a given investment that can be compensated is crucial. Useful criteria to distinguish regulatory measures from violation of the BIT provisions include the degree of interference (the extent, gravity and duration of the deprivation), and the character of the governmental measure (i.e. the purpose and the context of the governmental measure). Principles like proportionality, non-discrimination and due process of law are seen as interpretative tools in assessing whether a regulatory measure amounts to a taking. Given the vagueness of the conceptual divide between indirect expropriation and regulation that can be compensated,[29] the jurisprudence is often unpredictable.

The dispute settlement mechanisms

If an international dispute were to arise concerning public health measures adopted by a host state, several fora would be available. National courts always represent the first available option to foreign investors.[30] As property rights are territorial in nature, they are subject to the national laws of each individual country. At the regional level, the European Court of Justice (ECJ) and other regional economic integration courts have adjudicated many cases dealing with property. Even the European Court of Human Rights (ECtHR) has adjudicated on the clash between public health measures and private property, as property is protected under Article 1 of the first Protocol of the Convention.[31]

At the international level, states can recur to alternative dispute settlement mechanisms, such as negotiation, good offices and mediation. If these mechanisms are not successful, states can bring their dispute to the ICJ. With regard to environmental health, the ICJ has dealt with several cases involving environmental issues.[32] With regard to intellectual property disputes involving public health, it is worth pointing out that despite the reference to the ICJ in key treaties,[33] the ICJ has never been used to litigate an intellectual property case. There are several hypotheses to explain why states have preferred not to use the ICJ for intellectual property-related disputes. *First*, only recently has

---

29 The literature is extensive. See e.g. A. Newcombe, 'The Boundaries of Regulatory Expropriation in International Law', *ICSID Review-FILJ* 20, 2005, pp. 1–57 and S. Ratner, 'Regulatory Takings in Institutional Context: Beyond the Fear of Fragmented International Law', *AJIL* 102, 2008, pp. 475–528.

30 See for instance the *Carl Zeiss* case, concerning the use of trademark which was brought before UK courts and raised delicate international law issues concerning the recognition of the former German Democratic Republic. *Carl Zeiss Stiftung v. Rayner and Keeler Ltd* (no. 2) [167] AC 853; 431 ILR p. 42.

31 This point will be articulated more in detail in Chapter 4, Chapter 5 and Chapter 6. See generally, L. Helfer, 'The New Innovation Frontier? Intellectual Property and the European Court of Human Rights', *Harvard ILJ* 49, 2008, pp. 1–52.

32 These cases will be scrutinized in Chapter 6.

33 Paris Convention for the Protection of Industrial Property, lastly revised at Stockholm on July 14, 1967, and as amended on September 28, 1979. 828 UNTS 305.

intellectual property emerged as a topical issue in international relations; other economic sectors used to drive the economy before the advent of the post-industrial society. *Second*, the judicial remedies of the Court seldom include restoration to the original condition (*restitutio in integrum*) and do not include specific performance.[34] *Third*, the international law instruments governing intellectual property that preceded the TRIPS Agreement only provided 'very general provisions which made a justiciable dispute unlikely'.[35] *Fourth*, in some cases the enforcement of the ICJ decisions has been problematic, as some states have refused to comply with the judgments of this court.[36] Furthermore, even if article 94(2) of the UN Charter provides that failure of any Party 'to perform the obligations incumbent upon it under a judgment rendered by the Court' entitles the other Party to have 'recourse to the Security Council', such recourse is not likely. The veto power of the permanent members could make such recourse void of any practical significance.[37] *Finally*, international economic courts and tribunals seem to offer the most effective dispute settlement mechanism in the intellectual property area. In particular, WTO panels and the Appellate Body have already settled a number of intellectual property-related claims.[38]

The existence of a pending trade dispute does not impede the foreign investor from having recourse to arbitration. Nor does the existence of a pending investment dispute impede the home state from submitting such dispute to the WTO dispute settlement mechanism.[39] Under general international law there is no rule which prevents a parallel set of proceedings.[40] The 'phenomenon of a single measure being litigated under more than one regime has already occurred'.[41] For instance, the same Mexican measure

---

34 A.Z. Hertz, 'Shaping the Trident: Intellectual Property under NAFTA, Investment Protection Agreements and at the World Trade Organization', *Can.-U.S. L.J.* 23, 1997, pp. 271–2.

35 Ibidem, p. 269.

36 Ibidem, p. 273. For example, Hertz highlights that Albania refused to pay reparations to Great Britain in the *Corfu Channel* case; Iceland refused to obey an order of the Court in the *Fisheries Jurisdiction* case; Iran rejected the Court's order and judgment that it release the American hostages in *Diplomatic and Consular staff*; and the U.S. paid no compensation for injury caused by certain military and paramilitary activities in Nicaragua.

37 Ibidem, p. 274.

38 J. Pauwelyn, 'The Dog That Barked But Didn't Bite: 15 Years of Intellectual Property Disputes at the WTO', in J. de Werra (ed.), *La Resolution des Litiges de Propriété Intellectuelle*, Bruxelles: Bruylant, 2010, pp. 1–52.

39 The ICSID Convention provides that, where the parties have consented to the ICSID Arbitration, the consent operates to exclude any other forum or remedy. ICSID Convention, Article 26. However, the home state of the foreign investor may exercise diplomatic protection if the host state fails to comply with an award. ICSID Convention, Article 27.

40 G. Verhoosel, 'The Use of Investor-State Arbitration under Bilateral Investment Treaties to Seek Relief for Breaches of WTO Law', *JIEL* 6, 2003, p. 495.

41 M. Ewing-Chow, 'Thesis, Antithesis and Synthesis: Investor Protection in BITs, WTO and FTAs', *UNSW L.J.* 30, 2007, p. 550.

concerning soft drinks with non-sugar cane sweeteners was challenged both before the WTO and arbitral tribunals as well.[42] With regard to public health measures, compulsory licences have been challenged before arbitral tribunals and before the WTO.[43]

It is important to stress that even on similar matters, investment treaty disputes and trade disputes are not *identical*. Three elements are needed in order to have identical disputes: 1) *personae* (same parties); 2) *petitum* (same object); and 3) *causa petendi* (same legal grounds).[44] In this respect, not only do investment disputes and trade disputes have different parties, but they also present different *petita* and *causa petendi*. With regard to the parties, while trade disputes are inter-state disputes, investment arbitrations typically involve a state and a private actor, and inter-state arbitrations are rare. Furthermore, with regard to the object of the dispute, while WTO cases deal with inter-state trade, investment disputes deal with foreign investment in the host state. There may be a partial overlap in the object of given disputes where the concept of investment is interpreted in a broad fashion, but the remedies are different. While the Understanding on Rules and Procedures Governing the Settlement of Disputes (hereinafter Dispute Settlement Understanding or DSU)[45] aims at prompt compliance with recommendations or rulings of the Dispute Settlement Body (DSB) – thus having a prospective character – investment treaties allow the private party to obtain compensation for past wrongs by the host state.

With regard to the *causa petendi* or legal grounds of the disputes, the legal instruments to be interpreted and applied to the disputes are different. In the case of investment disputes, usually the parties can select the applicable law; in the absence of party agreement on the applicable law, arbitral tribunals will apply the law of the state party to the dispute and other rules of international law as may be applicable.[46] In the case of trade disputes, the DSU empowers the

---

42 *Mexico – Tax Measures on Soft Drinks and Other Beverages*, Report of the Appellate Body, WTO Doc. WT/DS308/AB/R. AB-2005–1 (2006). *Archer Daniels Midland Company and Tate & Lyle Ingredients Americas, Inc. v. United Mexican States*, Award of 21 November 2007 (ICSID Case No. ARB(AF)/04/5) and *Corn Products International, Inc. v. United Mexican States* (ICSID Case No. ARB(AF)/04/1).

43 For instance the US challenged the consistency of a Brazilian law allowing compulsory licences for pharmaceuticals with the TRIPS Agreement. However, the dispute was settled at the consultation stage of the DSB and hence did not reach the panel stage. See M. Dias Varella, 'The WTO, Intellectual Property and AIDS – Case Studies from Brazil and South Africa', *JWIP* 7, 2004, pp. 523–47. For an analysis of the relevant investment arbitrations, see below, Chapter 4.

44 The 'triple identity test' was identified by Judge Anzilotti in his Separate Opinion in the *Chorzów Factory* case. PCIJ, Ser. A. No. 13, at 23–7.

45 Understanding on Rules and Procedures Governing the Settlement of Disputes Apr. 15, 1994, Marrakesh Agreements Establishing the World Trade Organization, Annex 2, 33 I.L.M. 1226 (1994).

46 ICSID Convention, Article 42.

DSB to clarify the provisions of the covered agreements.[47] The fact that the intellectual property rules included in investment treaties partially overlap with the TRIPS provisions does not change the institutional and normative differences between the sources of international law norms. Companies filing an investor-state arbitration are not entitled to obtain a finding of TRIPS non-compliance from a BIT tribunal; nonetheless, claimants have often alleged violation of relevant TRIPS provisions to claim violation of fair and equitable treatment.[48]

What advantages does investor-state arbitration bring to foreign investors? *First*, recourse to investor-state arbitration does not require the exercise of diplomatic protection of the state of origin of a given corporation. Furthermore, the investor in an investor-state arbitration will have the greatest degree of control over its case. Instead, investors choosing the WTO forum will have to rely upon their home state's willingness to bring a claim. However, diplomatic protection constitutes a prerogative and not a duty for states which may exercise it at their will. When intellectual property violations are limited in scope and discriminate against a foreign investor only, its home state will be reluctant to initiate a trade dispute because of political and *de minimis* considerations. Even if the home state espoused the investor's claim, the dispute would be subject to 'the vagaries of other considerations in the relations between the two countries concerned'.[49] In addition, investment arbitration may be a suitable choice when the host state judiciary does not seem to ensure fair trial or impartiality. In such a circumstance, the foreign investor may directly circumvent the national courts, immediately referring the dispute to arbitration. Otherwise, the investor-state dispute settlement mechanism may constitute a last resort, when the case has already been discussed at the national level and the foreign investor is unsatisfied with the result because of discrimination or other reasons.

Second, foreign investors are not required to exhaust local remedies prior to pursuing an investor-state arbitration. This is in stark counterpoint to international human rights treaties, which generally oblige the claimants to resort to local courts in the first instance. Even where contracts between a company and a state expressly limit recourse to local diverse settlement options, claimants can directly bypass national jurisdictions and bring investment claims to arbitral tribunals in situations where the investor's home state and the host state have entered into a BIT.

Third, the remedies are different. While the DSU aims at prompt compliance with recommendations or rulings of the DSB[50] – thus having a prospective

---

47 DSU, Articles 3.2 and 19.2.
48 See *PMI v. Uruguay*, see below Chapter 5.
49 C. Gibson, 'A Look at the Compulsory License in Investment Arbitration: The Case of Indirect Expropriation', *TDM* 6, 2009, p. 41.
50 The primary remedy for a violation of WTO obligations is the recommendation to bring the inconsistent measure into conformity (DSU, Article 19). Compensation and the suspension of concessions or other obligations are temporary measures available in the event that the recommendations and rulings are not implemented within a reasonable period of

character – investment treaties allow the private party to obtain compensation for past wrongs inflicted by the host state.

Finally, the dispute settlement chapters of free trade agreements include *non-violation complaints* even with regard to intellectual property rights. Any measure that does not appear to directly violate treaty provisions, but is nevertheless disadvantageous to the investor's intellectual property, can fall within the category of non-violation complaints.[51] While the aim of the provision is to maintain the balance of benefits achieved during negotiations and is advantageous to foreign investors, the inclusion of *non-violation complaints* in the dispute settlement chapter of investment treaties and their applicability to intellectual property is a matter of concern.

In the parallel WTO system, extension of this clause to the intellectual property regulation was extremely controversial, during the TRIPS negotiations.[52] While Article 64.2 of the TRIPS Agreement provides for such a remedy, for the time being, WTO members have agreed not to use these complaints under the TRIPS Agreement, adopting a *moratorium*.[53] In examining the GATT/WTO jurisprudence relating to trade in goods, panels held that such a complaint 'should be approached with caution and should remain an exceptional remedy'[54] and that 'the reason for this caution is straightforward. Members negotiate the rules that they agree to follow, and only exceptionally would they expect to be challenged for actions not in contravention of these rules '[55] From a historical perspective, non-violation complaints were introduced into the GATT 1947 because of the general character of its obligations. However, the rules governing trade-related aspects of intellectual property are now outlined in detail in the TRIPS Agreement and other international conventions.

The introduction of non-violation complaints in the intellectual property sphere through international investment agreements may circumvent

---

time (DSU, Article 22.1). If no satisfactory compensation has been agreed within 20 days after the date of expiry of the reasonable period of time, any party having invoked the dispute settlement procedures may request authorization from the DSB to suspend the application to the Member concerned of concessions or other obligations under the covered agreements (DSU, Article 22.2).

51 See generally S. Cho, 'GATT Non-Violation Issues in the WTO Framework: Are They the Achilles' Heel of the Dispute Settlement Process?' *Harvard ILJ* 39, 1998, pp. 316–20.

52 Under Article XXIII:1(b) of GATT 1994, a Member state can file a suit even when the Agreement has not been violated, if it proves that it has been deprived of an expected benefit because of a government's action or any other circumstance.

53 Under Article 64.2, this moratorium (i.e. the agreement not to use TRIPS non-violation complaints) was to last for the first five years of the WTO, but it has been extended since then through the Doha Decision on Implementation-Related Issues and Concerns (¶ 11.1), the Decision adopted by the General Council on 1 August 2004 (¶ 1 h) and the Hong Kong Ministerial Decision (¶ 45).

54 *Japan – Measures Affecting Consumer Photographic Film and Paper*, adopted on 22 April 1998, WT/DS44/R ¶ 10.37.

55 Ibidem, ¶ 10.36.

multilateral agreement on the issue and raises important concerns with regard to public health.[56] The inherent ambiguity and the concomitant risk of misuse of non-violation complaints call for the non-inclusion of this remedy in sensitive domains such as intellectual property. For instance, pharmaceutical patents are a borderline area where a delicate balance has to be struck between the investor's interests on one side and access to medicines on the other. Unfortunately, aggressive negotiations have already determined the inclusion of these complaints in some recent international investment agreements with regard to such a delicate field.[57] Just how concretely all the interests concerned will be adequately balanced in an eventual arbitration remains to be seen.

Notwithstanding the mentioned advantages of investor-state arbitration (from an investor's perspective) to date, the known investment disputes concerning intellectual property are rare. This seems to be counter-intuitive, given the economic importance of intellectual property, the recent rise of intellectual property disputes at the WTO[58] and the flourishing of international intellectual property disputes among private parties.[59] To solve this puzzle, several considerations need to be taken into account.

56 In the application of the non-violation complaints, the public purpose does not exempt a given national measure from the review under the test of impairment of benefits, even when scientific evidence is unambiguous. *European Communities – Measures Affecting Asbestos and Asbestos-Containing Products*, Panel Report, released on 18 September 2000, WT/DS135/R, ¶ 8.257. The Appellate Body (AB) confirmed the panel's report, stating that 'the text [of Article XXIII 1(b)] does not distinguish between, or exclude, certain types of measures'. *European Communities – Measures Affecting Asbestos and Asbestos-Containing Products*, Report of the Appellate Body, 12 March 2001, WT/DS135/AB/R, ¶ 188. The AB further held that the EC's argument that Canada could not have legitimate or reasonable expectations of continued market access for products which are shown to pose a serious risk to human health and life, 'does not relate to the threshold issues [of the scope of application of Article XXIII:1(b)]. Rather [it] relates to the substance of [the] claim [. . .] whether a benefit has been nullified or impaired by a measure restricting market access for products posing a health risk.' *EC – Asbestos*, Report of the AB, ¶ 190.

57 See for instance, AUSFTA Article 21.2. See also Annex 22.2 of the United States-Chile FTA, Annex 20.2 of the CAFTA. A safeguard on non-violation complaints that both Agreements contain is that the benefits expected under the intellectual property chapter cannot be invoked with respect to measures taken under the general exception provisions under Article XX of GATT 1994.

58 *See* A. Di Blase, 'Human-Right-Related Aspects in the Settlement of International Disputes on Intellectual Property Rights', in G. Venturini *et al.* (eds), *Liber Amicorum Fausto Pocar*, Milan: Giuffrè, 2009.

59 The International Chamber of Commerce estimates that 10 per cent of its annual caseload involves intellectual property. WIPO has administered over 80 complex intellectual property arbitrations in recent years and some 25,000 domain name disputes since 2000. *See* S. Lamb and A. Garcia, 'Arbitration of Intellectual Property Disputes', *European and Middle Eastern Arbitration Review*, 2008, Section 3. Although the WIPO Centre's ADR services are appropriate for all types of commercial disputes, they have not had to date any investment dispute.

First, the available data may just represent the tip of the iceberg, given the limited transparency of investment arbitration.[60] While the ICSID makes the existence of all proceedings public and generally encourages the publication of the rendered awards, other facilities do not necessarily disclose their dockets of cases, and even when they do so, they do not publish the awards unless the parties agree to do so. Therefore, it is likely that the scarcity of cases in this matter is due not to an absence of conflicts, but to the lack of transparency of investment treaty arbitration.

Second, investment disputes are expensive. Initiating an investment dispute may be a suitable option only for large corporate actors. *Third*, knowledge about intellectual property is still too limited among investment lawyers. Not only is intellectual property considered to be a highly technical subject,[61] but it has entered the international law agenda only very recently. Similarly, the arbitrability of intellectual property-related disputes is restricted in certain jurisdictions.[62] Therefore, for the moment, investment disputes continue to focus mainly on tangible forms of investments, although this has started to change.

Public law and investment treaty arbitration

In the exercise of their sovereignty, states have the right to regulate a series of issues of public concern. However, through investment treaties they voluntarily limit their sovereignty and consent to submitting eventual disputes to arbitration. By doing so, states delegate some portions of the judicial function to private arbitrators, even with regard to matters concerning public law.[63] Arbitral tribunals have the jurisdiction to 'review' the conduct of the host state and to assess whether such conduct represents an infringement on investment treaty guarantees. This delegation constitutes a paradigm shift vis-à-vis the traditional prerogative of the national judge.

While investment treaty arbitration is usually depicted as a consensual adjudication between an investor and a state, or a sort of *stipulatio alteri* (i.e. stipulation for another),[64] it may also be viewed as 'a mechanism of

---

60 See generally F. Ortino, 'External Transparency of Investment Awards', *SIEL Working Paper No. 49/08*, 2008.

61 D. Vaver, 'Does the Public Understand Intellectual Property? Do Lawyers?', *Oxford Legal Studies Research Paper No. 23*, 2006.

62 On grounds of public policy, a small number of jurisdictions prohibit the resolution by arbitration of certain aspects of intellectual property disputes: a private adjudicator is not allowed to resolve a dispute that may affect society at large.

63 Public law can be defined as 'an assemblage of rules, principles, canons, maxims, customs, usages, and manners that condition and sustain the activity of governing'. M. Loughlin, *The Idea of Public Law*, Oxford: Oxford University Press, 2003, p. 30.

64 M. Sornarajah, 'The Neo-Liberal Agenda in Investment Arbitration: Its Rise, Retreat and Impact on State Sovereignty', in W. Shan, P. Simons and D. Singh (eds), *Redefining Sovereignty in International Economic Law*, Oxford: Hart, 2008, p. 210.

adjudicative review in public law'.[65] As a public law system, investor-state arbitration is used in settling disputes for the most part arising from the exercise of sovereign authority. Somehow, as judges in public law litigation,[66] arbitrators are asked to scrutinize 'the relationship between those who govern and those who are governed', and to determine 'matters such as the legality of governmental activity, the degree to which individuals should be protected from regulation, and the appropriate role of the state'.[67]

As Dworkin once said, 'the courts are the capitals of law's empire, and judges are its princes [. . .]'.[68] Indeed, when two parties in dispute ask a third party to help them, they build through a consensual act of delegation, 'a node of social authority, or mode of governance'.[69] When adjudicators resolve a dispute in which each of the parties pleads a legitimate value, it is the adjudicators' assessment of the situation – rather than treaty law *per se* – that determines the outcome. When it comes to balancing competing claims adjudicators necessarily become legislators and administrators. The reverse is also true: decisions push law makers and administrators into a judicial mode, requiring them to reason as a judge would, that is, to consider the merit and mode of their own activity.[70]

The business of arbitrators is to settle a specific dispute according to their mandate. However, compelling arguments stand in favour of assimilating arbitrators to international judges. From a historical perspective, adjudication traces its roots to arbitration. From a functional perspective, as Van Harten rightly puts it, 'both [judges and arbitrators] exercise the ultimate decision-making authority of the juridical sovereign in public law'.[71] In this regard, as one arbitrator put it, 'to some extent, arbitrators are expected to behave like judges in their concern for the public interest'.[72]

Therefore, while the internationalization of investment disputes may promote efficiency and depolarization, at the same time it may reduce the ability of states to control the activity of foreign investors and to enact regulation aimed at protecting public goods. In this regard, promoting efficiency should not be contemplated as the only consideration in international investment law and arbitration. Like judges, arbitrators are asked to safeguard vital community interests as well as to settle disputes in conformity with 'principles of justice and international law'.[73]

65 Van Harten, *Investment Treaty Arbitration and Public Law*, p. 45.
66 A. Chayes, 'The Role of the Judge in Public Law Litigation', *Harv L Rev* 89, 1976, p. 1281.
67 Van Harten, *Investment Treaty Arbitration and Public Law*, p. 70.
68 R. Dworkin, *Law's Empire*, Cambridge, MA: Harvard University Press, 1986, p. 407.
69 M. Shapiro and A. Stone Sweet, *On Law, Politics and Judicialization*, Oxford: Oxford University Press, 2002, chapter 4.
70 A. Stone Sweet, *Governing with Judges*, Oxford: Oxford University Press, 2000, chapter 7.
71 G. Van Harten, 'The Public-Private Distinction in the International Arbitration of Individual Claims Against the State', *ICLQ* 56, 2007, pp. 379–80.
72 W. Park, 'Private Disputes and the Public Good: Explaining Arbitration Law', *Am. U. Int'l L. Rev.* 20, 2004–2005, p. 905.
73 VCLT, Preamble.

Investment treaty arbitration as global administrative law

The rapid and continuing growth in investment arbitration has determined an increased interest in the matter by the public, lawyers and policy makers. Still, theoretical efforts to interpret and systematize this phenomenon are in a preliminary phase. In this context, the proposal to conceptualize investment treaty arbitration as a species of global administrative law deserves attention and scrutiny. According to some authors, investment treaty law may be conceptualized as a species of Global Administrative Law (GAL).[74] Since investment disputes arise from the exercise of public authority by the state and arbitral tribunals are given the power to review and control such an exercise of public authority settling what are in essence regulatory disputes, investment arbitration has been analogized to domestic administrative review.[75]

The comparison between arbitral tribunals and administrative courts and the claim that investment arbitration constitutes an example of GAL are based on several arguments. *First*, arbitral tribunals have an *international/global* character, because their authority derives from a treaty. *Second*, arbitral tribunals, like *administrative* courts, settle disputes arising from the exercise of public authority.[76] *Third*, the jurisdiction of arbitral tribunals extends to *legal* disputes.[77] This framework would give substance to the concept of global administrative law or *lex administrativa communis*,[78] which can be defined as '[the] process of a global homologation of principles of administrative, comparative and international law under different legal systems'.[79] As Van Harten and Loughlin put it '[investment treaty arbitration] may in fact offer the only exemplar of global administrative law, strictly construed, yet to have emerged'.[80]

However, this conceptualization may prove to be fragile as 'the defining features of global administrative law are rather fluid'.[81] Without a clear understanding of what is meant by GAL, any attempt to classify investment arbitration as a form of GAL remains a theoretical exercise. Furthermore, one may question whether international investment law may be reduced to a mere

---

74 G. Van Harten and M. Loughlin, 'Investment Treaty Arbitration as a Species of Global Administrative Law', *EJIL* 17, 2006, pp. 121–50.

75 Ibidem, pp. 121–3. See also B. Kingsbury, N. Krisch and R.B. Stewart, 'The Emergence of Global Administrative Law', *Law & Contemporary Problems* 68, 2005, p. 15.

76 S. Schill, 'Crafting the International Economic Order: The Public Function of Investment Treaty Arbitration and its Significance for the Role of the Arbitrator', *Leiden JIL* 23, 2010, pp. 401–30.

77 ICSID Convention, Article 25.

78 J. Robalino-Orellana and J. Rodríguez-Arana Muñoz (eds), *Global Administrative Law Towards a Lex Administrativa*, London: Cameron & May, 2010.

79 Ibidem.

80 Van Harten and Loughlin, 'Investment Treaty Arbitration as a Species of Global Administrative Law', p. 121.

81 Ibidem, pp. 121–2.

transnational form of administrative law. *First*, there is no such thing as a centralized system of administration in international law, rather, states retain their administrative functions.

Second, foreign investments are usually governed by a series of norms which are not limited to (national) administrative law but include international treaties, customs, general principles of law etc. Arbitral tribunals have expressly denied to be administrative courts. For instance, in *Generation Ukraine v. Ukraine*, the Arbitral Tribunal clarified that it was an international tribunal, applying international law to a question of international responsibility.[82] As many other cases confirm this distinction, this evidence questions the idea of a global administrative law.[83]

Third, the availability of a system of international adjudication should not be considered as a method of 'expropriating' the state of its judicial control over administrative matters. Instead, such an international mechanism should be viewed as complementary to the substantive guarantees provided by international investment treaties. International arbitration has traditionally involved horizontal relations between 'peers', that is, states versus states or private individuals versus private individuals. The fact that international investment treaty arbitration nowadays addresses a diagonal relationship between the host state and foreign investors reflects an evolution which is present in other sectors of international law such as human rights law. Therefore, if this mechanism parallels the local judicial review of the courts of the host state, it should not be conceived as a substitute of the same, but as a different and additional venue expressly provided by international investment treaties.

Fourth, conceiving international investment law and arbitration as a form of GAL risks decontextualizing it and making it a 'corporate bill of rights'[84] or a 'system of corporate rights without responsibility or liability'.[85] If BITs were the only sources of GAL, the resulting regime would be overbalanced becoming 'a charter of rights for foreign investors, with no concomitant responsibilities or liabilities, no direct legal links to promoting development objectives, and no protection for public welfare in the face of environmentally or socially destabilizing foreign investment'.[86]

Historically, foreigners have been amongst the vulnerable sectors of societies, easy object of reprisals, without vote and voice in the local political

---

82 *Generation Ukraine v. Ukraine*, (Merits) 16 September 2003, 44 ILM 404, ¶¶ 20.29–20.33.

83 J.A. Barraguirre, 'Los Tratados Bilaterales de inversion (TBIs) y el Convenio CIADI – La evaporación del derecho administrativo domestico?', *Res Pubblica Argentina* 3, 2007, p. 114.

84 T. Weiler, 'Balancing Human Rights and Investor Protection: A New Approach for a Different Legal Order', *TDM* 1, 2004, p. 2.

85 H. Mann, 'The Right of States to Regulate and International Investment Law: A Comment', in UNCTAD, *The Development Dimension of FDI: Policy and Rule-Making Perspectives*, New York and Geneva: UN, 2003, p. 215.

86 Ibidem, p. 212.

affairs.[87] Fundamentally, investment treaties aim at establishing a level playing field for foreign investors and a sort of shield against their discrimination and mistreatment by the host state.[88] In protecting property rights, international investment treaties do not have a revolutionary character. Since World War II, property rights and the parallel right to compensation for expropriation, have been enshrined in the Universal Declaration of Human Rights,[89] the first Protocol of the European Convention on Human Rights (ECHR)[90] and the American Human Rights Convention[91] as well as in the Constitutions of many states.[92] However, while national constitutions and international human rights instruments acknowledge the social function of property[93] and/or recognize its limits,[94] investment treaties do not have such a holistic approach, because they assume a pre-existing framework that is given by both national law and international law. In conclusion, emphasizing the GAL theory risks unduly emphasizing private interests at the expenses of the public wealth.

Conclusions

This chapter concludes Part I of this study which has defined and connected the two fields of investor rights and public health. In particular, after examining

87 See J. Paulsson, *Denial of Justice in International Law*, Cambridge: Cambridge University Press, 2005; F. Francioni, 'Access to Justice, Denial of Justice and International Investment Law', *EJIL* 20, 2009, pp. 729–47.
88 G. Starner, 'Taking a Constitutional Look: NAFTA Chapter 11 as an Extension of Member States' Constitutional Protection of Property', *Law and Policy of Int'l Business* 33, 2002, p. 405.
89 Article 17 of the UDHR affirms that 'everyone has the right to own property alone as well as in association with others. No one shall be arbitrarily deprived of his property'.
90 Article 1.1 of the First Protocol to the European Convention on Human Rights states 'Every natural or legal person is entitled to the peaceful enjoyment of his possessions. No one shall be deprived of his possessions except in the public interest and subject to the conditions provided for by law and by the general principles of international law. [. . .]'
91 Article 21.1 of the American Convention on Human Rights proclaims 'Everyone has the right to the use and enjoyment of his property [. . .]'
92 See, for instance, US Constitution, V Amendment; Italian Constitution, Article 42; Spanish Constitution, Section 33; South African Constitution, Article 25; Ukrainian Constitution, Article 14; Brazilian Constitution, Article 5.
93 See e.g. Article 14.2 of the German Constitution ('Property imposes duties. Its use should also serve the public weal') and Section 33.2 of the Spanish Constitution ('the social function of these rights [the right to private property and inheritance] shall determine the limits of their content in accordance with the law').
94 For instance, the European Convention on Human Rights recognizes 'the right of the state to enforce such laws as it deems necessary to control the use of property in accordance with the general interest or to secure the payment of taxes or other contributions or penalties'. First Protocol to the European Convention on Human Rights, Article 1.2. The American Convention on Human Rights similarly states that 'the law may subordinate [the] use and enjoyment [of property] to the interest of society'. American Convention on Human Rights, Article 21.1.

the two *corpora juris*, this part of the book has set up and illustrated the theoretical framework of their interaction. In the following chapters, these major themes will be expanded upon: Part II will explore the specific areas where the interplay between investor rights and public health may take place, and Part III will focus on the reconciliation of these values.

Part II

The interplay of foreign investment and public health in practice

Introductory note

The second part of the book examines the interplay of foreign investment and public health in practice. There is no such thing as a typical investment treaty dispute concerning public health as investment disputes involve a number of public health aspects. While many investment arbitrations have concerned environmental health,[1] this book will also focus on intellectual property disputes which concern other aspects of public health such as access to medicines and tobacco control.[2] This study selects access to medicines, tobacco control and environmental health as case studies, as these three key themes have received only limited analysis by scholars and have gained topical importance in current case law.[3]

Because investment treaty arbitrations are settled using a variety of different arbitral rules, not all of which provide for public disclosure of claims, there can be no accurate accounting of all such disputes. In addition to the known arbitrations, there is an unknown number of claims occurring under other auspices. Although anecdotal evidence discloses more and more of the proceedings of such investment treaty arbitrations, the fact that some portion of the iceberg remains hidden from view is a matter of concern given the public policy implications of such disputes.

In a preliminary way, two considerations may be put forward. First, these challenges against domestic regulation aimed at protecting public health have generated a storm of criticism. The central argument of this criticism focuses

---

1 See below Chapter 6.
2 See below Chapters 4 and 5.
3 In a broad sense, even a number of investment disputes concerning water distribution facilities and health services also relate to public health, as access to clean water and health services are among the determinants of public health. Water- and health services-related disputes are referred to by way of reference. See O. McIntyre, 'Private Investment in Water and Sanitation Services: Rights Based Approaches and International Investment Law – A Possible Way Forward', in J.R. Engel, L. Westra and K. Bosselmann (eds), *Democracy, Ecological Integrity and International Law*, Newcastle upon Tyne: Cambridge Scholars Publishing, 2010, pp. 321–45.

on the fact that investment treaties have shifted from being a protective 'shield' for defending corporations against unfair treatment, to a 'sword' used by those same corporations to query legitimate government regulation in the public interest.[4]

Second, although investment treaties share a philosophical affinity with civil and political rights (mainly protecting the economic freedom of foreign investors) their application has determined a dramatic increase of worldwide support for economic and social rights.[5] The economic dimension is not the only aspect concerned in relation to the discourse involving international investment treaties and related disputes. Inasmuch as increased prosperity and economic growth constitute essential elements in furthering broader societal interests, it may be said that investment treaties also feature an underlying, albeit indirect, social dimension. While a few writers have examined investment law from a human rights perspective,[6] scholars have rarely acknowledged the (unintended) transformation of international investment treaties into a vehicle for reconsideration of economic, social and cultural rights. In this sense, Professor Brower highlights that '. . . The application of Chapter 11 has shown widespread support for the right to health among the people and government of the United States.'[7]

Part II will proceed in three chapters. Chapter 4 will examine the interplay between the protection of intellectual property rights in international investment law and access to medicines. Chapter 5 will explore the linkage between tobacco control and the protection of foreign investment through BITs. Finally, Chapter 6 will analyze the interplay between environmental health and investor rights in investment treaty law and arbitration. These three apparently unrelated areas of research share more in common than they reveal at first sight. *First*, all these areas involve the clash of cultures between public health protection and foreign direct investment promotion. The reconciliation of these different goals, albeit in different areas, involves similar analytical tools. *Second*, Chapter 4 and Chapter 5 are closely interrelated as they present an analytical assessment of the interplay between certain intellectual property rights – namely pharmaceutical patents and trademarks – in relation

---

4 See R. Jones, 'NAFTA Chapter 11 Investor-to-State Dispute Resolution: A Shield to Be Embraced or a Sword to be Feared?', *Brigham Young University L Rev*, 2002, p. 527.

5 C.H. Brower II, 'NAFTA's Investment Chapter: Initial Thoughts about Second Generation Rights', *Vanderbilt Journal of Transnational Law* 37, 2003, pp. 1533–63.

6 See, *inter alia*, P.M. Dupuy, F. Francioni and E.U. Petersmann (eds), *Human Rights in International Investment Law and Investor-State Arbitration*, Oxford: Oxford University Press, 2009.

7 Brower, 'NAFTA's Investment Chapter', p. 1563, stressing that 'although international treaties typically characterize the right to health as an ESCR [economic, social and cultural right], it is possible that people . . . embrace this right because, in some respects, it promotes liberty. Although public health measures may restrict liberty for members of the regulated community, the beneficiaries of the measures may see them as a form of liberation from the harmful effects of industry.' Ibidem, footnote 149.

to public health. These chapters may seem detached from Chapter 6, which focuses on the interplay between property and environmental health, however, there is a clear analogy if not a substantial overlapping between the two linkages: 'intellectual property and public health' and 'property and public health'. It is submitted that indeed the two linkages reflect the fundamental dichotomy between property and public health. Notably, Chapter 6 offers a useful conceptual framework: while investment disputes concerning intellectual property have only recently emerged as a consequence of the increased international regulation in the area, investment disputes presenting environmental elements have an older pedigree. Analyzing the way these disputes have been addressed by arbitral tribunals offers food for thought as analogous arguments may be re-proposed in the context of intellectual property disputes.

4 Access to medicines in international investment law and arbitration

Introduction

In recent years, the flourishing of investment treaties in the form of all-encompassing treaties that include intellectual property (IP) as a form of investment has determined a paradigm shift in international knowledge governance.[1] In their vest of intellectual capital exporters, industrialized countries are interested in raising IP standards. Therefore, these countries have increasingly used regional and bilateral instruments in a strategic fashion to incorporate *TRIPS-plus* commitments that they would not be able to obtain in the World Trade Organization (WTO).[2] In their vest of intellectual capital importers, developing countries would benefit from laxer levels of protection. However, these countries generally accept higher IP standards in order to obtain favourable concessions in other areas.[3] The so-called TRIPS-plus provisions risk undermining the flexibilities provided at the multilateral level.[4]

---

1 International knowledge governance has recently become one of the more regulated sub-sets of public international law. Proprietary approaches to knowledge governance have become stronger than ever since the inception of the Agreement on Trade-Related Aspects of Intellectual Property Rights (TRIPS) under the World Trade Organization (WTO), and the growth of BITs. Agreement on Trade-Related Aspects of Intellectual Property Rights (TRIPS Agreement) Annex 1C to the Marrakesh Agreement Establishing the World Trade Organization, 33 ILM 1994, pp. 1197 ff. in force since 1 January 1995. For commentary, see for instance, D. Gervais, *The TRIPS Agreement: Drafting History and Analysis*, 3rd edn, London: Sweet & Maxwell, 2008; C. Correa, *Trade Related Aspects of Intellectual Property Rights. A Commentary on the TRIPS Agreement*, Oxford: Oxford University Press, 2007.
2 Agreement Establishing the World Trade Organization, 33 ILM 1994, 1144–53.
3 As Ryan points out, '[. . .] the key to getting agreement is getting the right mix of issues on the table, even if they are previously unrelated, so that they can be linked for bargaining purposes . . . Linkage-bargain diplomacy can be exploited in order to achieve treaties in politically difficult areas in which agreement would be otherwise elusive.' See M. Ryan, *Knowledge Diplomacy – Global Competition and the Politics of Intellectual Property*, Washington, D.C.: Brookings Institution Press, 1998, p. 92.
4 As Yamane points out 'Since the adoption of the Doha Declaration on the TRIPS Agreement and Public Health, adopted at the WTO Doha Ministerial Conference in November 2001, specific notions, such as compulsory licenses, exceptions to the rights conferred and the

This chapter will investigate the particular intersection between investment treaties, intellectual property and the access to medicines. As investment treaties regulate pharmaceutical patents, there are two questions that arise in relation to this connection. First, are investment treaties compatible with a hypothetical state international obligation to provide access to essential medicines? Second, if internal measures aimed to protect public health can be challenged by foreign investors, is investment treaty arbitration a suitable forum to protect public interests?

The argument will proceed in three parts. First, after defining access to medicines in relation to public international law, the international regulatory framework that disciplines pharmaceutical patents will be scrutinized. Second, the impact of investment treaty provisions on access to medicines will be assessed. Indeed, as investment treaties protect pharmaceutical patents as a form of investment, the book addresses the question as to whether an excessive protection of pharmaceutical patents under investment treaties and FTAs can limit the access of developing countries to essential medicines. Third, the issue as to whether national measures aimed at facilitating access to medicines can be considered as violation of investment treaty provisions will be examined. Finally, the relevant policy considerations will be addressed.

Access to medicines in international law

Almost two billion people lack access to essential medicines.[5] Traditionally, the problem has been perceived as being due to states' lack of funds and poverty, and therefore, as the exclusive domain of economists. Only recently have legal scholars analyzed access to medications from an international law perspective.[6] While some international law instruments have recognized the state duty to protect public health by ensuring access to essential medicines,[7]

freedom of the Members to establish their own regime for such exhaustion, have been thought of as TRIPS "flexibilities".' See H. Yamane, *Interpreting TRIPS – Globalization of Intellectual Property Rights and Access to Medicines*, Oxford: Hart Publishing, 2011, p. 246. Furthermore, as Yamane highlights, flexibility also indicates 'a method of TRIPS interpretation allowing the reduction of the level, the scope or the effects of IPR protection'. Ibidem, p. 247.

5 *WHO Medicines Strategy: Countries at the Core 2004–2007*, Geneva: WHO, 2004.

6 L.R. Helfer, 'Towards a Human Rights Framework for Intellectual Property', *UC Davis L Rev* 40, 2006–2007, pp. 971–1020; J. Gibson, *Intellectual Property, Medicine and Health: Current Debates*, Farnham: Ashgate, 2009, pp. 41 ff.; L.R. Helfer and G.W. Austin, *Human Rights and Intellectual Property*, Cambridge: Cambridge University Press, 2011, pp. 90 ff.

7 See, for instance, in the WTO context, the Doha Declaration on the TRIPS Agreement and Public Health, WT/MIN(01)/DEC/W/2, ¶ 4: 'We agree that the TRIPS Agreement does not and should not prevent Members from taking measures to protect public health. Accordingly, while reiterating our commitment to the TRIPS Agreement, we reaffirm that the agreement can and should be interpreted and implemented in a manner supportive of WTO members' rights to protect public health and, in particular, to promote access to medicines for all.'

others have conceptualized such access as a key component of the right to health and the right to life.[8] This double linkage has offered a new paradigm for understanding issues related to the availability and distribution of medicines and has provided a framework for influencing the way in which policy makers as well as other actors make decisions that affect access to medicines.

Scrutinizing access to medicines through human rights lenses means that states have not only moral responsibilities to ensure access to medicines, but they also have legal obligations. In turn, if states were not to meet these obligations, they would be legally responsible.[9] Also, a human rights framework places emphasis on the principles of equality and concern for the vulnerable components of society. The UDHR makes reference to the right to medical care[10] and the right to share in the benefits of scientific advancement.[11] While the ICESCR generally recognizes that everyone has a right to enjoy the highest attainable standards of physical and mental health,[12] the *General Comment No. 14* has further set out that states are bound to promote the right to health through ensuring access to affordable treatment.[13]

Also, the *General Comment* has recognized access to essential medicines – i.e. those that satisfy the priority health care needs of the population[14] – as part of the state's minimum *core obligations* under the ICESCR.[15] According to the human rights lexicon, core obligations are non-derogable and in many respects do not depend on a state's development level.[16] In particular, access to essential medicines has been connected to the right to life, which is a classic non-derogable human right, given that essential medicines are indispensable for life.[17] Not only is the right to life the legal foundation for all other rights,[18] but some international tribunals have pointed out that it has attained *jus cogens* status under international law.[19] In addition, some courts have linked access to

---

8 *General Comment No. 14*, ¶ 12.
9 See A. Chapman, 'Conceptualizing the Right to Health: A Violations Approach', *Tennessee L Rev* 65, 1998, p. 395.
10 UDHR, Article 25.
11 UDHR, Article 27.
12 ICESCR, Article 12,1.
13 *General Comment No. 14*, ¶ 12.
14 The WHO Model List of Essential Medicines has been updated every two years since 1977. The implementation of the concept of essential medicines is intended to be flexible and adaptable to many different situations; exactly which medicines are regarded as essential remains a national responsibility.
15 *General Comment No. 14*, ¶ 43.
16 *General Comment No. 14*, ¶ 47.
17 For an exhaustive analysis of the linkage between the right to life and access to medicines, see A. Ely Yamin, 'Not Just a Tragedy: Access to Medications as a Right Under International Law', *Boston University ILJ* 21, 2003, pp. 101–44.
18 ICCPR, Article 6(1).
19 For instance, the right to life was cited as *jus cogens* in the *Street Children Case (Morales v. Guatemala)*, Judgment of Nov 19, 1999 Inter-Am Ct H R (Ser. C) N0 63 ¶ 139.

medical treatment to the prohibition of inhuman treatment. For instance, the ECtHR has interpreted the prohibition of inhuman treatment under Article 3 of the ECHR so as to protect individuals against the withdrawal of medical treatment where the consequences of such withdrawal would be such that the person denied treatment would suffer in an inhuman or degrading way.[20] Both national and regional courts have elaborated significant jurisprudence on access to essential medicines, confirming the justiciability of access to essential medicines,[21] and implying that core contents of this right have gradually achieved prescriptive force. Even without conceptualizing health as a human right, public health requires states to provide access to essential medicines, albeit the extent of such access may be limited by resource considerations.

Pharmaceutical patent regulation in international economic law

The Agreement on Trade-Related Aspects of Intellectual Property Rights (TRIPS) under the World Trade Organization (WTO) is the first international instrument to introduce pharmaceuticals as patentable subject matter.[22] This move was very controversial as it is not certain whether an adequate balance between public and private interests has been achieved in the context of pharmaceutical patents. By providing the patent owner with twenty years of monopoly rights, pharmaceutical patents usually increase the price of medicines and this may result in a direct loss of patients' welfare.[23] The TRIPS Agreement attempts to strike a balance between the long term social objective of providing incentives for future inventions, and the short term objective of allowing people to use existing inventions and creations,[24] also providing for general exceptions and flexibilities.[25]

However, since the inception of the TRIPS, it has proven difficult for Member States to implement the flexibilities provided by the Agreement. The case that opened the debate on the linkage between pharmaceutical patents

---

20 In *D. v. UK*, the ECtHR affirmed that the withdrawal of treatment, and the manner of its withdrawal (in the deportation of an AIDS sufferer to St Kitts), would, if carried out, determine a violation of Article 3 of the ECHR as it 'would expose him to a real risk of dying under the most distressing circumstances and would thus amount to inhuman treatment'. (1997) 24 EHRR 423, ¶ 53.

21 See generally Ely Yamin, 'Not Just a Tragedy: Access to Medications as a Right under International Law'.

22 See generally N. Pires de Carvalho, *The TRIPS Regime of Patent Rights*, 3rd edn, Aalphen aan den Rijn: Wolters Kluwer, 2010.

23 D. Evans and A.J. Padilla, 'Excessive Pricing: Using Economics To Define Administrable Legal Rules', *Journal of Competition Law and Economics* 1, 2005, pp. 97–122.

24 TRIPS Agreement, Articles 7 and 8.

25 TRIPS Agreement, Articles 30 and 31.

and access to medicines is *South African PMA v. The Government of South Africa.*[26] In 1997, in response to the HIV/AIDS epidemic, the South African government enacted legislation to guarantee access to essential medicines through parallel imports[27] and compulsory licences.[28] However, the South African Pharmaceutical Manufacturers Association (PMA) challenged the legality of the *Medicines Act* in light of the South African Constitution and the TRIPS Agreement before the High Court of Pretoria. Because of pressures from NGOs and international public opinion, the court action was withdrawn. However, the case catalyzed the public opinion and raised the awareness of the problem of access to essential medicines in the light of the TRIPS provisions. The Doha Declaration,[29] and the subsequent Waiver[30] and proposed Amendment[31] of the TRIPS Agreement all attempted to better tune the TRIPS Agreement to the states' right to protect public health.

Nevertheless, from a legal perspective, the TRIPS Agreement sets international *minimum* standards for IP protection. While WTO Members cannot derogate or provide lower ceilings of protection, they still have the right to institute more extensive protection than that which is required by the Agreement, as long as they apply the general principles of the Most-Favoured-Nation (MFN) clause and national treatment under the Agreement.[32] Therefore, any intellectual property agreement which is negotiated after TRIPS and involves WTO members, can only create similar or higher standards – commonly known as *TRIPS-plus*. While IP rights in the WTO are virtually crystallized and the launching of multilateral negotiations on investment finds strong opposition, industrialized countries have increasingly used bilateral and regional negotiations to foster the protection of IP.

Investment treaties incorporate a broad definition of investment that generally covers both tangible and intangible property[33] thus including

---

26 *South African Pharmaceutical Manufacturers Association v. The Government of South Africa*, Case No 4183, 1998, High Court of Pretoria.

27 A parallel import is a non-counterfeit product imported from another country without the permission of the IP owner. K. Outterson, 'Pharmaceutical Arbitrage: Balancing Access and Innovation in International Prescription Drug Markets', *Yale Journal of Health Policy, Law & Ethics* 5, 2004, p. 10.

28 Compulsory licensing is when a government allows someone else to produce the patented product or process without the consent of the patent owner. It is one of the flexibilities on patent protection included in the TRIPS Agreement.

29 Declaration on the TRIPS Agreement and Public Health, IV Ministerial Conference, Doha, WT/MIN(01)/DEC/W/2, 20 November 2001.

30 Decision on Implementation of Paragraph 6 of the Doha Declaration on the TRIPS Agreement and Public Health, 30 August 2003 (document WT/L/540) at http://www.wto.org.

31 General Council, Amendment of the TRIPS Agreement, Decision of 6 December 2005, (document WT/L/641) at http://www.wto.org.

32 TRIPS Agreement, Article 1.1.

33 One of the first cases in which the violation of an intangible property right was deemed to be an expropriation was the *Norwegian Shipowners' Claims* case which dealt with the expropriation of shipbuilding contracts by the United States. *Norway v. US*, 1 RIAA 307, 332 (PCA 1922).

intellectual property.[34] The main policy justification for protecting pharmaceutical patents through investment treaties is that they induce foreign direct investment (FDI) in the research and development of new medicines, stimulating local inventive activities and encouraging transfer of technology into the country.[35]

FTAs, on the other hand, often provide for higher levels of IP protection than the TRIPS Agreement.[36] As Musungu and Dutfield point out, the concept of *TRIPS-plus* 'covers both those activities aimed at increasing the level of protection for right holders beyond that which is given in the TRIPS Agreement, and those measures aimed at reducing the scope or effectiveness of limitations on rights and exceptions under the TRIPS Agreement'.[37] Arguably, these *TRIPS-plus* standards reflect those of industrialized countries and this regime shift would lead to the progressive *feudalization* of knowledge and knowledge-based products.[38]

However, some authors stress that this regime export is inappropriate to the legal framework of developing countries which is less sophisticated and developed than that of their industrialized counterparts. According to these authors, IP regulations in industrialized countries are the outcome of long processes and are 'often supported and supplemented by other legal, judicial and institutional instruments and arrangements'.[39] This is not always the case in developing countries.

From a political science perspective, some authors contend that bilateralism and regionalism are undermining the world multilateral framework.[40] Extensive IP-related concessions made under a given investment treaty would throw away IP as a bargaining tool in the WTO with respect to other countries,

---

34 In the 1926 case of *German Interests in Polish Upper Silesia – the Chorzow Factory Case*, the Permanent Court of International Justice found that the seizure by the Polish government of a factory plant and machinery was also an expropriation of the closely interrelated *patents* of the company, although the Polish government at no time claimed to expropriate these. *F.R.G. v. Pol*, 1926 PCIJ (ser A) No 7 (May 1925).

35 In general terms, technology transfer can be described as the capacity to adopt, adapt and develop a technology, which ultimately leads to its consolidation in the receiving country. See generally, K.E. Maskus and J.H. Reichman (eds), *International Public Goods and Transfer of Technology under a Globalized Intellectual Property Regime*, Cambridge: Cambridge University Press, 2005.

36 J. Kuanpoth, 'TRIPS-Plus Rules under Free Trade Agreements: An Asian Perspective', in C. Heath and A. Kamperman Sanders (eds), *Intellectual Property and Free Trade Agreements*, Oxford and Portland: Hart Publishing, 2007, pp. 27–48.

37 S.F. Musungu and G. Dutfield, 'Multilateral Agreements and a TRIPS-Plus World: The World Intellectual Property Organization', Geneva: Quacker United Nations Office, 2003, p. 2.

38 See P. Drahos and J. Braithwaite, *Information Feudalism – Who Owns the Knowledge Economy?* New York: The New Press, 2003.

39 M. El Said, 'Surpassing Checks, Overriding Balances and Diminishing Flexibilities – FTA-IPRS Plus Bilateral Trade Agreements: From Jordan to Oman', *JWIT* 8, 2007, p. 250.

40 See M. El Said, 'The Road From TRIPS-Minus to TRIPS, to TRIPS-Plus: Implications of IPRs for the Arab World', *JWIP* 8, 2005, p. 61.

because the Most Favoured Nation clause would apply.[41] Thus, in the case in which advantageous conditions were granted to the members of a regional agreement, such conditions would have to be extended, automatically and unconditionally to all WTO Members. By contrast, other authors contend that regionalism and bilateralism in IP negotiations would be just a phase of a cycle and that sooner or later multilateralism would acknowledge and incorporate the standards developed through regionalism and bilateralism.[42] In conclusion, the flourishing of bilateral and regional investment treaties which include IP provisions may have a major impact on access to medicines. While the TRIPS Agreement and its impact on public health has been extensively analyzed,[43] the legal and economic consequences of IP regulation in investment treaties are less known and deserve scrutiny.

A taxonomy of claims in the patent area

Several kinds of potentially public health-related investment disputes may arise with regard to pharmaceutical patents.[44] In a preliminary way, some disputes will centre on the question as to which economic activities do amount to an investment. As an arbitral tribunal recently clarified, the mere sale of pharmaceutical products does not amount to an investment.[45] Next, although it may be very difficult, an affected patent owner may attempt to prove that state measures constitute an unlawful expropriation. In addition, claims could be made when a patent owner is dissatisfied with the determination of the level or mode of remuneration. Other claims can concern the alleged violation of the fair and equitable treatment standard or the alleged discrimination of the foreign investment.

---

41 TRIPS Agreement, Article 4. See C. Heath, 'The Most-Favoured Nation Treatment and Intellectual Property Rights', in C. Heath and A. Kamperman Sanders (eds), *Intellectual Property and Free Trade Agreements*, Oxford and Portland: Hart Publishing, 2007. pp. 127–54.

42 R. Okediji, 'Back to Bilateralism? Pendulum Swings in International Intellectual Property Protection', *University of Ottawa Law & Technology J* 1, 2003, p. 125.

43 E.g. F.M. Abbott, 'TRIPS and Human Rights: Preliminary Reflections', in F. Abbott, C. Breining-Kaufmann and T. Cottier (eds), *International Trade and Human Rights Foundations and Conceptual Issues*, Ann Arbor: University of Michigan Press, 2006; S. Musungu, 'The TRIPS Agreement and Public Health', in C. Correa and A.A. Yusuf (eds), *Intellectual Property and International Trade – The TRIPS Agreement*, 2nd edn., The Hague: Kluwer, 2008, pp. 421–69.

44 A French pharmaceutical company has currently filed an arbitration claim against Poland pursuant to the France–Poland BIT. As the case is proceeding with minimal publicity, and the claims are not known, it is not possible to scrutinize this case in this section. See L.E. Peterson, 'France's Second Largest Pharmaceutical Company Quietly Pursues Arbitration Against Republic of Poland', *IAR* 4, 18 August 2011.

45 *La Republique d'Italie v. La Republique de Cuba*, Arbitrage ad hoc, Sentence Finale, 2008, ¶ 219, available at http://www.iareporter.com/downloads/20110901_1. This case was an inter-State investment treaty arbitration initiated by the Republic of Italy so as to espouse the claims of Italy's allegedly injured nationals.

Expropriation

With regard to the first claim, the arbitration will be concerned with the issue as to what acts of the state may be characterized as amounting to taking, and with the circumstances in which such taking would be considered unlawful. Albeit rare, cases of direct confiscation of foreign IP rights have taken place in the past. For instance, during World War I, the German-owned Bayer trademark for aspirin was assigned to an unrelated US company.[46] In the *Norwegian Shipowners* case, an international arbitral tribunal found that the US authorities had to pay compensation not only for the requisition of all ships (tangible property) but also for the affected contract rights of Norwegian shipowners (intangible property).[47] In *German Interests in Polish Upper Silesia*, the Permanent Court of International Justice found that a Polish statute which transferred to the Polish Treasury all the properties of the German Reich located in the territory annexed to Poland amounted to a taking not only of the Chorzów factory, but of certain patents which were affected by the legislation.[48] At the end of World War II, Belgium confiscated the German-owned Hag coffee trademark which was assigned to a Belgian company.[49]

A more difficult enquiry is the question as to whether regulatory measures which do not require the outright seizure of patents can nonetheless amount to a *regulatory taking* or *indirect expropriation*. While *direct expropriation* refers to the nationalization or taking through formal transfer of title or outright seizure, *indirect expropriation* indicates measures that do not directly take investment property, but which interfere with its use, depriving the owner of its economic benefit.[50] Both direct and indirect expropriations are not *per se* wrongful under customary international law or investment treaties unless certain other conditions are met.[51] For instance, NAFTA Article 1110 does not define expropriation, but puts forward certain conditions under which expropriation becomes lawful:[52] (a) a public purpose; (b) a non-discriminatory

---

46 A.Z. Hertz, 'Shaping the Trident: Intellectual Property under NAFTA, Investment Protection Agreements and at the World Trade Organization', *Can.-U.S. L.J.* 23, 1997, p. 276.

47 *Norwegian Shipowners' Claims* (*Norway v. United States*) 1 U.N.R.I.A.A. (1922) 307.

48 *Chorzów Factory Case* (*Germany v. Poland*) 1927 PCIJ Series A No. 7 at 44, Judgment of 25 May 1926.

49 Hertz, 'Shaping the Trident', p. 276.

50 B. Stern, 'In Search of the Frontiers of Indirect Expropriation', in A. Rovine (ed), *Contemporary Issues in International Arbitration and Mediation*, Leiden: Martinus Nijhoff Publishers, 2008, p. 35.

51 As Comeaux and Kinsella have pointed out 'A State may always expropriate property of investors within its borders; however, for such an expropriation to be "legal", it must be non-discriminatory against the investor, it must be for a public purpose, and it must be accompanied by compensation . . .' P. Comeaux and N. Kinsella, *Protecting Foreign Investment Under International Law*, New York: Oceana Publications, 1997, pp. 77–8.

52 North American Free Trade Agreement between Canada, the United States and Mexico, signed on Dec 8–14, 1992 and entered into force on January 1, 1994, 32 ILM 289 (1993).

basis; (c) accordance with due process of law and fair and equitable treatment; and (d) compensation.[53]

In particular, the central question raised by the so-called indirect expropriation is how to draw the line between legitimate regulations that do not give rise to compensation and regulatory takings that do.[54] There is no settled approach to cases where investors allege that certain regulatory measures constitute a form of expropriation that can be compensated. Scrutinizing the existing jurisprudence, two different doctrines have emerged regarding indirect expropriation.[55] The first approach, the *sole-effect doctrine*, favours investor's interests, as it puts emphasis on the expropriatory effect of the given regulatory measure.[56] Therefore, the *bona fide* public policy purpose of the taking may be presumed but it still requires compensation.[57] The second approach, the *police powers* doctrine, favours the right of the state to regulate and gives weight to the purpose and the circumstances of the governmental action. Thus, according to this theory, the effect of the regulatory measure is placed into a broader framework which allows a weighing and balancing of other factors. There is no single definition of police powers, but this concept is generally understood to include measures taken by government to protect the environment, public health, and so on.[58] A common feature of this doctrine is that these measures are designed to protect the public, or public goods in general, from harm or nuisance that may arise from the acts of the regulated party. According to such doctrine, 'harm prevention' ought not to be compensated, but 'benefit extraction' generally should.[59] A hypothetical example may help in clarifying the issue at stake. Let us imagine a ban on highway advertising: has the government acquired a property right or is it regulating a noxious use of property that causes accidents? Professor Michelman famously argued that similar prohibitions can be classified either as preventing harm or providing a public benefit.[60]

Thus far, neither of the two doctrines can be characterized as dominant or as representing the mainstream of international thinking.[61] While the arbitral jurisprudence is inconsistent on how to treat exercise of regulatory power

---

53 NAFTA, Article 1110.1.

54 V. Lowe, 'Regulation or Expropriation?', *Current Legal Problems* 55, 2002, p. 447.

55 M. Brunetti, 'Indirect Expropriation in International Law', *International Law Forum du Droit International* 5, 2003, p. 151.

56 R. Dolzer, 'Indirect Expropriations: New Developments?', *NYU Environmental L.J.* 11, 2003, p. 90.

57 B. Appleton, 'Regulatory Takings: The International Law Perspective', *NYU Environmental L.J.* 11, 2003, pp. 35–48.

58 See also Chapters 5 and 6.

59 S. Rose-Ackerman and J. Rossi, 'Disentangling Deregulatory Takings', *Virginia L. Rev.* 86, 2000, p. 1435; J.L. Sax, 'Takings and the Police Power', *Yale LJ* 74, 1964–1965, p. 36.

60 F.I. Michelman, 'Property, Utility, and Fairness: Comments on the Ethical Foundations of "Just Compensation" Law', *Harvard L.R.* 80, 1967, p. 1165.

61 See Chapter 6 below.

depriving an investment of some of its value, but which is aimed at protecting policy objectives, doctrinal studies have attempted to clarify the conceptual landscape between indirect expropriation and the right to regulate. Notably, some authors and arbitrators have elaborated a two-fold test to verify whether regulatory measures may be deemed to be indirect expropriation or a legitimate exercise of police power.[62] According to the proposed procedure, *first*, it must be ascertained whether a deprivation of property has occurred, because of the effect of the measure taken. The answer to this question would be given through an essentially quantitative approach. *Second*, the conclusion that a given measure is potentially expropriatory may be modified through an essentially qualitative approach. In other words, 'one should take into account both sides of the coin, and that the challenge is precisely to know where to draw the line in balancing the conflicting interests of investors and states'.[63]

With regard to pharmaceutical patents the question has emerged as to whether compulsory licences and parallel imports can amount to an unlawful expropriation under relevant investment provisions.[64] Compulsory licensing is a regulatory tool that allows governments to temporarily authorize the production of a patented invention without the patent owner's consent for public policy reasons.[65] Compulsory licences may help preventing abuses of the IP system as well as coping with health emergencies. As WTO members have experienced difficulties in reconciling patent protection with access to essential medicines, the Doha Declaration on the TRIPS Agreement and Public Health has clarified the content of this flexibility stating that each WTO member has the right to grant compulsory licences,[66] the freedom to

62 H. Mann and J. Soloway, 'Untangling the Expropriation and Regulation Relationship: Is There a Way Forward?' Report to the Ad Hoc Expert Group on Investment Rules and the Department of Foreign Affairs and International Trade, Canada (2002).

63 Stern, 'In Search of the Frontiers of Indirect Expropriation', p. 44. This point will be articulated more in detail in Chapter 7.

64 C. Correa, 'Implications of Bilateral Free Trade Agreements on Access to Medicines', *Bull. WHO* 84, 2006, pp. 399–404.

65 The TRIPS Agreement does not specifically list the reasons that might be used to justify compulsory licensing as the TRIPS negotiators could not agree on this point. However, Article 31 of the TRIPS Agreement lists eleven conditions for issuing compulsory licences. In particular, companies applying for a licence have to negotiate a voluntary licence with the patent holder on reasonable commercial terms. Only if this fails can a compulsory licence be issued. Compulsory licensing cannot be given exclusively to licensees (e.g. the patent-holder can continue to produce), and it should be subject to legal review in the country. In cases of 'national emergencies', 'other circumstances of extreme urgency' or 'public non-commercial use' (or 'government use') or anti-competitive practices, there is no need to make an initial attempt to negotiate. When a compulsory licence has been issued, the patent owner has to receive adequate remuneration, taking into account the economic value of the authorization. As the TRIPS Agreement does not define adequate remuneration or economic value, in case a dispute arises on this point, the authorities in the country concerned will decide whether the payment is adequate.

66 Doha Declaration on the TRIPS Agreement and Public Health, ¶ 5 b.

determine the grounds on which such licences are granted,[67] and the right to determine what constitutes a national emergency or other circumstances of extreme urgency.[68]

In turn, parallel trade occurs when a product covered by intellectual property rights has been placed in a first market by or with the permission of the patent holder and then imported into a second market without the permission of the patent holder.[69] As parallel trade tends to force price convergence across markets, it normally increases economic welfare by permitting consumers in importing countries to benefit from lower prices realized by more efficient producers in exporting countries. Thus, parallel trade can be an important tool for developing countries to have access to medicines by importing patented medicines from other countries where they are available at lower prices.[70]

Obviously, regulatory measures such as compulsory licences and parallel trade cannot be categorized as a case of *direct expropriation*. Indeed, the patent owner maintains the title of the property and the possibility to commercialize the pharmaceutical product although non-exclusively. However, it may be asked whether measures such as compulsory licences and parallel imports can effectively neutralize the enjoyment of property of the foreign investor and thus constitute *indirect expropriation*.[71]

The economic impact of these measures on the economic value of the investment can be consistent. However, if one considers the nature of compulsory licences, a fundamental question raised is whether they constitute a violation or rather an exception or derogation with respect to IP norms.[72] If compulsory licences are conceived as inherent limits to IP and therefore constitute not a violation of the rule, but a *natural boundary* of the right, there

---

67 Ibidem.
68 Ibidem, ¶ 5 c.
69 From a legal perspective, parallel imports are based on the principle of *international exhaustion*. The countries which follow this principle accept that placing a product on a market anywhere in the world exhausts the patent rights in their market, even where the patent owner has prohibited further commercialization by contract. This means that once the product has been sold, the patent owner has no further rights regarding the additional commercialization of the product.
70 The TRIPS Agreement does not set a standard for parallel trade, but leaves it to the regulatory autonomy of member states. TRIPS Agreement, Article 6.
71 In *Middle East Cement Shipping and Handling Co. v. Egypt*, indirect expropriation was described as a 'measure taken by a state the effect of which is to deprive the investor of the use and benefit of his investment even though he may retain nominal ownership of the respective rights'. See *Middle East Cement Shipping and Handling Co. v. Egypt* (2002) ICSID ARB 99/6, ¶ 107.
72 Several authors deem compulsory licences as an exception. See Pires de Carvalho, *The TRIPS Regime of Patent Rights*, p. 428; Musungu, 'The TRIPS Agreement and Public Health', p. 436. Others seem to consider compulsory licences as limitations of patent rights. See C. Correa, *Trade Related Aspects of Intellectual Property Rights. A Commentary on the TRIPS Agreement*, Oxford: Oxford University Press, 2007, p. 314 ('. . . The TRIPS Agreement simply recognizes the right of WTO Members to limit the patent owners' rights under compulsory licenses and government use. . .').

is no violation of treaty provisions provided that the due process required for the issuance of a compulsory licence is respected. The conditions for lawfully granting a compulsory licence are listed in Article 31 of the TRIPS Agreement.[73] As long as these requirements are fulfilled (and they include adequate remuneration), no violation of intellectual property occurs. If no violation of IP occurs, no international responsibility arises. The text of the TRIPS Agreement seems to confirm this reading by not considering compulsory licences as *limited exceptions*[74] but as *other uses without authorization*[75] of the patent holder.

Regional and national courts have confirmed this conceptualization of compulsory licences as inherent limits to property rights. For instance, in the *Smith Kline* case, the former European Commission on Human Rights (ECommHR) held that the granting under Dutch law of a compulsory licence on a patented medicine was not a violation of Article 1 of Protocol 1 to the ECHR which protects the right to property, but the licence was lawfully issued to pursue a legitimate aim.[76] Similarly, in the Philippine case *Smith Kline and French Laboratories LTD v. Court of Appeals, Bureau of Patents*,[77] the Court rejected the petitioner's claim that a compulsory licence on a patented medicine amounted to expropriation and that the compensation was not fair. The Supreme Court affirmed *in toto* the challenged decision of the Court of Appeal, stating that the award of a compulsory licence is a valid exercise of the police powers of the state.

Turning our attention to investment treaty disputes, a case, registered at the ICC, involved a pharmaceutical company contesting a compulsory licence issued by an East European country. Nothing else, however, is known. Clearly, due to the confidentiality requirements, lawyers could not disclose any information to the author. Still, it may be questioned whether shedding some light on the process would be preferable.[78]

More recently, a Canadian manufacturer of generic medicines filed a claim against the US alleging, *inter alia*, expropriation.[79] In 2003, the company, Apotex Inc., filed an application with the US Food and Drug Administration to obtain the approval of a generic version of Pfizer's antidepressant Zoloft, before Pfizer's patent expired in 2006. In doing so, Apotex triggered an

---

73 TRIPS Agreement, Article 31.

74 TRIPS Agreement, Article 30.

75 TRIPS Agreement, Article 31.

76 ECtHR (Commission Report), *Smith Kline and French Laboratories Ltd. v. the Netherlands*, Appl. No 12633/87, 4 October 1990, (1990) 66 Decisions and Reports 70.

77 *Smith Kline and French Laboratories Ltd v. Court of Appeals, Bureau of Patents, Trademarks and Technology Transfer and Doctors Pharmaceuticals Inc*, Supreme Court of Manila, G.R. No. 121867, 24 July 1997.

78 V. Vadi, 'Mapping Uncharted Waters: Intellectual Property Disputes with Public Health Elements in Investor-State Arbitration', *TDM*, 2009, pp. 1–22.

79 *See Apotex Inc. v. the Government of the United States of America*, Notice of Arbitration under the Arbitration Rules of the UNCITRAL and the NAFTA, 10 December 2008.

'artificial' act of patent infringement, in an effort to draw Pfizer into a dispute that would provide a judgment, one way or the other, on the legality of Apotex's application to sell the antidepressant. When Pfizer declined to file a suit, Apotex filed for a declaratory judgment asserting that it was not infringing on the patent, which is allegedly a common legal tactic in patent litigation. However, US Federal Courts refused to rule on the matter, deeming that they lacked a 'reasonable apprehension' that Pfizer would launch a suit for patent infringement. In its notice of arbitration, Apotex argues that the US courts 'misapplied' statutory and constitutional law. According to the claimant, the reasonable apprehension doctrine creates a sort of bottleneck, delaying the expeditious development and manufacture of generics and thus is contrary to public welfare.[80]

The US contested that 'the reasonable apprehension of suit standard had been applied in hundreds of cases by federal courts throughout the United States over the course of several decades in declaratory judgment actions involving intellectual property'.[81] More interestingly, the U.S. *inter alia* argued that *Apotex* made no effort to establish the basis – other than legal error – on which these decisions violated the NAFTA: 'This Tribunal does not sit as a court of appeals for the courts of the United States, and in any event "legal error" by a court when applying U.S. law does not give rise to a violation of the NAFTA'.[82] As the case is still pending, it is not possible to foresee how the arbitral tribunal will settle the dispute.

In a parallel dispute,[83] Apotex claimed that the United States breached, *inter alia*, NAFTA Article 1110 (Expropriation and Compensation).[84] Again the dispute involves the submission of a medicine application seeking approval for a generic version of a heart medication. In order to obtain the approval of its application, Apotex had sued the patent owner, Bristol Myers Squibb (BMS), to obtain the guarantee that it would not file a claim for patent infringement after the launch of Apotex medicines on the market. In response, BMS moved to dismiss for lack of subject matter jurisdiction on the grounds that it had no intention of suing Apotex for infringement. The Court dismissed Apotex's declaratory judgment action for lack of subject matter jurisdiction. According

---

80 See E.L. Peterson, 'Canadian Pharmaceutical Maker Files Notice of Arbitration against the United States', *IAR* 2, 5 January 2009.

81 *Apotex Inc. v. United States of America*, Statement of Defense – Respondent United States of America, 15 March 2011, available at http://www.state.gov/documents/organization/159488.pdf , ¶ 13.

82 Ibidem ¶ 21.

83 Although there are two different statements of claims and the U.S. Department of State maintains two different webpages for the documents relating to this other dispute, there shall be one arbitration dealing with the two different claims. See Joint Letter to the Tribunal, 10 August 2010, available at http://www.state.gov/documents/organization/146083.pdf.

84 *Apotex Inc. v. the Government of the United States of America*, Notice of Arbitration under the Arbitration Rules of the UNCITRAL and the NAFTA, 4 June 2009, ¶ 32.

to the claimant, the administrative decision of the Food and Drug Administration, the U.S. District Court for the District of Columbia, and the US Court of Appeals each violated U.S. statutory law and prior controlling precedent.[85] Apotex claims that because the United States had no "public purpose" for interfering with its property rights and did not provide compensation, the company is entitled to compensatory damages.[86] It is too early to foresee how these disputes will evolve;[87] however, they deserve scrutiny as they concern the interpretation and application of patent regulations which may favour the entry of generics into the market. They also shed light on state responsibility for the decisions of its judicial organs, a theme that has emerged in other investor-state arbitrations.[88]

Compensation

A consequential argument relates to the amount of compensation that should be paid or not paid in the case in which a compulsory licence were to be granted. The right of the state to regulate and even to expropriate in the public interest is not questioned under international law. The issue is whether compensation should be paid.[89] The rule is explicit in relation to the payment of compensation in the case of direct expropriation and transfer of property. It is not quite so clear in the case of regulation that does not involve such a transfer.[90] The issue can be further refined as the determination of who is to pay for the economic cost of attending to the public interest involved in the measure in question. Is it to be society as a whole, represented by the state, or the owner of the affected property?[91]

First and foremost, IP norms already provide compensation for the IP owner in case of compulsory licensing. If one accepts the thesis that compulsory licences are not *per se* a violation of IP but admissible derogations to the same, additional compensation should not be granted in the context of arbitral proceedings. If however, the issuance of compulsory licences was unlawful, i.e.

---

85 Ibidem ¶ 66.

86 Ibidem ¶¶ 78–80.

87 See L.E. Peterson, 'Investor Withdraws Stay Request, and Plans to Proceed with Two NAFTA Arbitration Claims', *IAR* 4, 13 January 2011, pp. 9–10.

88 For instance, in *Saipem v. Bangladesh*, the arbitral tribunal held Bangladesh liable under a BIT for unlawfully expropriating Saipem's right to ICC arbitration through the interference of Bangladeshi courts. *Saipem v. Bangladesh*, ICSID Case No. ARB/05/7, decision on the merits, 30 June 2009, available at the ICSID website.

89 See, generally, S. Ripinsky, *Damages in International Investment Law*, London: BIICL, 2008.

90 As Professor Schreuer points out, today the most difficult question for a judge faced with an allegation of expropriation is not so much whether the requirements for a legal expropriation have been met, but whether there has been an expropriation in the first place. C. Schreuer, 'The Concept of Expropriation under the ETC and other Investment Protection Treaties', *TDM* 2, 2005, p. 3.

91 R. Higgins, 'The Taking of Property by the State: Recent Developments in International Law', *Rec. des Cours* 176, 1982, p. 259.

issued in the absence of the requirements listed in Article 31 of the TRIPS Agreement, there would be a violation of the patent owner's rights; thus the arbitral tribunal could award compensation. For instance, the patent owner could claim that no negotiations were held or that the compensation was not paid.

Second, claims can be made, for instance, when a patent owner is dissatisfied with the determination of the level or mode of remuneration. Standards of compensation for the patent owner may vary from jurisdiction to jurisdiction, but in assessing the adequacy of a given compensation, arbitrators should bear in mind the economic rationale of compulsory licensing and the public policy goal furthered by the national measure. The terms of the compulsory licences 'should be given a humanitarian reading, guided also by the broader human rights context'.[92] It would be illogical to impose huge compensation on a developing country which is issuing compulsory licences to obtain affordable medicines. If over-compensation is likely to occur, then promoting socially valuable goals may become unsustainable. Developing countries will need to develop rules and procedures adapted to their own circumstances for setting royalty rates, but the implication of the experiences of other countries is that royalty rates need not be very high.[93] For example, the Supreme Court of the Philippines affirmed that the royalty at 2.5 per cent of the net wholesale price is a fair compensation.[94] In another case, the Court deemed that the royalty rate of 2.5 per cent was reasonable and thus did not amount to a taking of the claimant's property without due process.[95] In the U.K., authorities have set the royalty in the pharmaceutical sector at about 18 per cent of the sale price but in Canada these rates were considerably lower – at ten per cent or at four per cent.[96]

Expropriation rules, if found applicable, may in some cases be more beneficial to the patent owner than the compulsory licence rules, particularly because the obligation to pay will rest with the government. If one adopts the *sole effects* doctrine, thus focusing on the economic effect of the regulatory measures on the patent, compulsory licences may *prima facie* appear as indirect expropriations. Customary compensation rules, uniformly enshrined in investment protection treaties, do not differentiate between various public purposes of expropriations, posing a single standard instead. The full

---

92 A. Taubman, 'Rethinking TRIPS: "Adequate Remuneration" for Non-Voluntary Patent Licensing', *JIEL* 11, 2008, p. 963.

93 Ibidem.

94 *Smith Kline & French Laboratories Ltd v. Court of Appeals, Bureau of Patents, Trademarks and Technology Transfer and Doctors Pharmaceuticals Inc.*, July 24, 1997, G.R. No. 121867, available at http://www.lawphil.net/judjuris/juri1997/jul1997/gr_121867_1997.html.

95 *Barry John Price v. United Laboratories*, Supreme Court of Manila, 29 September 1988, G.R. 82542 available at http://www.lawphil.net/judjuris/juri1988/sep1988/gr_82542_1988.html.

96 J. Watal, 'Pharmaceutical Patents, Prices and Welfare Losses: Policy Options for India Under the WTO TRIPS Agreement', *World Economy* 23, 2002, p. 743.

compensation is often described as having the characteristics of promptness, adequacy and effectiveness according to the so-called Hull formula.[97] Usually arbitral proceedings do not take into account the public dimension or the lawfulness of the measure to establish the exact amount of compensation.[98] For instance, in *Compania del Desarollo de Santa Elena v. Republic of Costa Rica*[99] the arbitral tribunal concurred with the claimant that the particular public policy objective pursued by the expropriation could not *per se* affect the level of compensation. In other words, the question of compensation was not linked to the legality of the taking.

Again, it is worth pointing out that compulsory licences are not a violation of IP; rather they should be seen as a derogation or internal limit thereof. Therefore, the amount of compensation should be in conformity of consistent IP practice worldwide.[100] An additional argument could be made that, since compulsory licences on pharmaceuticals can be viewed as a specialized form of exercise of state regulatory powers, they are justified by overwhelming public interest; thus, no compensation should be provided besides that already awarded under IP rules. Under the *police powers* doctrine, no compensation has to be paid for *bona fide* government regulations enacted for the protection of public health, safety, morals or welfare that are non-discriminatory and within the commonly accepted police powers of the state.[101]

In conclusion, as Professor Gibson points out, 'those who would argue that [compulsory licences] can never be considered an expropriation overstate their claim, while those who suggest that it must always be considered an expropriation commit an overstatement from the opposing side of the argument'.[102] Instead, the determination of whether a compulsory licence amounts to a *de facto* or *indirect* expropriation must be made case by case. The

97   The Hull formula is named after the American Secretary of State, Cordell Hull, who described a full compensation standard as 'prompt adequate and effective' in a diplomatic exchange of notes with Mexico in 1930. Letter from U.S. Secretary of State Cordell Hull to the Mexican Ambassador (F. Castillo Najera) Washington D.C. July 21, 1938) in 5 Foreign Relations of the United States, Diplomatic Papers 1938 at 674, 678 (1954).

98   Restitution may play a role in order to overcome this impasse. Indeed, pharmaceutical patents could be prolonged after their deadline if being suspended for health emergencies during their life. However, the notion of returning to the *status quo ante* is always subject to the condition that doing so does not place a disproportionate burden on the state. In the context of investment disputes, 'the impracticality of requiring restitution has been observed in many cases' and arbitral tribunals are reluctant to order it against a sovereign state. See A. Cohen Smutny, 'Some Observations on the Principles Relating to Compensation in the Investment Treaty Context', *ICSID Review-FILJ* 22, 2007, p. 9.

99   *Compañía del Desarollo de Santa Elena v. Republic of Costa Rica*, ICSID Case No. ARB/96/1, Final Award of 17 February 2000, *ICSID Review-FILJ* 15, 2000, pp. 169–204.

100 D.R. Cahoy, 'Confronting Myths and Myopia on the Road from Doha', *Georgia L Rev* 42, 2007–2008, pp. 131ff.

101 A. Newcombe, 'The Boundaries of Regulatory Expropriation in International Law', *ICSID Rev.-FILJ* 20, 2005, p. 23.

102 C. Gibson, 'A Look at the Compulsory License in Investment Arbitration: The Case of Indirect Expropriation', *Am. U. Int'l L. Rev.* 25, 2010, p. 393.

adoption of a compulsory licence aimed at protecting public health cannot necessarily be deemed to be a violation of investment treaty provisions *per se*. The burden of proof lies on the investors: they have to demonstrate that a given national measure is in violation of their rights as provided by treaty law. The mere fact that the regulatory measure may have an adverse economic effect on an investment, in and of itself, does not establish that a *de facto* or *indirect* expropriation has occurred. In this sense, one has to enquire into the nature of such a measure.[103] Is such measure enacted to protect public health? Is such measure discriminatory vis-à-vis foreign producers? Is such measure reasonable with regard to the stated objective? While arbitrators address these and similar questions when scrutinizing the conformity of state measures with the fair and equitable treatment and the non-discrimination standards, such assessment may also be of relevance when establishing whether an indirect or regulatory expropriation has taken place.

Fair and equitable treatment

With regard to the alleged violation of fair and equitable treatment, claims will concern the fairness of the state's measures, the alleged violation of the investor's legitimate expectations and/or denial of justice claims. For instance, with regard to possible claims that the issuance of a compulsory licence has violated the fair and equitable treatment (FET) standard, arbitrators will investigate whether or not the government in carrying out its process to determine whether it was necessary to issue a compulsory licence or similar measure, conducted such process in an independent manner. For example, if the chairman of a generic pharmaceutical company was also the chairman of the health committee which issued the compulsory licence, this may give rise to doubt as to the fairness of the regulatory process. In a situation involving discrepancies in the issuance of compulsory licences only of foreign medicines, national policies would have to be justified according to reasonable and objective criteria. This would be the case if there was a health emergency and no national company was producing a specific or analogous medical treatment. In such circumstance, compulsory licences of foreign medicines in favour of national (and foreign) producers would be reasonable. However, the issuance of compulsory licences on the mere ground that the patent is not 'worked' locally – i.e. the medicines are not produced in the host state – and irrespective of public health needs, might be deemed controversial by arbitral tribunals in the light of existing international standards.[104]

103 See, e.g. R. Bird and D.R. Cahoy, 'The Impact of Compulsory Licensing on Foreign Direct Investment: A Collective Bargaining Approach', *American Business L.J.* 45, 2008, p. 306 (questioning Egypt's stated rationale for issuing a compulsory licence on Viagra 'to benefit the poor').

104 See Article 27 of the TRIPS Agreement stating, *inter alia*, that 'patents shall be available and patent rights enjoyable without discrimination as to . . . whether products are

On the other hand, questions arise as to the protection of the patent holder's legitimate expectations under the FET standard. For instance, the issuance of a compulsory licence can disrupt the investment-backed expectation of the patent holder.[105] In the NAFTA case *Signa S.A. v. Canada*,[106] a Mexican generic pharmaceutical company challenged a Canadian measure concerning the duration of pharmaceutical patents, claiming that the longer patent life span imposed by the new Canadian legislation frustrated its legitimate expectations under Article 1105 of the NAFTA. As the parties quickly settled this case, there is no publicly available information on the dispute. This withdrawal was probably due to the inception of the TRIPS Agreement that extended the pharmaceutical patent protection to twenty years. Whether the filing of the Notice of Intent to Arbitrate had any strategic or other impact is unknown.

Finally, denial of justice claims have been raised with regard to the regulation of pharmaceutical patents. Denial of justice indicates cases in which national courts have released manifestly unjust judgments in violation of international law. For instance, in the pending *Apotex* case, the claimant alleged that the U.S. courts '[rendered] manifestly unjust decisions by misapplying statutory and common law. . .'.[107] The case has not been decided yet.

Non-discrimination

With regard to the fourth type of claim, relating to non-discrimination, had there been a BIT between India and the U.S., the well known case *Novartis v. Union of India and Others* might have been adjudicated before an investment treaty tribunal, and the investor might have alleged *inter alia* violation of the non-discrimination principle. Instead, as there is no such BIT, the case was adjudicated before the High Court in Madras, which rejected the challenge by Swiss Novartis against Section 3(d) of the 2005 Indian Patent law. The Indian Patent Law blocks the patenting of minor improvements of known molecules for evident public health reasons.[108] After rejection of its patent application on a leukaemia drug, on the grounds that the new medicine was insufficiently

---

imported or locally produced'. In 2001 the U.S. withdrew its WTO claim against Brazil concerning the law requiring the local manufacture of HIV/medicines. Under the agreement between the two countries, 'should Brazil seek to issue a compulsory license on grounds of failure to work the patent locally, it would consult the US before doing so'. D. Matthews, *Intellectual Property, Human Rights and Development*, Cheltenham: Edward Elgar, 2011, p. 38.

105 Bird and Cahoy, 'The Impact of Compulsory Licensing on Foreign Direct Investment', p. 284.

106 *Signa v. Canada* Notice of Intent to Submit a Claim to Arbitration, 4 March 1996.

107 *Apotex v. United States*, Notice of Arbitration, 4 June 2009, op. cit., ¶ 73.

108 *Novartis AG and another v. Union of India and Others*, unreported 2007, High Court of Judicature at Madras, 6 August 2007.

different from the previous version,[109] the company filed the case, challenging the constitutionality of section 3(d) and arguing *inter alia* that by requiring 'enhancement of the known efficacy', the clause was not sufficiently defined and conferred unguided power to the patent examiner who could decide applications on a case by case basis. Allegedly, because of its vagueness and arbitrariness, Section 3(d) contravened the equality principle affirmed by Article 14 of the Indian Constitution. The Court rejected the claim, stating that the goal of the provision was clear: for a patent to be granted, it must be shown that the medicine has a better therapeutic effect. If the Madras Court had ruled the other way, Indian companies would have been prevented from manufacturing generic versions of the medicine.

In the pending *Apotex* case, Apotex challenges that the U.S. courts committed errors in interpreting federal law and that these errors, *inter alia*, are in violation of NAFTA Article 1102.[110] Allegedly, as these errors prevented Apotex from obtaining a judgment of patent non-infringement, Apotex was unable to commercialize its generic products and its investment was not treated in the same fashion as the investments of U.S. investors.[111] While the United States has rejected such allegations in its Statement of Defense,[112] the case has not been decided yet.

Reconciling patent rights with public health in investment law

Foreign direct investment, intellectual property and human rights have been deemed to exist in quasi-hermetical isolation: they are treated as separate areas, subject to their own norms and institutional structures. These subject matter areas are considered as a part of general international law, but often presented as self-contained and disconnected from one another. However, as the case studies mentioned above have shown, norms arising in different subject areas increasingly can, and do, interact. This section addresses the question as to whether it is possible to enhance coherence between different treaty regimes.

Interpretation

The Vienna Convention on the Law of Treaties (VCLT)[113] establishes a framework which governs the interplay between different international law

---

109 See A. Gentleman, 'Setback for Novartis in India Over Drug Patent', *New York Times*, 7 August 2007.

110 *Apotex v. United States*, Notice of Arbitration 4 June 2009, op. cit., ¶¶ 68–70.

111 Ibidem, ¶ 70.

112 *Apotex v. United States*, Statement of Defense, Respondent United States of America, 15 March 2011, available at http://www.state.gov/documents/organization/159488.pdf .

113 Vienna Convention on the Law of Treaties, done in Vienna on 23 May 1969, entered into force on 27 January 1980, United Nations Treaty Series vol. 1155, p. 331.

rules.[114] In particular, it addresses three different relationships: 1) the relationship between two or more treaties relating to the same subject matter; 2) that between a treaty and *jus cogens* norms; and 3) that between a treaty and other relevant rules of international law. With regard to the relationship between treaties governing the same subject matter, the VCLT reaffirms the principle *lex posterior derogat priori*.[115] However, as Professor Sands points out, the Convention does not define what constitutes the same subject matter, and this issue may be a matter of debate.[116] For instance, it is clear that investment treaties do not entirely overlap and in fact some FTAs go beyond the IP requirements of the TRIPS Agreement. However, some International Investment Agreements (IIAs) expressly refer to the TRIPS Agreement. If there is a *renvoi matériel*, the TRIPS Agreement and the Doha Declaration on the TRIPS Agreement and Public Health are part of the applicable law in that they will be relevant in interpreting and applying investment treaty standards, as required by the *renvoi*. If there is no such incorporation, the TRIPS Agreement and the Doha Declaration can be relevant under article 31(3)(c) of the VCLT.

With regard to the relationship between a treaty and *jus cogens* norms, Article 53 of the VCLT states that a treaty shall be void if at the time of its conclusion it conflicts with a peremptory norm of general international law. As mentioned previously, access to essential medicines has been deemed to be part of the right to health and the right to life. An argument has been made that components of these rights have reached the status of *jus cogens* norms. If one accepts such argument, the necessary consequence would be the nullity of investment treaties that conflict with such a peremptory norm. However, intellectual property promotes medical research. The argument that investment treaties or that some of their norms are incompatible *tout court* with access to medicines proves too much. Rather, the interpretation of intellectual property as an absolute right may be incompatible with access to medicines. Therefore, as such interpretation would determine the incompatibility of the investment treaty with a *jus cogens* norm (if one accepts the hypothesis that access to medicines already belongs to *jus cogens*), it should be avoided.

With regard to the third relationship between a treaty obligation and other international law sources, international law comes into play under any investment treaty pursuant to Article 31(3)(c) of the VCLT, which provides that the treaty interpreter shall take into account 'any relevant rules of

---

114 The literature on treaty interpretation is extensive. See, for instance, R. Gardiner, *Treaty Interpretation,* New York: Oxford University Press, 2008; A. Orakhelashvili, *The Interpretation of Acts and Rules in Public International Law*, Oxford: Oxford University Press, 2008.

115 VCLT, Article 30.

116 See P. Sands, 'Sustainable Development: Treaty, Custom and the Cross-Fertilization of International Law', in A. Boyle and D. Freestone (eds), *International Law and Sustainable Development*, Oxford: Oxford University Press, 1999, p. 49.

international law applicable in the relations between the parties'. As stated by Sinclair, pursuant to Article 31(3)(c), '[e]very treaty provision must be read not only in its own context, but in the broader context of general international law, whether conventional or customary'.[117] International law serves as a relevant context and colours the interpretation of the investment treaties. According to Professor Sands, Article 31(3)(c) reflects a 'principle of integration': 'It emphasizes both the "unity of international law" and the sense in which rules should not be considered in isolation of general international law'.[118]

Interpretation by analogy with the WTO is relevant because the TRIPS Agreement most notably provides a comprehensive discipline of IP. However, other international organizations such as the World Health Organization also play an active role in international IP regulation.[119] If the TRIPS Agreement is duly taken into account in interpreting investment treaties,[120] conceptually there is no reason to object to the consideration of other international law norms, provided that they are relevant.[121]

Negotiation and mediation

Negotiation and mediation are dispute settlement methods alternative to judicial settlement and arbitration. Such processes may occur on an *ad hoc* basis or even in the context of arbitral institutions such as the ICSID.[122] As negotiation generally creates a situation where both parties cooperate to reach a satisfactory result,[123] it may amplify the advantages and chances of both parties. For instance, Thailand negotiated with some foreign pharmaceutical companies to obtain essential medicines at a considerably reduced price. The

---

117 I. Sinclair, *The Vienna Convention on the Law of Treaties*, Manchester: Manchester University Press, 1984, p. 139.

118 See Sands, 'Sustainable Development', p. 49.

119 The extent to which external concerns can be taken into account in the interpretative processes has been much considered among international economic law scholars. On the WTO jurisprudence, see for instance, P. Mavroidis, 'No Outsourcing of Law? WTO Law as Practised by WTO Courts', *AJIL* 102, 2008, p. 421; G. Marceau, 'A Call for Coherence in International Law – Praises for the Prohibition Against Clinical Isolation in WTO Dispute Settlement', *JWT* 33, 1999, pp. 87–152; and J. Pauwelyn, 'The Role of Public International Law in the WTO: How Far Can We Go?', *AJIL* 95, 2001, p. 535. On the investment case law, see R. Hofmann and C. Tams, *International Investment Law and General International Law*, Baden: Nomos, 2011.

120 On the use of WTO analogies for investment disputes, see N. Di Mascio and J. Pauwelyn, 'Non-Discrimination in Trade and Investment Treaties: Worlds Apart or Two Sides of the Same Coin?' *AJIL* 102, 2008, pp. 48–89.

121 See Chapter 7.

122 See S. Franck, 'Challenges Facing Investment Disputes: Reconsidering Dispute Resolution in International Investment Agreements', in K. Sauvant (ed.), *Appeals Mechanism in International Investment Disputes*, Oxford: Oxford University Press, 2008, pp. 143–92.

123 See H. Raiffa, *The Art and Science of Negotiation*, Cambridge, MA: Harvard University Press, 1982; A. Plantey, *International Negotiation in the Twenty-First Century*, London: Routledge, 2007.

agreement went much beyond price reduction though, as it included the donation of pharmaceuticals for the terminally ill and the poor.[124]

It is interesting to point out that in the context of negotiations, both developing and developed countries have used the threat of compulsory licences to reduce medicine prices. For instance, in 2001, the Government of Brazil was able to obtain a price reduction of up to 70 per cent for AIDS medicines. It is notable that, in that circumstance, Brazil successfully used the threat of compulsory licensing in price negotiations, without issuing a compulsory licence.[125] Similarly, the United States obtained a drastic reduction in the price of stockpiled *Cipro* during the anthrax scare in 2001 by threatening to impose a compulsory licence for government use. In the end, an agreement was reached with Bayer.[126]

Mediation may also play a useful role in this context. Where the degree of animosity between the parties is so great that direct negotiations are unlikely to lead to a dispute settlement, the intervention of a third party to reconcile the parties may be a suitable option.[127] Mediation involves the good offices of a neutral third party which facilitate communication between the discussants. Like negotiation, mediation is guided by the goal of finding a win-win situation for all parties through a creative process that focuses on the interests of the parties, rather than on their positions, and searches for creative alternatives to solve the dispute. As the mediator does not have the authority to make a binding decision and does not follow a fixed procedure, the procedure allows for flexible and dynamic dialogue.

Time is another intrinsic advantage of negotiation and mediation, as these instruments usually achieve results in a short time frame. Importantly, these methods are not required to deal with the past: they require the parties to focus their future and reshape their duties and responsibilities towards each other. Foreign investors thus participate in the decision-making process that will ultimately affect them and become aware of the local population interests. In these proceedings all the different interests are explored and discussed. Furthermore, experience shows that agreements entered into through a voluntary process stand out for their durability, because of the parties' high identification with the achieved result.

However, these characteristics should not lead to the over-emphasis of these alternative dispute resolution methods. Indeed, these methods can be

---

124 'Thailand: Latest Talks with Patent Owners of Cancer Drugs Show Positive Results', *IP Watch*, 5 November 2007.
125 Brazil awarded compulsory licences on other medicines though. See T. Gerhardsen, 'Brazil Takes Steps To Import Cheaper AIDS Drugs Under Trade Law', *IP Watch*, 7 May 2007.
126 'US and Bayer Settle Anthrax Row', *BBC News*, 24 October 2001.
127 J. Collier and V. Lowe, *The Settlement of Disputes in International Law: Institutions and Procedures*, Oxford: Oxford University Press, 1999, p. 29; C. Bürhing-Uhle, L. Kirchhoff and G. Scherer, *Arbitration and Mediation in International Business*, The Hague: Kluwer, 1996; E. Carroll and K. Mackie, *International Mediation – The Art of Business Diplomacy*, The Hague: Kluwer, 2006.

extremely useful in those situations where both contracting parties have equal or similar bargaining power. This is the case when the host state is an industrialized country or a country with manufacturing capacity. On the contrary, negotiation or other alternative dispute resolution methods do not seem to be effective when developing and least developed countries are involved; these countries need foreign investments to foster development and growth.[128] Because of this endemic need and other systemic characteristics, these countries may have an incentive to lower health standards (i.e. *race to the bottom*) to attract foreign investment flows. The threat of litigation by investors can create a chilling effect on policy makers. For instance, in Thailand, NGOs campaigned invoking the use of compulsory licences to reduce the prices of DDI, an anti-retroviral drug against AIDS. However, the threat of trade sanctions prevented Thailand from pursuing the idea.[129]

Legal drafting

Some investment treaties anticipate possible disputes by providing safeguard clauses with regard to compulsory licensing. For instance, NAFTA provisions on expropriation and compensation provide an exception with regard to compulsory licences.[130] Also, the new Article 6(5) in the U.S. Model BIT of 2004 on expropriation and compensation clarifies that 'This Article does not apply to the issuance of compulsory licenses granted in relation to intellectual property rights in accordance with the TRIPS Agreement.'[131] Analogously, the 2004 Canadian Model FIPA excludes the application of the provision on expropriation to the issuance of compulsory licences or the revocation, limitation or creation of intellectual property rights to the extent that such issuance, revocation, limitation or creation is consistent with the WTO Agreement.[132]

Similarly, the *side letter* to the U.S.–Morocco FTA governs eventual conflicts between different treaty regimes, stating that 'Nothing in the intellectual property chapter of the agreement shall affect the ability of either party to take

128 Bird and Cahoy argue that 'Developing nations, however, may attempt to use their compulsory license strategically by acting collectively with countries that have similar interests.' Bird and Cahoy, 'The Impact of Compulsory Licensing on Foreign Direct Investment', p. 330.

129 See E. Ghanotakis, 'How the US Interpretation of Flexibilities Inherent in TRIPS Affects Access to Medicines for Developing Countries', *JWIP* 7, 2004, pp. 563–91.

130 NAFTA, article 1110.7: 'This article [on expropriation and compensation] does not apply to the issuance of compulsory licenses granted in relation to IPRs, or to the revocation, limitation or creation of IPRs, to the extent that such issuance, revocation, limitation or creation is consistent with Chapter Seventeen (Intellectual Property)'. See also U.S.–Australia FTA, Article 11.7.5.

131 For analogous language, see India–Singapore FTA Article 6.5.6; Chile–U.S. FTA, Article 10.9.5; U.S.–Uruguay BIT, Article 6(5).

132 Canadian Model FIPA (2004) Article 13(5).

necessary measures to protect public health by promoting access to medicines for all, in particular concerning cases such as HIV/AIDS, tuberculosis, malaria, and other epidemics as well as circumstances of extreme urgency or national emergency.'[133] The side letter also clarifies that the IP chapter of the FTA will not prevent the effective utilization of the waiver allowing developing countries that lack pharmaceutical manufacturing capacity to import drugs under compulsory licence.

However, the legal value of side letters or understandings is unclear. Such clauses may be virtually meaningless if interpreted as declaratory statements and not as legally binding instruments. If the clause is considered to have a merely interpretative value, many problems arise with regard to its implementation. The hierarchy of these statements vis-à-vis other investment treaty provisions is extremely ambiguous. Moreover, express reference to these issues made only in some recent investment treaties and not in others indicates that the ones in which such reference is absent are in fact limiting public health regulation.[134]

In this sense, the approach adopted by the U.S. and Canadian Model BITs does not bar any consideration of the compulsory licences in investment treaty arbitration, but demands the arbitrators to ascertain that the host state's issuance of the licence or analogous measure is in compliance with the TRIPS Agreement.[135] In order to verify that a compulsory licence is in compliance with the TRIPS Agreement, the arbitral tribunal will have to interpret the detailed Article 31 of the TRIPS Agreement in the context of other relevant provisions, such as Articles 7 and 8 of the TRIPS Agreement,[136] and the Doha Declaration on the TRIPS Agreement and Public Health.[137] In this sense, the provisions of the U.S.–Colombia FTA, U.S.–Panama FTA and the U.S.–Korea FTA expressly state that 'a Party may take measures to protect public health in accordance with the Declaration on the TRIPS Agreement and Public Health'.[138]

In conclusion, investment treaties need to maintain the balance between private and public interest that is implicit in the protection of pharmaceutical

---

133 Side letter to the U.S.–Morocco FTA Agreement. For analogous language see also the Side Letter to the U.S.–Central America FTA (CAFTA).

134 R. Castro Bernieri, 'Intellectual Property Rights in Bilateral Investment Treaties and Access to Medicines: The Case of Latin America', *JWIP* 9, 2006, p. 553.

135 See Gibson, 'A Look at the Compulsory License in Investment Arbitration', p. 34.

136 TRIPS Agreement, Articles 7 and 8. Article 7 of the TRIPS Agreement provides that IP rights should contribute to the promotion of technological innovation and/or the transfer and dissemination of technology, to the mutual advantage of producers and users. Article 8 specifies that Members, in formulating their laws and regulations, may adopt measures necessary to protect public health.

137 See H. Hestermeyer, *Human Rights and the WTO, The Case of Patents and Access to Medicines*, Oxford: Oxford University Press, 2007.

138 U.S.–Colombia FTA, Article 16.10; U.S.–Panama FTA, Article 15.10; U.S.–Korea FTA, Article 18.9.

patents.[139] Medicines are not mere investments destined to enhance private profit, but being related to health and life, they also serve a social function.[140] Thus, it is important to take into account not only their proprietary dimension, but also their impact on public health. Still, the extent to which the new less stringent IP language will apply to future investment treaties is unclear and will be the subject of continued negotiations.

Conclusions

This chapter has explored the interplay between patent protection, international investment law and public health, highlighting the potential negative impact that an excessive patent protection may have on public health policies. This may seem paradoxical as pharmaceutical patents are usually associated with positive effects on scientific research and consumer well-being. By providing incentives and remuneration to the patent owner, pharmaceutical patents promote medical research and ultimately public welfare. However, in case of health emergencies, the flexibilities which are provided by the patent system need to be fully implemented. In this respect, the Doha Declaration on the TRIPS Agreement and Public Health has clarified the importance and the extent of the flexibilities within the TRIPS Agreement.

International investment treaties can generate grey areas which can be used to challenge national measures even if they are TRIPS-consistent. Thus, in the absence of a conflict clause, it is important to read investment treaties in the light of current international law, including public health instruments, human rights law, and the Doha Declaration, which clearly reaffirmed the right of WTO Members to use the flexibilities of the TRIPS 'to promote access to medicines for all'.[141]

De jure condendo, *ad hoc* investment treaty provisions might clarify and/or restate the flexibilities available to the host state in the implementation of IP regulation. In this regard, while the *General Comment No. 14* has stressed that 'State parties should ensure that the right to health is given due attention in international agreements [. . .]',[142] the UN Commission on Human Rights has called upon states, at the international level, to take steps to ensure that their actions as members of international organizations 'take due account of the right of everyone to the enjoyment of the highest attainable standard of [. . .] health and that the application of international agreements is supportive of public health policies which promote broad access to [. . .] pharmaceutical

---

139 See P. Drahos, *A Philosophy of Intellectual Property*, Dartmouth: Ashgate, 1996, p. 199.
140 *General Comment No. 17*, The Right of Everyone to Benefit from the Protection of the Moral and Material Interests Resulting from Any Scientific, Literary or Artistic Production of Which He Is the Author (Art. 15(1)(c), UN Doc. E/C.12/GC/17, 12 January 2006, ¶ 35).
141 Doha Declaration on TRIPS and Public Health, ¶ 4.
142 *General Comment No 14*, ¶39.

products'.[143] Importantly, access to essential medicines may be considered as part of the traditional prerogative of states to protect the public health of their citizens. Even those countries which are not party to the ICESCR and, thus, are not bound by its provisions, have the duty to adopt measures to facilitate access to essential medicines and have concretely done so in cases of health emergencies.

In the absence of such clauses, arbitral tribunals should be expected to map the interactions between multiple sources of law. Pursuant to customary rules of treaty interpretation, treaty terms must be interpreted not only according to their strict textual meaning, but also in good faith, in context and in the light of their object and purpose. Moreover, terms must be interpreted taking into account any relevant rules of international law applicable in the relations between the parties. Investment treaties should not be considered as isolated from public international law.

---

143 CHR Resolution 2003/29, *Access to Essential Medicines in the Context of Pandemics such as HIV/AIDS, Tuberculosis and Malaria* (E/CN.4/2003/L.11/Add. 3), adopted on 22 April 2003.

5 Trademark protection v. tobacco control in international investment law

Introduction

According to the World Health Organization (WHO), tobacco consumption causes the death of five million people each year and this figure could rise to more than eight million by 2030 unless measures are taken to control the tobacco epidemic.[1] Countries have massively adhered to the WHO Framework Convention on Tobacco Control (FCTC),[2] which has established 'cognitive and normative consensus' for promoting global public health through tobacco control.[3]

Despite these approaches, international investment governance risks undermining the goal of tobacco control, by increasing competition and thus lowering the prices of tobacco products.[4] In addition, tension exists when a state adopts tobacco control measures interfering with foreign investments, as such a regulation may be considered as tantamount to a violation of investment treaty provisions protecting the trademarks of tobacco companies. As investment treaties provide foreign investors with direct access to investment arbitration, foreign investors can directly challenge tobacco control measures and can seek compensation for the impact of such regulation on their business. As a result, the mere threat of an investor-state dispute may have a chilling effect on policy makers. Again, several questions arise in this context. Are investment treaties compatible with states' obligations to protect public health? Are there any limits to the power of states to enact tobacco control regulations?

---

1 WHO, Tobacco Fact Sheet No. 339/2010, May 2010, available at http://www.who.int/mediacentre/factsheets/fs339/en/index.html.
2 World Health Organization Framework Convention on Tobacco Control, WHA Res. 56.1, World Health Assembly, 56th Ass 4th plenary meeting, Annex WHO Doc. A56.VR/4, 21 May 2003, 42 ILM 3 (2003) 518–39 [hereinafter FCTC]. The Convention entered into force on 27 February 2005.
3 B. Mason Meier, 'Breathing Life into the Framework Convention on Tobacco Control: Smoking Cessation and the Right to Health', *Yale J. of Health Policy & Ethics* 5, 2005, p. 137.
4 *See* P. Jha and F. Chaloupka (eds), *Tobacco Control in Developing Countries*, Oxford: Oxford University Press, 2000.

In the light of parallel developments before other fora, this chapter scrutinizes and critically assesses the clash between trademark protection and tobacco control before investment treaty tribunals and offers a systematic and updated analysis of the recent case law. The chapter then concludes with some policy options that may help policy makers and adjudicators to reconcile the different interests at stake. The argument will proceed in three parts. First, the international law instruments concerning tobacco control will be sketched out. Second, this chapter will explore the conflict areas between international investment law and tobacco control, examining some recent cases. This survey will show that, in some cases, the regime established according to investment treaties does not strike an appropriate balance between the different interests concerned. Lastly, this chapter offers a series of legal tools available to policy makers and adjudicators in order to reconcile the different interests at stake.

Global health governance and tobacco control

Tobacco control is an important aspect of contemporary public health governance. Whatever its conceptualization, be it considered a human rights issue or a mere public policy objective, the legitimacy of such a goal is uncontested.[5] This section explores the multi-level legal framework that governs tobacco control and proceeds as follows. First, it explores the conceptualization of tobacco control as a component of the right to health, assessing the pros and cons of this theory. It then scrutinizes the more neutral conceptualization of tobacco control as a public health objective and examines the relevant legal framework.

Tobacco control as a human rights issue

Tobacco control has been conceptualized as 'a human rights issue',[6] and in particular as a component part of the right to health. This argument is based on several grounds. In a preliminary fashion, scientific evidence has proven that tobacco use is not a mere behavioural choice,[7] but constitutes a physiological addiction largely outside the control of the individual.[8] Furthermore, as tobacco consumption harms not only active smokers, but also the passive ones, tobacco control should not be considered a paternalistic

5 World Bank, *Tobacco Control Policy: Strategies, Successes and Setbacks*, Washington, DC: WB, 2003, p. 10.
6 *See* V. Leary, 'Concretizing the Right to Health: Tobacco Use as a Human Right Issue', in F. Coomans, F. Grünfeld, I. Westendorp and J. Willems (eds), *Rendering Justice to the Vulnerable: Liber Amicorum in Honour of Theo van Boven*, The Hague: Kluwer Law International, 2000, p. 161.
7 The right to health does not address individual lifestyle choices. *General Comment No 14*, ¶ 8.
8 See K.-O. Fagerström, 'Measuring Degree of Physical Dependence to Tobacco Smoking with Reference to Individualization of Treatment', *Addictive Behaviours* 3, 1978, pp. 235–41.

issue,[9] but a public good, which requires public action both at the national and international levels. Other considerations follow.

First, at the international level, the Committee on Economic, Social and Cultural Rights has construed Article 12 of the International Covenant on Economic, Social and Cultural Rights on the right to the highest attainable standard of health to require states parties to implement certain tobacco control measures.[10] In particular, states are encouraged to undertake information campaigns regarding the adverse consequences of cigarette smoking, with the aim of discouraging tobacco use.[11] By failing to undertake tobacco control initiatives, governments violate their human rights obligations to protect public health.[12] Indeed *General Comment No. 14* expressly states that: 'Violations of the obligation to protect [the right to health] follow from the failure of a State to take all necessary measures to safeguard persons within their jurisdiction from infringements of the right to health by third parties. This category includes such omissions as the failure to regulate the activities of individuals, groups or corporations so as to prevent them from violating the right to health of others; the failure to protect consumers . . . from practices detrimental to health, e.g. by . . . the failure to discourage production, marketing and consumption of tobacco. . .'[13] Although General Comments are not a primary source of law, they are deemed to be authoritative interpretations of treaty text, thus contributing to the clarification and development of the living law or *droit vivant*.

Second, at the regional level, the ECtHR has affirmed the human rights dimension of tobacco control, according a wide margin of appreciation to national governments regarding the precise parameters of a tobacco regulatory regime.[14] In *Wöckel v. Germany*, the European Commission on Human Rights (ECommHR) provided guidance concerning the scope of states parties' obligations to protect non-smokers from environmental smoke.[15] In particular, as the German government had imposed restrictions on tobacco advertising and prohibited smoking in certain public areas, the ECommHR held that the applicant's right to life and to respect for private and family life had not been violated, interpreting Articles 2 and 8 of the Convention as not requiring Germany to do more than it had already done. In *Novoselov v. Russia*, the Court considered that the conditions of detention had to be compatible with the

---

9 A. Weale, 'Invisible Hand or Fatherly Hand? Problems of Paternalism in the New Perspective on Health', *Journal of Health Politics, Policy and Law* 7, 1983, pp. 784–807.

10 See *General Comment No. 14*.

11 *General Comment No 14*, ¶ 15.

12 For commentary, see M. Crow, 'Smokescreens and State Responsibility: Using Human Rights Strategies to Promote Global Tobacco Control', *Yale JIL* 29, 2004, p. 211.

13 *General Comment No 14*, ¶ 51.

14 European Convention for the Protection of Human Rights and Fundamental Freedoms, 4 November 1950, 213 UNTS 222.

15 *Wöckel v. Germany*, App. No. 32165/96, ECommHR 1998.

prisoner's human dignity, health and well-being.[16] Thus, the lack of adequate ventilation, aggravated by a general tolerance of smoking in the cell was an element that ultimately led the Court to find a violation of Article 3 of the Convention.

Third, even national constitutional courts have adjudicated on the scope of governments' obligations in relation to tobacco control and linked this issue to the human rights discourse. Some courts have held that constitutional human rights norms require governments to undertake tobacco control measures.[17] For instance, in *Deora v. India*, the Indian Supreme Court held that the Union of India had violated the constitutional right to health of its citizens by failing to undertake adequate tobacco control measures.[18] Similarly, the Bangladeshi Supreme Court banned the advertising of tobacco products in the mass media, to ensure protection of the right to health and human dignity, as required by the Bangladeshi Constitution.[19] Other national courts have deemed second-hand smoke a violation of the right to life and to a clean healthy environment.[20]

The exponents of the theory which subsumes tobacco control under the umbrella of the right to health stress that, on the one hand, this conceptualization concretizes the right to health.[21] On the other hand, it brings 'considerable attention and rhetorical force to the issue'.[22]

However, while there is scientific consensus on the lethal effects of tobacco smoke, there is less agreement on the need for some states to ratify the ICESCR.[23] In addition, there was virtually no discussion of human rights during the course of the negotiations that led to the inception of the FCTC. As one author highlights, 'repeated arguments made during the negotiations that public health should be prioritized over international trade were based upon the sovereign right to protect public health, not the human right to health'.[24] Other than a vague reference in the preamble to Article 12 of the ICESCR as well as the Convention on the Rights of the Child and CEDAW, the final text of the FCTC contains no other reference to human rights.

---

16 *Novoselov v. Russia*, App. No 66460/01, ECtHR (2 June 2005) ¶ 39.
17 There is an emerging jurisprudence on the scope of governments' obligations to regulate the activities of tobacco companies within their jurisdictions. For an exhaustive account of this case law, see for instance Crow, 'Smokescreens and State Responsibility'.
18 *Murli S. Deora v. Union of India*, AIR 2002 S.C. 40, http://www.elaw.org/node/1834.
19 *Nurul Islam v. Bangladesh*, WP Nos. 1825/99, 4521/99, 7 February 2000, http://www.elaw.org/node/1768.
20 *Environmental Action Network Ltd v. Attorney General and National Environment Management Authority* (High Court of Uganda) Misc App n. 39 of 2001.
21 Leary, 'Concretizing the Right to Health', p. 162.
22 Ibidem, p. 169.
23 Notably, the United States has signed but not ratified the ICESCR.
24 A.L. Taylor, 'Trade, Human Rights, and the WHO Framework Convention on Tobacco Control: Just What the Doctor Ordered?', in T. Cottier, J. Pauwelyn and E. Bürgi Bonanomi (eds), *Human Rights and International Trade*, Oxford: Oxford University Press, 2005, p. 329.

Whatever the position adopted on this issue,[25] scholars recognize the interdependence of human rights and the protection of public health. Also, the national and regional case law shows that there is a scientific consensus over the need for tobacco control and an increasing jurisprudential trend towards linking this to human rights.[26] Although the above-mentioned cases are not formal precedents, they may have an impact on the reasoning of other courts and tribunals.[27]

The Framework Convention on Tobacco Control (FCTC)

Tobacco control epitomizes a typical public health issue as it highlights the special responsibility of states in public health matters and requires regulation of individuals who may pose a risk to the public health.[28] When the World Health Organization (WHO) adopted the FCTC,[29] this move represented a major breakthrough in international public health law, as the WHO had never before adopted conventions;[30] only soft law instruments such as recommendations, and regulations.[31] This new approach reflects the cognitive consensus on the lethal effects of tobacco smoke.[32] Due to the uncertain political viability of obtaining consensus on a conventional treaty structure, the World Health Assembly opted for a Framework Convention to institute a structure for further course of action.[33] While the FCTC sets general objectives, it can be supplemented by specialized protocols.

The main objective of the FCTC is to protect present and future generations from the health, social and economic consequences of tobacco

---

25 Some authors even argue that there would be an emerging human right to tobacco control. See C. Dresler and S. Marks, 'The Emerging Human Right to Tobacco Control', *Human Rights Quarterly* 28 (2006), pp. 599–651.

26 R. De Silva de Alwis and R. Daynard, 'Reconceptualizing Human Rights to Challenge Tobacco', *Michigan State JIL* 17, 2008–2009, pp. 354 ff.

27 On judicial dialogue see below, Chapter 7.

28 L. Gostin, *Public Health Law: Power, Duty, Restraint*, Berkeley: University of California Press, 2000, p. 4.

29 See A. Taylor, 'Global Health Governance and International Law', *Whittier Law Review* 25, 2003, pp. 261–2.

30 WHO Constitution, Article 19.

31 On the 'soft law ethos' of the WHO, see M. Prabhu and S. Atapattu, 'The WHO Framework Convention on Tobacco Control: When the WHO Meets the WTO', in M.C. Cordonier Segger and C.G. Weeramantry (eds), *Sustainable Justice: Reconciling Economic, Social and Environmental Law*, Leiden: Brill, 2005, p. 367.

32 K. Shibuya et al., 'WHO Framework Convention on Tobacco Control: Development of an Evidence Based Global Health Treaty', *BMJ* 327, 2003, pp. 154–7.

33 Framework conventions establish a system of governance for an issue area, in order to facilitate the development of consensus about the relevant facts and the appropriate international response. This is followed by the development of more specific commitments in subsequent treaties, the Protocols, which supplement the original Convention and require states to undertake specific legal obligations. See J.K. Setear, 'An Iterative Perspective on Treaties: A Synthesis of International Relations Theory and International Law', 37 *Harvard ILJ*, 37, 1996, p. 217.

use.[34] The Convention covers a wide range of issues, including measures relating to the reduction in the demand and supply of tobacco such as price and tax measures, regulation and disclosure of the contents of tobacco products, packaging and labelling, education, communication, and ban and restriction on tobacco advertising.[35] Among the measures aimed at reducing the supply of tobacco are: the elimination of the illicit trade of tobacco products, restriction on sales to and by minors, and technical and financial assistance for tobacco growers and workers to move to alternative occupations. In addition, the FCTC encourages parties to implement measures beyond those required by the Convention.[36]

As the regulation of the manufacture and advertising of tobacco products necessarily involves both free market and public health concerns, the FCTC provides that its provisions 'shall in no way affect the right of parties to enter into bilateral or multilateral agreements, . . . on issues relevant or additional to the Convention and its protocols, provided that such agreements are compatible with their obligations under the convention and its protocols'.[37] Where a dispute arises among states parties concerning the interpretation and application of the FCTC, the states parties should make a good faith attempt to settle it through negotiation. If negotiation fails, the Parties might submit the dispute to *ad hoc* arbitration.[38]

In the case of disputes concerning the linkage between tobacco control regulation and the protection of foreign investments, will investment treaty tribunals take into account the provisions of the FCTC? The FCTC is one of the most widely supported treaties in the history of the United Nations.[39] If the FCTC is not applicable to the parties,[40] it may be questioned whether its existence amounts to scientific evidence or consensus over the lethal effects of tobacco. One can also wonder whether the FCTC might be considered evidence of an emerging *opinio juris* which – if backed by state practice – can lead to the crystallization of customary international law that would be binding on non-parties.[41] Another interesting question is whether adjudicators will consult the WHO.

34 See generally N. Devillier, 'La Convention cadre pur la lutte anti-tabac de l'Organisation Mondiale de la Santé', *Revue Belge de Droit International* 38, 2005, pp. 701–28.
35 See e.g. FCTC, Articles 11 and 13.
36 FCTC, Article 2(1).
37 FCTC, Article 2(2).
38 FCTC, Article 27.
39 The FCTC has 174 parties and 168 signatories as of 24 October 2011. http://www.who.int/fctc/signatories_parties/en/index.html.
40 Besides the states which have never signed the Convention, Argentina, Cuba, the Czech Republic, El Salvador, Ethiopia, Haiti, Morocco, Mozambique, Saint Kitts and Nevis, the United States and Switzerland signed but never ratified the Convention. http://www.who.int/fctc/signatories_parties/en/index.html.
41 The provisions of multilateral treaties can evolve into universally applicable norms of customary international law when supported by widespread state practice upholding those norms.

The 'tobacco wars': case studies in international investment law

Investment treaties protect trademarks and good will as a form of investment.[42] As countries are gradually implementing tobacco control measures, a number of disputes have arisen with regard to these regulations. In a preliminary way, three types of investment disputes concerning tobacco may be outlined. First, an affected intellectual property (IP) owner may claim that an unlawful expropriation has taken place and/or contest the adequacy of the amount of compensation. For instance, trademark owners may argue that labelling regulations constitute an indirect expropriation. In parallel, the compulsory disclosure of ingredients may be deemed to be a violation of a trade secret. Second, the IP owner may also allege violation of the principles of fair and equitable treatment. Third, some claims may concern the prohibition of unreasonable measures and/or the alleged discrimination suffered by the foreign investor. The following sections will describe and assess this emerging investment-related jurisprudence, focusing on investment arbitral awards, but also shedding some light on conflicts that have been settled at a more informal level.

Expropriation

With regard to the first type of claim, three subsidiaries of Philip Morris International (hereinafter PMI) have recently filed an arbitration claim against the Republic of Uruguay, alleging, *inter alia*, expropriation of their IP rights under the Switzerland–Uruguay BIT.[43] Presidential Decree No. 287/2009 required that at least 80 per cent of each side of cigarette boxes be covered by graphic images of the possible detrimental effects of smoking,[44] and extended the prohibition on the use of product names (such as 'light' and 'mild'), to restrict the use of different shades or colours on tobacco packaging.[45] To implement the decree, the Ministry of Public Health issued Ordinance 514 which required each cigarette brand to have a single presentation and prohibited different packaging or presentations for cigarettes sold under a given brand.[46]

---

42 See, for instance, Article 1 of the Switzerland–Pakistan BIT and Article 1 of the Finland–Uzbekistan BIT.

43 *FTR Holding S.A. (Switzerland), Philip Morris Products S.A. (Switzerland) and Abal Hermanos S.A. (Uruguay) v. Oriental Republic of Uruguay (PMI v. Uruguay)* (ICSID Case No. ARB/10/7), case registered on 26 March 2010. The Switzerland-Uruguay BIT was signed on 7 October 1988 and entered into force on 22 April 1991.

44 Presidential Decree N° 287/009 promulgated on 15 June 2009 and entered into force on 12 December 2009.

45 Presidential Decree N° 287/009, Article 12. *PMI v. Uruguay*, Request for Arbitration, 19 February 2010, available at http://ita.law.uvic.ca/documents/PMI–Uruguay NoA.pdf, ¶ 21.

46 Ministry of Public Health Ordinance N° 514, issued on 18 August 2009 and entered into force on 14 February 2010, Article 3. *PMI v. Uruguay*, Request for Arbitration, ¶ 24.

Admittedly, the claimants do not contend the government's sovereign right to promote and protect public health,[47] but claim that in the alleged furtherance of public health goals 'the Government cannot abuse that right'.[48] According to the claimants, the combined effect of the enacted regulations amounts to an indirect expropriation.[49] The claimants point out that no compensation was provided, and contend that the measures were not taken under due process of law.[50]

According to the Claimants, being 'highly shocking'[51] the pictograms that are purported to illustrate the adverse health effects of smoking undermine the good will associated with PMI protected trademarks,[52] 'thereby depriving them of their commercial value'.[53] Furthermore, PMI claims that 'because of its size, the 80 per cent health warning coverage requirement . . . effectively deprives the Claimants of their right to use the trademarks'.[54] Finally, the claimants hold that Ordinance 514 forced them to remove from the market seven of the twelve cigarette products it previously sold, allegedly wiping out the commercial value of the IP rights in the discontinued product varieties.[55] Thus, the companies sought both compensation for losses to their investments in Uruguay and suspension of the application of Uruguay's recent regulatory measures.[56]

More recently, as Australia announced its legislation requiring 'plain packaging' for cigarettes,[57] Philip Morris Asia Ltd filed a notice of claim on the Federal Government stating that it intended to file an investor-state arbitration over the legislation under the Hong Kong–Australia BIT.[58] Plain packaging means that 'trademarks, graphics and logos are removed from cigarette packs with the exception of the brand name which is displayed in a standard font'.[59] While the stated goal of plain packaging is to reduce tobacco consumption, by making cigarette packs less attractive and making health warnings more visible, the company contends that plain packaging constitutes

---

47 *PMI v. Uruguay*, Request for Arbitration, ¶ 7.
48 Ibidem.
49 Ibidem, ¶ 82.
50 Ibidem.
51 Ibidem, ¶ 4.
52 Ibidem, ¶ 4.
53 Ibidem, ¶ 48.
54 Ibidem, ¶ 47.
55 Ibidem, ¶ 44.
56 See L.E. Peterson, 'Philip Morris Files First-Known Investment Treaty Claim against Tobacco Regulations', *IAR*, 3 March 2010.
57 The *Tobacco Plain Packaging Bill* mandates plain packaging of tobacco by 1 December 2012. The Bill is available at http://www.aph.gov.au/house/committee/haa/billtobacco package/documents/doc01.pdf. The Bill received Royal Assent on 1 December 2011.
58 C. Kenny, 'Big Tobacco Ignites Legal War', *The Australian*, 27 June 2011.
59 A. Alemanno and E. Bonadio, 'The Case of Plain Packaging of Cigarettes', *European Journal of Risk Regulation*, 2010, p. 268.

an indirect expropriation.[60] According to the claimants 'there is no credible evidence that plain packaging reduce smoking prevalence'.[61] Furthermore, the company contests the case for plain packaging, as this policy could ease trade in counterfeit cigarettes.[62]

In its Response, Australia highlights that plain packaging forms part of a comprehensive tobacco control policy and is 'a legitimate exercise of the Australian's Government's regulatory powers to protect the health of its citizens'.[63] Australia also pinpoints that its efforts are 'consistent with trends in other countries around the world' and with the FCTC, which is 'one of the most widely ratified treaties'.[64] More specifically, Australia contends that plain packaging requirements are non-discriminatory measures of general application designed to protect public health. Therefore, according to Australia, they do not amount to expropriation and do not give rise to a duty of compensation.[65]

In a previous case, *Grand River v. United States*, the arbitral tribunal held that tobacco control measures did not amount to an indirect expropriation.[66] Although the case did not concern trademarks, it is relevant for our discussion as it illustrates that certain tobacco measures do not amount to indirect expropriation but to a legitimate regulation. Grand River Enterprises Six Nations, Ltd. (a Canadian corporation) and members of Canadian First Nations filed a claim against the United States concerning the claimants' distribution and sale of tobacco products in the United States. The claimants alleged that the Master Settlement Agreement (MSA)[67] between U.S. states and major tobacco companies requiring tobacco companies to make cash payments to a central account in respect of each cigarette sold *inter alia* amounted to indirect expropriation of their investment.[68] According to the

---

60 *Philip Morris Asia Ltd v. The Commonwealth of Australia*, Notice of Claim, 15 July 2011, http://www.dfat.gov.au/foi/downloads/dfat-foi-11–20550.pdf, ¶ 10(a). See also *Philip Morris Asia Ltd v. The Commonwealth of Australia*, Notice of Arbitration, 21 November 2011, available at http://italaw.com/documents/PhilipMorrisAsiaLimited_v_Australia_NOA_21Nov2011.pdf.

61 *Philip Morris Asia Ltd v. the Commonwealth of Australia*, Notice of Claim, ¶ 35.

62 Ibidem.

63 *Philip Morris Asia Limited v. The Commonwealth of Australia*, Australia's Response to the Notice of Arbitration, 21 December 2011, http://www.transnational-dispute-management.com/legal-and-regulatory-detail.asp?key=6985 ¶ 3.

64 Ibidem, ¶ 16.

65 Ibidem, ¶ 46.

66 *Grand River Enterprises Six Nations Ltd et al. v. United States*, Award, 12 January 2011, http://www.state.gov/documents/organization/156820.pdf.

67 In 1998, several attorneys general entered into the *Master Settlement Agreement* (MSA) with major tobacco companies to settle legal claims that the states had filed seeking to recoup costs incurred for treating smoking-related illnesses. In exchange for payments, the states dropped all antitrust and consumer protection lawsuits. In order to avoid free riding by competitors not participating in the initiative, opting-out firms had to contribute a percentage of their sales to non-refundable escrow accounts. Ibidem, ¶¶ 8, 10, 13–14.

68 Ibidem, ¶¶ 7–9.

claimants, the requirement to make payments into state accounts would constitute an expropriation in violation of NAFTA Article 1110, because it would raise prices by an amount that would neutralize cost advantages.[69]

The arbitral tribunal rejected the expropriation claim in its entirety.[70] Relying on previous NAFTA cases, the tribunal also stated that NAFTA Article 1110 requires 'a complete or very substantial deprivation of owners' rights in the totality of the investment.'[71] As the claimants' business had remained 'profitable',[72] the tribunal concluded that there was no expropriation.[73]

The *Marvin Feldman Karpa* case[74] concerned the application of certain tax laws by Mexico to the export of tobacco products by CEMSA, a company owned and controlled by Marvin Feldman Karpa, a U.S. citizen. In it, Karpa claimed that Mexico's refusal to rebate taxes applied to cigarettes exported by CEMSA resulted *inter alia* in an *indirect expropriation* of his investment in breach of Article 1110 of NAFTA.[75] The arbitral tribunal questioned whether the actions of the Mexican government constituted an expropriation stating that: 'if there is a finding of expropriation, compensation is required *even if* the taking is for a public purpose, non-discriminatory and in accordance with due process of law'.[76] However, it held that 'non-discriminatory, bona fide *general* taxation does not establish liability',[77] and 'not every business problem experienced by a foreign investor is an indirect or creeping expropriation under Article 1110'.[78] Thus, the award finally dismissed the claim of expropriation.[79] More importantly, the arbitral tribunal affirmed that 'governments must be free to act in the broader public interest through . . . tax regimes, . . . and the like. Reasonable governmental regulation of this type cannot be achieved if any business that is adversely affected may seek compensation . . .'[80]

69 Ibidem, ¶ 18.
70 The Tribunal held that it did not have jurisdiction over the claims of Grand River Enterprises Six Nations, Ltd., Jerry Montour and Kenneth Hill because these Claimants did not have an investment in the United States. With regard to the claims of Arthur Montour Jr., the Tribunal held that the legislative measures in question did not constitute an expropriation of his investment. Ibidem, ¶¶ 125–6.
71 Ibidem, ¶ 148.
72 Ibidem, ¶ 153.
73 Ibidem, ¶ 155.
74 *Marvin Roy Feldman Karpa v. United Mexican States*, Award, 16 December 2002, ICSID Case No ARB (AF)/99/1.
75 Ibidem, ¶ 1.
76 Ibidem, ¶ 98.
77 Ibidem, ¶ 106.
78 Ibidem, ¶ 112.
79 Ibidem, ¶ 153.
80 Ibidem, ¶ 103.

Non-discrimination

One of the main objectives of BITs is to prevent discrimination based on the nationality of an investor.[81] While detecting direct discrimination is a relatively easy task as this involves discriminating against companies on the basis of their nationality; ascertaining indirect discrimination is a complex task as it involves state measures that, without making reference to the nationality criterion, *de facto*, affect foreigners vis-à-vis national companies. Disguised discrimination is more difficult to spot than direct discrimination because it requires distinguishing between the legitimate exercise of government authority and discrimination.[82]

In the *Marvin Feldman Karpa* case,[83] the arbitral tribunal upheld the claim of violation of national treatment. Mexican law imposed a tax on the production and sale of cigarettes in the domestic market and applied a zero tax rate to cigarette exports under certain circumstances.[84] In particular, rebates were applied only to cigarette producers, but were denied to resellers, such as CEMSA, the company owned and controlled by Mr. Feldman Karpa.[85] CEMSA initiated an action before the Mexican courts, alleging that these measures infringed upon the constitutional principle of tax equity.[86] The Mexican Supreme Court of Justice ruled in favour of CEMSA, finding unanimously that measures allowing rebates only to producers violated the constitutional principle of 'equity of taxpayers'.[87] Since Mexican authorities nonetheless asked CEMSA to fulfil other requirements,[88] Mr. Feldman Karpa filed an arbitration request to the ICSID on behalf of his company.[89] The claimant did not believe that the Mexican government policy of limiting cigarette exports was justified by public policy grounds, particularly in light of the stated purpose of the law, which was to encourage Mexican exports of tobacco products.[90] The arbitral tribunal upheld the discrimination claim.[91]

Fair and equitable treatment

Other cases have arisen relating to the fair and equitable treatment (FET) standard. This standard requires that foreign investors be accorded a minimum

---

81 A. Newcombe and L. Paradell, *Law and Practice of Investment Treaties*, The Hague: Kluwer Law International, 2009, p. 148.
82 N. Di Mascio and J. Pauwelyn, 'Non-Discrimination in Trade and Investment Treaties: Worlds Apart or Two Sides of the Same Coin?', *AJIL* 102, 2008, pp. 48–89.
83 *Feldman Karpa v. United Mexican States*, Award, op. cit.
84 Ibidem, ¶ 7.
85 Ibidem, ¶¶ 9–10.
86 Ibidem, ¶ 11.
87 Ibidem.
88 Ibidem, ¶ 17.
89 Ibidem, ¶ 24.
90 Ibidem, ¶ 89.
91 Ibidem, ¶ 187.

standard treatment 'in accordance with international law'.[92] Although there is no commonly accepted definition of this standard,[93] it is generally deemed to include access to justice, due process (in judicial and administrative decision making), good faith, and the respect of the legitimate expectations of the investor. In this respect, if a state makes a specific or implicit representation to a foreign investor, and the investor relies on such representation in making his or her investment and the state then frustrates the expectation it previously raised, then this would be considered to be a breach of the FET standard.[94] However, in assessing whether legitimate expectations exist, arbitral tribunals have to scrutinize the relevant circumstances in the respondent country at the time the investment was made 'including not only the facts surrounding the investment, but also the political, socioeconomic, cultural and historical conditions prevailing in the host state'.[95]

In the *Grand River* case, the claimants argued that their investment was harmed by the U.S. MSA and alleged a violation of the FET standard.[96] As one of the individual claimants was a member of the Six Nations of Native Americans, he alleged that his business activity involved trade among sovereign indigenous peoples.[97] According to the claimant, Article 1105 of the NAFTA required respect of international law including customary law.[98] More specifically, the claimant argued that an emerging norm of customary international law requires states to actively consult with indigenous peoples before taking regulatory action that will substantially affect their interests.[99]

The tribunal, with the exception of one member, found that state legal officers 'acted less than optimally' in working together to discuss and develop the proposed regulatory measures. It also considered that 'First Nations or tribal governments, particularly those in the United States whose regulatory authority is or may be implicated by application of the MSA, should have been included in these discussions.'[100] Nonetheless, the tribunal held that 'whatever unfair treatment was rendered to [the claimant] or his business enterprise, it did not rise to the level of an infraction of the fair and equitable treatment'.[101]

---

92 See NAFTA Article 1105.
93 See I. Tudor, *The Fair and Equitable Treatment Standard in the International Law of Foreign Investments*, Oxford: Oxford University Press, 2008.
94 See, e.g., *Grand River Enterprises Six Nations Ltd et al. v. United States of America*, Award, 12 January 2011, ¶ 140.
95 *Suez, Sociedad General de Aguas de Barcelona S.A., and Vivendi Universal S.A. v. the Argentine Republic*, Decision on Liability, ICSID Case No. ARB/03/19, 30 July 2010, ¶ 230 (internal quotations omitted).
96 See *Grand River v. United States of America*, Award, ¶ 127.
97 Ibidem, ¶ 128.
98 Ibidem, ¶ 180.
99 Ibidem, ¶ 182.
100 Ibidem, ¶ 185.
101 Ibidem, ¶ 187.

Similarly, in *PMI v. Uruguay*, the claimants contend that 'while a host State has the sovereign right to change its regulatory framework, including changes for the purpose of pursuing its public health policies, such changes must be fair and equitable in light of the investor's legitimate expectations'.[102] *In casu*, the claimants argue that the 'Respondent failed to maintain a stable and predictable framework consistent with [the claimants'] expectations'.[103] According to the claimants, not only did the host state fail to comply with its own law and respect private property,[104] but it also adopted measures incompatible with Uruguay's treaty obligations under the TRIPS Agreement as well as the Paris Convention for the Protection of Industrial Property.[105] Analogously, in *Philip Morris Asia v. Australia*, the claimant alleges the purported violation of Australia's international obligations under the TRIPS Agreement, the Paris Convention and the WTO Agreement on Technical Barriers to Trade.[106] While Uruguay's response is not publicly available, and thus it is not possible to refer to its arguments in this early phase of the proceedings, Australia has objected to the jurisdiction of the arbitral tribunal, alleging *inter alia* that such claims are 'plainly outside the scope of protection of the BIT' as a matter of the fair and equitable treatment standard.[107]

It is still too early to predict how this case will be settled; however, if the argument that the host states have to maintain a stable and predictable framework *consistent with the claimants' expectations* were to be upheld by the arbitral tribunals, then this would pave the way to other cases being filed against a number of countries adopting tobacco control measures. Developing countries and emerging markets would be particularly targeted as their legal framework is still evolving; but industrialized countries would be affected as well, as tobacco control policies have only recently emerged in regulatory settings. The existence of international standards such as Guidelines elaborated under the aegis of the WHO, and similar regulations adopted by a number of other nations would be factors to take into account.[108] One may wonder, however, whether such predictability test would have to be in conformity with best regulatory practice, rather than in accordance with investors' expectations only. Regulatory efforts need to adequately deal with new scientific evidence, and new regulatory techniques should not be dismissed *a priori* because never tested before. Accepting such a line of argument would freeze regulation and isolate it from technological developments and new scientific evidence.

---

102 *PMI v. Uruguay*, Request for Arbitration, ¶ 84.
103 Ibidem.
104 Ibidem.
105 Ibidem ¶ 85.
106 *Philip Morris Asia Ltd v. Australia*, Notice of Claim, ¶ 10(b).
107 *Philip Morris Asia Ltd v. Australia*, Australia's Response to the Notice of Arbitration, ¶ 34.
108 On the need of comparative surveys of best regulatory practices, see P. Eeckhout, 'The Scales of Trade – Reflections on the Growth and Functions of the WTO Adjudicative Branch', *JIEL* 13, 2010, pp. 3–26.

The prohibition of unreasonable measures

Some BITs also prohibit the adoption of 'unreasonable or discriminatory measures' 'that impair . . . the management, maintenance, use, enjoyment, extension, sale and . . . liquidation' of foreign investments.[109] While some authors have noted that 'unreasonable' can be equated with 'unfair'[110] and state regulatory measures have been scrutinized in the light of the more common FET standard, other authors wonder whether the prohibition of unreasonable measures can be analogized to the anti-discrimination provisions.[111] If this were the case, 'a separate prohibition on impairment by unreasonable . . . measures would to some extent appear to be superfluous'.[112] Adopting a literary interpretation, however, if such a provision is inserted in a BIT, it must have an autonomous *raison d'être*. In this sense, some arbitral tribunals have assessed the conduct of states in light of the reasonableness standard, giving this provision an autonomous meaning.[113]

As the term 'reasonable' is not defined in BITs, one has to consider its ordinary meaning. Reasonable regulatory measures would surely include logical, consequential and well-founded measures reflecting good governance. In this sense, 'unreasonabless' is very close to 'arbitrariness' which, under international law, involves a breach beyond the ordinary meaning of reason, an act which shocks, or at least surprises, a sense of juridical propriety.[114]

Despite the apparent simplicity of this concept, reasonableness is at the centre of legal debate. The fundamental dilemma is: should reasonableness be measured against the expectations of the parties to the BIT rather than as a function of the means chosen by a state to achieve its goals? In the *BG v. Argentina* case, the arbitral tribunal held that reasonableness should be measured against the expectations of the Parties to the BIT.[115] For instance, withdrawal of undertakings and assurances given in good faith to investors as an inducement to their making an investment is by definition unreasonable and a breach of the treaty.[116]

If reasonableness had to be measured against the best regulatory practices, the arbitral tribunals would need to rely on comparative surveys of best regulatory approaches. The problem with this theory is given by the identification of the relevant comparators. Should we consider tobacco

---

109 See e.g. Argentina–UK BIT, Article 2.2.
110 Newcombe and Paradell, *Law and Practice of Investment Treaties*, p. 304.
111 See T. Weiler, 'Philip Morris v. Uruguay – An Analysis of Tobacco Control Measures in the Context of International Investment Law', Report for Physicians for a Smoke Free Canada, 28 July 2010, p. 14.
112 Newcombe and Paradell, *Law and Practice of Investment Treaties*, p. 304.
113 *Tecmed* Award, ¶ 122.
114 *Contra*, *BG Group Plc v. Argentina*, UNCITRAL (UK/Argentina BIT), Award, 24 December 2007, ¶ 341.
115 Ibidem., ¶ 342.
116 Ibidem, ¶ 343.

products as an autonomous category or should we compare them to other products? Comparators could be alcoholic beverages or 'fat' products which may cause drunkenness or illness such as cardiovascular diseases, obesity and diabetes respectively. If tobacco products were assimilated to these other categories of products, any basic regulation could be deemed to be excessive. 'Fat' products do not include health warning let alone pictorial warnings. By contrast, their packaging could not be more colourful and glossy. These analytical difficulties however should not be overestimated. Since the inception of the FCTC, tobacco control has achieved an autonomous standing in regulatory efforts. In conclusion, given the unsettled jurisprudence on the matter and the vagueness of the reasonableness text, 'the determination of reasonableness is in its essence a matter for the arbitrator's judgment'.[117]

In *PMI v. Uruguay*, the claimants contend that prohibiting the use of colours to identify and differentiate brand packs[118] constitutes a breach of the prohibition of unreasonable measures under the BIT because the measure applies regardless of whether the trademarks create a false impression as to the harmfulness of the product.[119] According to the claimants, the single presentation requirement arbitrarily reduces the number of available product varieties without any rational public health justification.[120] Tobacco companies argue that colours are used to identify and differentiate different brand packs, not to communicate whether one product is less harmful than another.[121] Finally, the claimants note that 'no other jurisdiction has adopted a single presentation requirement like the one in Ordinance 514'.[122]

The claimants also allege that the 80 per cent warning requirement does not bear any rational relationship to a legitimate governmental policy.[123] The claimants argue that the protection of public health could have been achieved with a narrower and more tailored measure.[124] Finally the claimants contend that pictograms 'are neither necessary nor justified to warn consumers of the health risks associated with smoking'.[125]

Undeniably tobacco control is a legitimate public health objective. In order to assess the reasonableness and rationality of regulatory measures such as those adopted by Uruguay, the arbitral tribunal will have to consider whether the regulatory measures are adopted in good faith or whether the host state measure has a protectionist aim. *In casu*, as a Party to the FCTC, Uruguay

---

117 Ibidem, ¶ 342.
118 Ordinance 514, Article 3.
119 *PMI v. Uruguay*, Request for Arbitration, ¶ 78.
120 Ibidem, ¶ 79.
121 See D. Wilson, 'Coded to Obey Law, Lights Become Marlboro Gold', *New York Times*, 19 February 2010.
122 Ibidem, ¶ 25.
123 Ibidem, ¶ 81.
124 Ibidem.
125 Ibidem.

is bound by its provisions which require health warnings.[126] Health warnings are particularly helpful for consumers who are in vulnerable situations, such as children, teenagers and low-income consumers.[127] Article 11(1)(b) of the FCTC indicates that no less than 30 per cent of the display area must be reserved for health warnings, and that such areas 'should take up 50 per cent of the principal display area . . .'[128] As a general clause, FCTC Article 2 allows the Parties to implement measures beyond those required by the FCTC.[129] Furthermore, the FCTC Guidelines urge the Parties to 'cover as much of the principal display areas as possible'.[130] While national courts have recognized the reasonableness of health warnings,[131] even regional courts have ruled that a total ban on advertising that constituted a restriction on services was justified to protect public health.[132] As one study

126 FCTC, Article 11(1)(b).
127 A.R. Salazar, 'NAFTA Charter 11, Regulatory Expropriation, and Domestic Counter-Advertising Law', *Ariz. J. Int'l & Comp. L.* 27, 2010, p. 53.
128 FCTC, Article 11(1)(b).
129 Article 2 of the FCTC states that 'nothing in [the FCTC and its protocols] shall prevent a Party from imposing stricter requirements that are consistent with their provisions and are in accordance with international law'.
130 Guidelines for Implementation of Article 11 of the WHO Framework Convention on Tobacco Control (Packaging and Labeling of Tobacco Products) in Third Session of the Conference of the Parties of the WHO Framework Convention on Tobacco Control, Durban, South Africa, 17–22 November 2008, available at http://www.who.int/fctc/guidelines/article_11/en/index.html.
131 For instance, in *Canada Attorney General v. JTI-Macdonald Corp.*, the Supreme Court of Canada recently held that a requirement that 50 per cent of the principal display surface of a package be devoted to a warning of the health hazards of a product was a 'reasonable measure'. *Canada (Attorney General) v. JTI-Macdonald Corp.*, [2007] 2.S.C.R. 610, 2007 SCC 30 (Can.). In *Commonwealth Brands Inc. et al. v. United States of America et al.*, the Court held that the *Family Smoking Prevention and Tobacco Control Act* which mandated the use of warning for cigarette packages that occupy 50 per cent of the front and rear panels of packaging and include colour graphics depicting negative health consequences of smoking did not unjustifiably and unduly burden the commercial speech of the claimants. The Court held that the government's goal was to 'ensure that the health risk message [was] actually seen by consumers in the first instance' (at p. 24). The judge stated that the Congress '. . . relied on the international consensus reflected in the World Health Organization's Framework Convention on Tobacco Control. . .' (p. 26). The judge concluded that the challenged measures '[seemed] eminently reasonable . . . since every other tool in the government's arsenal [was] made less effective and more costly by plaintiffs' use of advertising to stimulate . . . demand' (p. 41). *Commonwealth Brands Inc. et al. v. United States of America et al.*, United States District Court Western District of Kentucky, Bowling Green Division, Memorandum Opinion and Order, 1 May 2010.
132 Court of Justice of the European Communities, Judgment of the Grand Chamber in Cases C-262/02 and C-429/02 (13 July 2004), *Bacardi France SAS, v. Télévision française 1 SA (TF1), Groupe Jean-Claude Darmon SA and Girosport SARL*. A French producer of alcoholic beverages filed a claim against television companies which put pressure on foreign clubs to refuse its brand names to appear on advertising hoardings around sports stadia. The Court held that 'it is for the Member States to decide on the degree of protection which they wish to afford to public health and on the way in which that protection is to be

shows, 'no nation has compensated any company for the loss of brand identity in this process'.[133]

Under Article 11 of the FCTC, health warnings may be in the form of, or include, pictures. Pictorial warnings, whose images differ in their content, but refer to the multiple negative effects of tobacco smoke and include lung disease, damaged brain, etc., are particularly effective as the pictures are hard to ignore and alert potential smokers to danger every time they look at a pack even in countries and communities with low literacy rates.[134] The WHO urged governments to require that all tobacco packages include pictorial warnings to show the sickness and suffering caused by tobacco use.[135] In 2010 almost 40 states had adopted pictorial warnings[136] and the number is on the rise.

Plain packaging, on the other hand, that requires the removal of all colours, brand imagery, corporate logos and trademarks, permitting manufacturers to only print the brand name in a mandated size, font and place, in addition to required health warnings and other legally mandated product information such as toxic constituents, is a more controversial measure.[137] The FCTC does not address plain packaging directly; rather it requires Parties to 'ensure that tobacco product packaging and labeling do not promote a tobacco product by any means that are . . . likely to create an erroneous impression about its characteristics . . . including any term, descriptor, trademark, figurative or any other sign that directly or indirectly creates the false impression that a particular tobacco product is less harmful than other tobacco products'.[138] Read in conjunction with FCTC Article 2 which encourages the Parties to implement measures beyond those required by the FCTC, this provision can be interpreted as to establish a rational connection between the stated objectives i.e. tobacco control and the plain packaging measures.

While plain packaging is not mentioned in the treaty text of the FCTC, it is addressed in the Guidelines to both Articles 11 (Packaging and

achieved. They may do so, however, only within the limits set by the Treaty and must, in particular, observe the principle of proportionality' (at ¶ 33). The Court admitted that 'rules on television advertising such as those at issue in the main proceedings constitute a restriction on freedom to provide services within the meaning of Article 59 of the Treaty' (at ¶ 35) but held that such rules 'pursue an objective relating to the protection of public health . . .' (at ¶ 37). Finally, the Court concluded that such rules were 'appropriate to ensure their aim of protecting public health' (at ¶ 38).

133 B. Freeman, S. Chapman and M. Rimmer, 'The Case for Plain Packaging of Tobacco Products', *Addiction* 103, 2008, pp. 580–90.

134 G. Fong, D. Hammond, and S.C. Hitchman, 'The Impact of Pictures on the Effectiveness of Tobacco Smoking', *Bull. WHO* 87, 2009, pp. 640–3.

135 WHO, *Call for Pictorial Warnings on Tobacco Packs* 29 May 2009, available at http://www. who.int/mediacentre/news/releases/2009/no_tobacco_day_20090529/en/index.html.

136 Canadian Cancer Society, *Cigarette Package Health Warnings International Status Report* (2010) p. 3 available at http://www.tobaccolabels.ca/factshee/cigarettepackagehealth warningsinternationalstatusr.

137 See e.g. Alemanno and Bonadio, 'The Case of Plain Packaging of Cigarettes', op.cit.

138 FCTC, Article 11(1)(a).

Labelling of Tobacco Products) and 13 (Tobacco Advertising, Promotion and Sponsorship) of the FCTC.[139] The guidelines recommend that Parties consider plain packaging 'to eliminate the effects of advertising or promotion on packaging' and that 'packaging [. . .] should carry no advertising or promotion, including design features that make products attractive'.[140]

Reconciling investor rights and tobacco control in investment law

Having examined the conflict area between the law of foreign investment and tobacco control measures, it seems that investment protection and public health are not to be deemed incompatible or irreconcilable. None of the provisions of the FCTC are inherently inconsistent with respect to international investment law. Therefore, as the real issue is the co-ordination between the FCTC and international investment law, the different norms arising from these different treaty regimes need to be reconciled through a series of legal and interpretative tools. This chapter illustrates three different methods: 1) negotiation/mediation; 2) interpretation; and 3) stipulating ad hoc safeguards.

Negotiation/mediation

While the FCTC provides for consensual mediation or conciliation for disputes among Member States,[141] BITs typically include a negotiation or consultation period, the so-called 'cooling-off period', before a claim may be initiated.[142] The period is usually anywhere from three to six months from the date in which the dispute arose or was formally notified by the investor to the host state, at the end of which arbitration proceedings may be commenced.[143] The

---

139 The legal status of the Guidelines is a matter of debate. See S. Foster Halabi, 'The World Health Organization's Framework Convention on Tobacco Control: An Analysis of Guidelines Adopted by the Conference of the Parties', *Ga. J. International and Comparative Law* 39, 2010, p. 1. Guidelines are deemed to be 'recommendations' adopted by the Conference of the Parties (COP), and form part of the context of the FCTC. Thus, guidelines matter when interpreting the relevant provisions of the FCTC under customary rules of treaty interpretation. Whatever their legal status, they become a 'benchmark for judging State Party compliance'. R. Haffajee and G. Bloche, 'The FCTC and the Psychology of Tobacco Control', 5 *Asian J. WTO & Int'l Health L. & Pol'y* 5, 2010, p. 92. The FCTC Conference of the Parties adopted guidelines for implementation of Articles 11 and 13 of the WHO FCTC at its second and third session held in Bangkok, Thailand, 30 June–6 July 2007 and Durban, South Africa, on 17–22 November 2008 respectively. The text of the guidelines is available at http://www.who.int/fctc/guidelines/article_11.pdf and http://www.who.int/fctc/guidelines/article_13.pdf.
140 Guidelines to the implementation of Article 13, at ¶ 17.
141 FCTC, Article 27.
142 See, for instance, Hong Kong–Australia BIT, Article 10.
143 See, U.S.–Ecuador BIT, Article VI.

practical purpose of the 'cooling off period' is two-fold. On the one hand, the host state is granted 'the right to be informed about the dispute at least six months before it is submitted to arbitration', and 'an *opportunity* to redress the problem before the investor submits the dispute to arbitration'.[144] On the other hand, the cooling-off period aims to facilitate settlement before positions become entrenched. Failure to observe a treaty's cooling-off period results in a tribunal declining jurisdiction.[145] As an arbitral tribunal recently clarified, the obligation to negotiate is an obligation of means, not of results.[146]

Negotiation and mediation are useful dispute resolution methods alternative to judicial settlement and arbitration, and are both based on cooperative and interest-based approaches. In abstract terms, they create a situation where both parties cooperate to reach a satisfactory result, looking at their underlying interests, rather than at their stated legal positions. These processes may also produce more successful outcomes than the adversarial 'winner takes all' approach.[147] Where the degree of animosity between the parties is so great that direct negotiations are unlikely to lead to a dispute settlement, the mediator may facilitate communication between the discussants.

These alternative dispute resolution methods usually achieve results in a short time frame as they are not necessarily required to deal with the past: they ask the parties to look at their future and to reshape their duties and responsibilities towards each other. Foreign investors thus participate in the decision-making process that will ultimately affect them, and, in so doing, they also become aware of the interests of the local population. In addition, experience shows that agreements entered into through a voluntary process stand out on account of their durability, because the parties highly identify with the agreement achieved. At the national level, in some cases, negotiation between tobacco companies and the state has led to positive results. For instance, in the U.S., the MSA between states and tobacco companies has settled thousands of disputes.

However, the advantages of alternative dispute resolution (ADR) mechanisms should not lead us to overestimate these methods. While they can be extremely useful in those situations where both contracting parties have equal or similar bargaining power – for instance in commercial disputes among private parties – agreements between host states and foreign investors may lead to unsatisfactory results as they offer no guarantees of an even playing

---

144 *Burlington Resources Inc. v. Republic of Ecuador* (ICSID Case No. ARB/08/5), Decision on Jurisdiction of 2 June 2010, ¶ 315.
145 *Murphy Exploration and Production Company International v. Republic of Ecuador*, ICSID Case No. ARB/08/4 – award on jurisdiction, available at http://icsid.worldbank.org/ICSID/FrontServlet?requestType=CasesRH&actionVal=showDoc&docId=DC1811_En&caseId=C267.
146 Ibidem, ¶ 135.
147 See R. Fisher and W. Ury, *Getting to Yes: Negotiating Agreement Without Giving In*, New York: Penguin Books, 1983.

field. Critics correctly argue that mediation does not provide the procedural safeguards of more structured dispute settlement mechanisms, particularly where an imbalance in bargaining power exists between the parties.[148] Concretely, unbalanced negotiation or mediation may lead states to accept unnecessary limits on their regulatory power. For instance, an agreement between the Mexican government and the tobacco industry which *inter alia* conditioned the disclosure of ingredients in respect of industrial secrets and confidential information was criticized because it contrasted with the key articles of the FCTC, which Mexico ratified and which requires unconditional disclosure of ingredients.[149]

As developing and least developed countries need foreign investments to foster development and growth, these countries may have an incentive to lower health and environmental standards (i.e. *race to the bottom*) to attract foreign investment flows.[150] Reportedly, this happened in Uzbekistan, where a foreign tobacco company lobbied and obtained a series of regulatory benefits as part of its investment conditions. Advertising bans were replaced by an advertising code drafted by the tobacco industry, and smoke-free restrictions were scaled back to cover only healthcare facilities and kindergartens and schools.[151]

The existence of investment treaty obligations and the threat of an investor-state dispute by a foreign investor may have a chilling effect on policy makers. Proposals to introduce plain packaging of tobacco products in the United Kingdom have raised the protests of major tobacco companies which decried such proposals as a form of expropriation.[152] In general, industrialized countries seem to resist such pressures. When Canadian health officials were to issue a new regulation on cigarette labelling, a tobacco company is known to have threatened to use the NAFTA investment chapter to challenge the proposed rules on cigarette packaging.[153] In the end, Canada adopted the labelling system and no investment claim was filed.[154] When Australia considered

148 See M. Cappelletti, 'Alternative Dispute Resolution Processes Within the Framework of the World-Wide Access to Justice Movement', *Modern L Rev* 56, 1995, p. 288.

149 J. Samet, H. Wipfli, R. Perez-Padilla and D. Yach, 'Mexico and the Tobacco Industry: Doing the Wrong Thing for the Right Reason?', *BMJ* 332, 2006, pp. 353–4.

150 E. Sebrié and S.A. Glantz, 'The Tobacco Industry in Developing Countries has Forestalled Legislation on Tobacco Control', *BMJ* 332, 2006, pp. 313–14.

151 A. Gilmore, J. Collin and M. McKee, 'British American Tobacco's Erosion of Health Legislation in Uzbekistan', *BMJ* 332, 2006, pp. 355–8.

152 L.E. Peterson, 'Plain Packaging of Tobacco Products Decried as Expropriation, Contrary to Treaties; Long-Running Debate Rejoined', *IAR* 3, 9 February 2010.

153 L.E. Peterson, *Bilateral Investment Treaties and Development Policy Making*, Winnipeg: IISD, 2004, p. 37.

154 Canadian measures to ban 'light' and 'mild' descriptors on tobacco packs were implemented through court-enforceable agreements with the industry, notwithstanding the initial opposition of the industry to such measures. M.C. Porterfield and C.R. Byrnes, 'Philip Morris v. Uruguay: Will Investor-state Arbitration Send Restrictions On Tobacco Marketing Up In Smoke?', *ITN* 4, July 2011, p. 3.

adopting plain packaging,[155] its relevant authorities reportedly announced they 'made no apology for the measures'.[156] When Philip Morris Asia Ltd announced its intention to file an investor-state arbitration against Australia, Australian Prime Minister, Julia Gillard stated: 'We are not going to be intimidated by big tobacco tactics . . . We are not taking a backward step. We have made the right decision and we'll see it through.'[157] She also reaffirmed that 'We are confident of our reforms – confident we can deliver them and confident that they will make a difference to the number of people who smoke . . .'[158]

The threat of an investment dispute, however, may prove potent in less industrialized countries.[159] When Philip Morris filed an ICSID claim against Uruguay, it was reported that Uruguay was going to water down tobacco control legislation.[160] Serendipitously, in November 2010, Mayor Michael R. Bloomberg of New York pledged his financial assistance to the state's legal defence.[161]

Acknowledging the special nature of tobacco products, Article 5.3 of the FCTC requires that 'in setting and implementing their public health policies with respect to tobacco control, Parties shall act to protect these policies from commercial and other vested interests of the tobacco industry in accordance with national law'.[162] This reflects the Parties' 'need to be alert to any efforts by the tobacco industry to undermine or subvert tobacco control efforts . . .'.[163] In this sense, the guidelines to the implementation of Article 5.3 of the FCTC acknowledge the 'fundamental and irreconcilable conflict between the tobacco industry's interests and public health policy interests',[164] and recommend that 'the Parties should interact with the tobacco industry only when and to the extent strictly necessary to enable them to effectively regulate the tobacco industry and tobacco products'.[165] Where interactions with the tobacco industry are necessary, Parties should ensure that such interactions are conducted transparently.[166] More interestingly, the guidelines also recommend that Parties should not accept, support or endorse partnerships

155 'Roxon Introduces Plain Packaging Bill', *ABC News*, 6 July 2011.
156 'Australia to Ban Cigarette Logos', *BBC News*, 29 April 2009.
157 'Julia Gillard Stands Firm on Cigarette Plain Packaging', *Herald-Sun*, 27 June 2011.
158 'Philip Morris Launches Legal Battle Over Australian Cigarette Packaging', *Bridges Weekly Trade News Digest* 15, 29 June 2011, p. 6.
159 See E. Sebrie et al., 'Tobacco Industry Successfully Prevented Tobacco Control Legislation in Argentina', *Tobacco Control* 14, 2005, p. 2.
160 'Uruguay to Relax Tobacco Laws to Combat Philip Morris Claim', *Global Arbitration Review Briefing*, 28 July 2010.
161 D. Wilson, 'Bloomberg Backs Uruguay's Anti-smoking Laws', *New York Times*, 15 November 2010.
162 FCTC, Article 5.3.
163 FCTC, Preamble.
164 Guidelines for implementation of Article 5.3 of the WHO FCTC, Principle 1.
165 Ibidem, ¶ 20.
166 Ibidem, ¶ 17.

and non-binding or non-enforceable agreements as well as any voluntary arrangement with the tobacco industry.[167]

It may be argued that Article 5.3 of the FCTC and respective guidelines are irreconcilable with the cooling-off provisions of BITs. However, while the text of Article 5.3 of the FCTC does not prohibit consultations, the guidelines are not binding. In turn, the cooling-off provisions of BITs put forward obligations of means and not of results. Good faith requires the investor to clarify its positions, explaining why it deems state regulation to be in violation of BIT provisions. On the other hand, the host state may eventually provide the investor information concerning the state obligations under the FCTC and refer to relevant scientific studies. Under the cooling-off provision the host state is not obliged to make any concession but may show that its conduct conforms to the rule of law and international standards of fairness. If a protocol were to be adopted by the FCTC Conference of the Parties with regard to Article 5.3 prohibiting any voluntary arrangements with the tobacco industry, then the content and scope of the cooling-off period would be sensibly reduced. Nonetheless, the ratio of the cooling-off period is not necessarily to reach an amicable solution, rather, it serves the function of providing the host state the right to be informed in advance of the forthcoming dispute and to facilitate the dialogue between the parties.

In conclusion, while negotiation and mediation may represent useful means to settle disputes between foreign investors and the host state, where there is no equal bargaining power, approaches of a more legal character are preferable. In this respect, in the following sections, treaty interpretation and legal drafting will be examined.

Interpretation

Customary rules of treaty interpretation, as restated by the VCLT, offer the adjudicators the conceptual and legal framework to settle disputes 'in conformity with the principles of justice and international law'.[168] Customary rules of treaty interpretation are applicable to investment treaties because investment treaties are international law treaties. Furthermore, some investment treaties expressly mention these rules.[169] According to the *general rule of interpretation*, which comprises several sub-norms, 'a treaty shall be interpreted in good faith in accordance with the ordinary meaning to be given to the terms of the treaty in their context and in the light of its object and purpose'.[170] As a matter of convenience, the following analysis will follow the order in which these norms generally appear.

167 Ibidem, ¶ 21, recommendation 3.1.
168 VCLT, Preamble.
169 See, e.g., AUSFTA Article 21.9.2.
170 VCLT, Article 31.1.

Textual interpretation

According to the principle of textuality, treaties are to be interpreted on the basis of their actual text. In examining the literal terms of treaty norms, the Preamble of the FCTC states that the contracting parties are determined 'to give priority to the right to protect public health'.[171] On the other hand, recent free trade agreements which include chapters on investments expressly provide general clauses allowing public health measures. NAFTA Article 1114(2) concisely states that:

> The parties recognize that it is inappropriate to encourage investment by relaxing domestic health, safety or environmental measures. Accordingly, a party should not waive or otherwise derogate from, or offer to waive or otherwise derogate from, such measures as an encouragement for the establishment, acquisition, expansion, or retention in its territory of an investment of an investor. If a party considers that another party has offered such an encouragement, it may request consultations with the other party and the two parties shall consult with a view to avoiding any such encouragement.[172]

In a more detailed fashion, Annex 10-C(4)(b) of the Central America Free Trade Agreement (hereinafter CAFTA)[173] expressly states: 'Except in rare circumstances, non-discriminatory regulatory actions by a party that are designed and applied to protect legitimate public welfare objectives, such as public health, safety and the environment, do not constitute indirect expropriations.'

With regard to intellectual property (IP), investment treaties usually build upon the relevant provisions of the TRIPS Agreement. For instance, the CAFTA makes clear reference to the TRIPS Agreement, as it states that '. . . the parties affirm their existing rights and obligations under the TRIPS Agreement . . .'[174] Thus, such FTA incorporates the relevant provisions of the TRIPS Agreement which become applicable or may provide guidance in the context of investment disputes.

In a preliminary way, in the specific intellectual property jargon, trademarks do not offer their owners positive rights to actually use the sign, but just a *jus excludendi alios*, that is, the negative right to prevent third parties from using

---

171 FCTC, Preamble.
172 NAFTA Article 1114, ¶ 2.
173 The Dominican Republic – Central America Free Trade Agreement encompasses the United States and the Central American countries of Costa Rica, El Salvador, Guatemala, Honduras, Nicaragua and the Dominican Republic. The final text was signed on 5 August 2004, and is available at http://www.ustr.gov/assets/Trade_Agreements/Bilateral/CAFTA/CAFTA-DR_Final_Texts/asset_upload_file747_3918.pdf.
174 CAFTA, Article 15.1.7.

the asset in question.[175] With regard to plain packaging, some authors have suggested that this form of packaging does not infringe trademarks 'as no positive right to use trademarks is offered by TRIPS to trademark holders'.[176]

Furthermore, Article 8 of the TRIPS Agreement seems to provide space for reconciliation between private and public interest in IP regulation. Notoriously, Article 8 of the TRIPS Agreement expressly governs the interface between public health protection and IP, stating that WTO Members 'may, in formulating or amending their laws and regulations, adopt measures necessary to protect public health and nutrition, and to promote the public interest in sectors of vital importance to their socio-economic and technological development, provided that such measures are consistent with the provisions of this Agreement'.[177] Furthermore, the Doha Declaration on the TRIPS Agreement and Public Health has clarified the relevance of Article 8 of the TRIPS Agreement for the interpretation of the whole agreement.[178]

However, the measures to be adopted must be consistent with the TRIPS Agreement. *Prima facie*, this clause may be interpreted as to give precedence to intellectual property over other interests. But, at a closer glance, it merely requires taking the whole agreement into account when adopting measures necessary to protect public health. In a sense, it reaffirms the need of interpreting the treaty 'in accordance with the ordinary meaning to be given to the terms of the treaty *in their context and in the light of its object and purpose*' (emphasis added).[179]

Teleological interpretation

The method of teleological interpretation searches for the purpose of a norm to clarify uncertainties in its exact content. In interpreting investment treaty provisions protecting trademarks as an intellectual property right and thus as an investment, interpreters and adjudicators need to take into account the fact that the protection of trademarks can be seen as serving two main purposes. The first function is to indicate the producer, so that the linkage between a producer and its product is clear (*Origin function*). The second function, which is strictly related to the first one, is to protect the consumers from deception, that is, to prevent the public from purchasing inferior goods in the mistaken belief that they originate from another trader (*Quality or guarantee function*). By knowing that a product is produced by a certain company, the consumer immediately assumes certain product qualities or characteristics. In other

---

175 TRIPS Agreement, Article 16(1).
176 A. Alemanno and E. Bonadio, 'Do You Mind My Smoking? Plain Packaging of Cigarettes Under the TRIPS Agreement', *John Marshall Review of Intellectual Property Law* 10, 2011, p. 452.
177 TRIPS Agreement, Article 8.
178 On the Doha Declaration, see Chapter 4 (with regard to pharmaceutical patents).
179 VCLT, Article 31.1.

words, the trademark reassures the consumer about the quality of the product.[180]

In protecting trademarks as proprietary rights, the risk is that of over-emphasizing the first essential function of trademark protection, that is the identifying function, while diminishing the worth of the second function, that is consumer protection. In other words, as an author highlights, arbitral tribunals should not replace the traditional rationale for trademark law with a conception in which 'trademark owners are given strong rights over the marks without much regard for the social costs of such rights.'[181] Like other intellectual property rights, trademarks offer an intrinsic dichotomy between private and public interests. Although these interests often go hand in hand – high-quality products build the producer's reputation – in some contexts, however, there may be a divergence between these polarities. In fact, the object of trademark protection presents a dichotomy between private and public interests. If one puts too much emphasis on the proprietary aspects of trademarks, the risk is that the public interest will be jeopardized.

In particular, Professor Gervais and Professor Geiger suggest the recognition of two equilibria within intellectual property.[182] While the *intrinsic equilibrium* concerns the very structure or architecture of IP norms, the *extrinsic equilibrium* indicates the search for a balance between IP and other rights as established by different treaty regimes. The intrinsic equilibrium is evident in the conceptual matrix of certain norms of the trademark regime, such as TRIPS Article 20 which forbids unjustifiable special requirements for trademarks. Such a provision does not forbid special requirements *tout court*, but it gives a certain margin of appreciation to policy makers and adjudicators to determine what a justifiable requirement is. Therefore, Article 20 of the TRIPS Agreement 'presents no obstacle to the requirements to print large health warnings on cigarette packets'.[183] In other words, by presenting a certain degree of flexibility, the same trademark regime does not offer an absolutist paradigm, but an intrinsic equilibrium.[184]

---

180 A third function of trademarks would be the investment or advertising function. Through this function, trademarks advertise a certain product or service, enhancing the efficiency of the consumer's choice and creating an incentive for trademark holders to invest in quality to create reputation. See V. Vadi, 'Trademark Protection, Public Health and International Investment Law: Strains and Paradoxes', *EJIL* 20, 2009, pp. 773–803.

181 M. Lemley, 'The Modern Lanham Act and the Death of Common Sense', *Yale L.J.* 108, 1999, p. 1697.

182 See C. Geiger, '"Constitutionalising" Intellectual Property Law? The Influence of Fundamental Rights on Intellectual Property in the European Union', *IIC Int'l Rev Intellectual Property and Competition L* 37, 2006, p. 351; D. Gervais, 'The Changing Landscape of International Intellectual Property', in C. Heath and A. Kamperman Sanders (eds), *Intellectual Property and Free Trade Agreements*, Oxford and Portland: Hart Publishing, 2007.

183 D. Rogers, 'The TRIPS Regime of Trademarks and Designs', *European Intellectual Property Review*, 2007, p. 77.

184 As Geiger notes, 'Already in the 13th century, the theologian and philosopher Thomas Aquinas held the opinion that "positive rights" (*ius positivum*) could be regarded only as

In parallel, the extrinsic equilibrium appears in the *telos* or ultimate goal of IP. According to Articles 7 and 8 of the TRIPS Agreement private remuneration should not be given more weight than the social welfare, but a harmonious balance between different interests needs to be struck.[185] In other words, if one adopts an instrumentalist view of IP, the international IP system should function for the good of all. According to Professor Gervais, 'one should not protect beyond what is necessary to achieve policy objective(s) because the risk of a substantial general welfare impact is too high'.[186] Similarly, Professor Cornides points out that 'property is not an end in itself. Obviously, it must be used in a way that contributes to the realisation of the higher objective of human society.'[187]

Subsidiary means of treaty interpretation

The instrumental or functional conceptualization of property has been adopted by a variety of courts at both national and regional levels. This case law may provide a rich source of comparative understanding regarding the linkage between tobacco control and the investment treaty regime. Although there is no binding precedent in international law and, according to the ICJ Statute, judicial decisions are recognized only as *subsidiary* means of interpretation,[188] in most cases, precedent can be persuasive. A systematic study of the case law of international tribunals suggests the 'tendency to chart a coherent course within law',[189] and highlights a path coherence by which arbitrators look at previous arbitral awards, and at the jurisprudence of other international courts and tribunals.[190] In particular, reference is made not only to the ICJ jurisprudence and the WTO Dispute Settlement Body case law, which have dealt with the protection of foreign investments and international trade law respectively, but also to the case law of regional courts and tribunals.

In this sense, a review of the jurisprudence of the ECHR and the ECJ concerning tobacco control may provide some useful reference. The ECJ

fair and legitimate as long as they aimed for general well-being . . . Where this is no longer the case, property must be limited; otherwise it will lose legitimacy.' See Geiger, 'Constitutionalizing Intellectual Property Law', p. 374.

185   TRIPS Agreement, Articles 7 and 8.

186   Gervais, 'The Changing Landscape', op.cit.

187   See J. Cornides, 'Human Rights and Intellectual Property, Conflict or Convergence?', *JWIP* 7, 2004, p. 143.

188   According to Article 38(1)(b) of the Statute of the ICJ, the sources of international law include international conventions and international customs, as well as general principles and, as a subsidiary means of interpretation, judicial decisions and the teachings of the most highly qualified publicists of international law.

189   C. McLachlan, 'The Principle of Systemic Integration and Article 31(3)(c) of the Vienna Convention', *ICLQ* 54, 2005, p. 289.

190   V. Vadi, 'Towards Arbitral Path Coherence and Judicial Borrowing: Persuasive Precedent in Investment Arbitration', *TDM* 5, 2008, pp. 1–16.

stated in the famous *Tobacco Products Judgment*[191] that the right to property is not absolute and that 'its exercise may be restricted, provided that those restrictions in fact correspond to objectives of general interest . . . and do not constitute a disproportionate and intolerable interference, impairing the very substance of the rights guaranteed.'[192] The case concerned some provisions of Directive 2001/37, which required cigarette packets to carry indications of the levels of harmful substances and warnings concerning the risks to health, and required larger health warnings.[193] Some tobacco companies claimed that the large size of the new health warnings required by Article 5 of the Directive would dominate the overall appearance of tobacco product packaging, thus curtailing or even preventing the use of their trademarks.[194] The companies also complained that the absolute ban on the use of terms such as *mild* or *light* amounted to a trademark infringement, as these terms were incorporated into the trademark.[195]

The Court found that the imposed measures did not prejudice the substance of companies' trademark rights, but constituted a proportionate restriction on the use of the right to property to ensure a high level of health protection.[196] In particular, the prohibition on using a trademark incorporating *mild* or similar descriptors did not keep tobacco manufacturers from distinguishing their products by using other distinctive signs.[197] The restrictions on the trademark right caused by the Directive did in fact correspond to an objective of general interest pursued by the Community and did not constitute a disproportionate and intolerable interference, impairing the very substance of that right.[198]

The ECJ decision fully conforms to the trademark protection rationale. As mentioned above, trademarks can be conceived as tools of information about ownership or origin, but also as instruments of consumer protection.[199] In this sense, public health considerations help overcome the dysfunctions of the trademark system, especially when it is used excessively and contrary to its rationale.[200]

---

191   *The Queen v. Secretary of State for Health (ex parte British American Tobacco Investments Ltd and Imperial Tobacco Ltd)* [hereinafter *Tobacco Products Judgment*], Case C-491/01, 10 December 2002 [2002] ECR I-11453.

192   *Tobacco Products Judgment*, ¶ 149.

193   Directive 2001/37 on the approximation of the laws, regulations and administrative provisions of the Member States concerning the manufacture, presentation and sale of tobacco products, [2001] OJ L 194/26, Article 5.

194   *Tobacco Products Judgment*, ¶ 143.

195   Ibidem, ¶ 144.

196   Ibidem, ¶ 150.

197   Ibidem, ¶ 152.

198   Ibidem, ¶ 153.

199   B. Sodipo, *Piracy and Counterfeiting GATT, TRIPS and Developing Countries*, London: Kluwer Law International, 1997, pp. 74–81.

200   See L. Helfer, 'Towards a Human Rights Framework for Intellectual Property', *UC Davies L Rev.* 40, 2006–2007, pp. 972–1020, at p. 1017.

In a more recent case, the ECJ dismissed an action brought by Germany for the annulment of two articles of the EC directive on banning tobacco advertising in the press and tobacco sponsorship in radio programmes.[201] In its judgment, the Court clarified that the prohibition of tobacco advertisement did not constitute a disproportionate restriction of the freedom of the press.[202] The Court considered that with regard to political, social and economic choices affecting fundamental human rights, the Community legislature enjoyed wide discretion, and the advertising ban was not inappropriate to achieve its objective.

In the *Swedish Match* cases,[203] the ECJ recognized that the prohibition of the marketing of tobacco for oral use restricted the freedom to pursue a trade,[204] but stressed that such a regulation was intended to protect a high level of health which is an objective of general interest.[205] The ECJ considered that in the exercise of the power conferred by Article 95 of the EC Treaty, the Community legislature must adopt a high level of health protection.[206] As scientific evidence has shown that tobacco products for oral use can cause cancer of the mouth, the Court held the Legislature fully entitled to prohibit the commercialization of these new products.[207] The Court also noted that the measure was necessary and appropriate, as tobacco products for oral use were particularly attractive to young people, and the risk of their developing an addiction to nicotine was high.[208]

The United States' Supreme Court adopted an almost identical approach in *Austin v. Tennessee*.[209] In this seminal case, the Court held: 'Without undertaking to affirm or deny their evil effects, we think it within the province of the legislature to say how far cigarettes may be sold or to prohibit their sale entirely . . . and there is no reason to doubt that the act in question is designed for the protection of public health'.[210]

---

201 ECJ, *Germany v. European Parliament and Council*, Case C-380/03, judgment of 12 December 2006.
202 Ibidem, ¶ 156–8.
203 Joined Cases C-210/03 and C-434/02: Case C-210/03, *Swedish Match AB, Swedish Match UK Ltd v. Secretary of State for Health* [2004] ECR I-11893; Case 434/02, *Arnold André GmbH & Co. v. Landrat des Kreises Herford* [2004] ECR I-11825. The case concerned a Swedish manufacturer and a German trader who wanted to commercialize tobacco products for oral use, called *snus*, in the United Kingdom and Germany respectively. As their activities were prevented by national laws in accordance with a 2001 Directive, the two companies brought actions against the decisions taken by national authorities before national courts, claiming that the Directive breached several principles of Community law. The Courts deferred a number of questions to the ECJ for a preliminary ruling.
204 *Swedish Match*, at ¶ 73.
205 Ibidem, ¶ 74.
206 Ibidem, ¶ 56.
207 Ibidem, ¶ 49.
208 Ibidem, ¶ 49.
209 *William B. Austin v. State of Tennessee*, 179 U.S. 343 (19 November 1900).
210 Ibidem.

The ECtHR's consistent case law on the right to property might provide useful guidance to arbitrators facing expropriation claims,[211] especially with regard to the amount of compensation that should be paid or not paid in case of regulatory measures concerning tobacco control. In this regard, the ECtHR has taken a relatively sophisticated approach to the wisdom of requiring compensation for regulatory activity that incidentally diminishes the value of property. The Court has stated that the notion of public interest is extensive and that states have a wide margin of appreciation to consider what is in the public interest.[212] In particular, an important public interest will weigh in the balance to justify the control of the use of property without compensation. In assessing whether a fair balance of public and private interests has been achieved, the Court looks at the nature and proportionality of the interference and at the legitimate expectations of the private owners.[213]

For instance, in *Fredin v. Sweden*, the Court held that environmental legislation had a public interest goal to protect nature, and that it was thus proportionate, notwithstanding there was no payment of market compensation.[214] In *Pinnacle Meat Processors Co. v. United Kingdom*,[215] the applicants conducted a business involving the de-boning of cattle heads and claimed that regulation prohibiting the commercialization of meat extracted from cattle heads violated their property rights. Such a regulation, which aimed to prevent the possibility of contracting the human form of Bovine Spongiform Encephalopathy (BSE) from infected beef, had forced the claimants out of business. In evaluating whether there was a fair balance between the protection of the public and private interests, the Commission observed that protecting people against a potentially fatal disease was a pre-eminent interest. Thus the Commission held that the applicants' loss was neither a formal nor a *de facto* expropriation and declared the case inadmissible.[216]

Systemic interpretation

If referring to the object and purpose of the treaty does not help, another criterion of treaty interpretation requires adjudicators to take into account 'any relevant rules of international law applicable in the relations between the

---

211 E. Freeman, 'Regulatory Expropriation Under NAFTA Chapter 11: Some Lessons From the European Court of Human Rights', *Columbia Journal of Transnational Law* 42, 2003–2004, pp. 177–215; H. Ruiz-Fabri, 'The Approach Taken by the European Court of Human Rights to the Assessment of Compensation for "Regulatory Expropriations" of the Property of Foreign Investors', *NYU Environmental L J* 11, 2002–2003, pp. 148–74.

212 *James v. United Kingdom*, 98 ECtHR (ser A) 9, 32 (1986).

213 H. Mountfield, 'Regulatory Expropriations in Europe: The Approach of the European Court of Human Rights', *NYU Environmental L J* 11, 2002–2003, p. 142.

214 *Fredin v. Sweden*, 192 ECtHR (Ser A) (1991).

215 *Pinnacle Meat Processors Co. v. United Kingdom*, App. No.33298/96, 27 European H. R. Rep. 217 (1998) (Commission Report).

216 *Pinnacle* at 223.

parties'.[217] In this regard, the ICJ has recognized that an adjudicator's interpretation cannot remain unaffected by subsequent developments of law and 'an international instrument has to be interpreted and applied within the framework of the entire legal system prevailing at the time of interpretation'.[218]

Many public health principles which belong to national constitutional orders have already been translated in international law. Some such norms have become rules of customary international law; others have been codified in a series of international treaties, and are binding on the states which ratified them. If the states, parties to the BIT, were also parties to the FCTC, the provisions of the FCTC could be examined and taken into account by the arbitrators when adjudicating an investment dispute. As some authors point out, 'a conflict between the FCTC and the BIT might be avoided by adopting a harmonious interpretation of the two treaties'.[219] If the applicable law was the law of the host state, and the host state was a party to the FCTC, this Convention again would become relevant regardless of whether the home country of the investor is a party to the FCTC.[220] It is also worth recalling that Article 18 of the VCLT requires the signatories to a Treaty not to defeat the object and purpose of a treaty prior to its entry into force.[221] Thus, the FCTC is of relevance also for those states which have signed but not ratified it.[222] Furthermore, as Weiler points out, the home state of the investor could notify its views about the interpretation of both the BIT and the FCTC to an arbitral tribunal 'either by way of an amicus submission to the Tribunal or by agreeing to an exchange of diplomatic notes between itself and the [host country] agreeing to a shared interpretation of the mutual obligations under the BIT and the FCTC'.[223]

217 VCLT, Article 31(3)(c).
218 ICJ Advisory Opinion of 21 June 1971, *Legal Consequences for States of the Continued Presence of South Africa in Namibia (South-West Africa) Notwithstanding Security Council Resolution 276 (1970)*, ICJ Reports (1971) 16.
219 T. Voon and A. Mitchell, 'Implications of International Investment Law for Tobacco Flavouring Regulation', *JWIT* 12, 2011, p. 12.
220 The WTO case law on the possibility to take external (non-WTO) norms into account in interpretation of WTO law if both parties to the second treaties are not parties to the first, is far from settled. For instance, in *EC – Approval and Marketing of Biotech Products*, the panel rejected the EC argument that its measures were fully justified by the Cartagena Protocol on Bio-Safety, an instrument that had been ratified by 142 states. Instead the panel took the view that since the instrument at hand had not been ratified by all WTO Members, it was legally irrelevant for the purpose of the litigation before it. See Chapter 7 below.
221 VCLT, Article 18.
222 Not by coincidence, although the United States did not ratify the FCTC, it recently mentioned the Convention in its first written submission before the WTO in the *United States – Measures Affecting the Production and Sale of Clove Cigarettes* case. DS 406 First Written Submission of the United States of America, 16 November 2010, ¶¶ 141–3.
223 Weiler, *Philip Morris v. Uruguay – An Analysis of Tobacco Control Measures in the Context of International Investment Law*, p. 35.

Although arbitral tribunals cannot issue a finding of compliance or non-compliance with the FCTC or the TRIPS Agreement because this ultimately falls outside their mandate,[224] they can evaluate the legitimacy and good faith character of a given regulatory measure in the light of international 'objective standards' such as those elaborated in the FCTC. As Sands puts it, 'those charged with interpreting and applying treaties on the protection of foreign investment need to take into account the values that are reflected in norms that have arisen outside the context of the investment treaty which they are applying'.[225]

Stipulating ad hoc safeguards

Having analyzed the *ex post* approach to the interplay between tobacco control and international investment governance in the context of litigation, this section scrutinizes an *ex ante* or legislative approach to tobacco control in investment treaties. Both approaches – the preventive and the jurisprudential one – can be used cumulatively, as they aim to achieve the same objective: reaching an equilibrium between the protection of foreign direct investment and public health.[226]

In general, public health goals are more directly achievable through the political and legal processes than through litigation. Therefore, it is crucial to critically assess the impact that investment treaties may have on public policy measures *before* signing them. Such a critical assessment does not merely play a negative role, in that it may prevent a country from adhering to certain international obligations, but may also play a positive role, in that it leads the parties to introduce new terms and safeguard clauses in their conventional practice. While a number of BITs already mention public health in their preambles, there is no certainty as to the legal meaning of such provisions.[227] As investment treaties are periodically re-negotiated, the discretion and uncertainty of arbitral tribunals may be narrowed through the use of much more detailed treaty language. For instance, at the European level, the Treaty of Lisbon[228] includes a provision on tobacco control.[229]

---

224 The principle *nec ultra petita* or *nec ultra fines mandati* requires the arbitral tribunal to limit itself to the scope of power allowed, and its violation is widely recognized as a cause for the annulment of the arbitral award. New York Convention, article V.1(c).

225 See P. Sands, 'Searching for Balance: Concluding Remarks', *NYU Environmental LJ* 11, 2002, p. 202.

226 See W.B. Hamida, 'La prise en compte de l'intérêt général et des impératifs de développement dans le droit des investissements', *Revue trimestrielle de droits de l'homme* 19, 2008, p. 1002.

227 See J. Crook, 'New Investment and Dispute Settlement Provisions in U.S.–Peru Trade Agreement,' *AJIL* 103, 2009, p. 768.

228 Treaty of Lisbon Amending the Treaty on European Union and the Treaty Establishing the European Community, signed on 13 December 2007, OJ C306/135 of 17 December 2007. The Treaty entered into force on 1 December 2009.

229 Treaty of Lisbon, Article 127 d (iv).

Should tobacco products be excluded *tout court* from investment treaties? Setting up an exception to investment protection for the tobacco trade would be a feasible option. This approach has already been adopted in the context of the U.S.–Vietnam Free Trade Agreement, which excludes tobacco from its tariff regulation and reduction scheme.[230] In parallel, investment treaties might exclude the tobacco trade from their application scope. According to such an exemption, if an investor invoked dispute settlement to challenge any regulatory measure taken by the state under this provision, an arbitral tribunal would not have jurisdiction.

Should investment treaties recognize the need to promote policy regulation aimed at tobacco control? Theoretically, there is no need for such a specific provision, as protecting public health is a traditional police power of a given state.[231] The police power of a state stems from the concept that good governance aims at public welfare and it may restrain private property for the protection of public safety and health. Where a deprivation of property or other economic loss arises out of *bona fide* general regulation aimed at preventing nuisance, it should be considered within the boundaries of acceptable exercise of police powers and would be unable to be compensated. Scrutinizing the arbitral jurisprudence, arbitral tribunals have accepted as a principle of customary international law that a state is not responsible for *bona fide* regulation that falls within the scope of a generally recognized *police power*.[232]

Furthermore, in examining most constitutional traditions and regional treaties,[233] it appears that property rights are not absolute;[234] rather their owners can enjoy them within the limits established by the law.[235] The concept of property includes the use, enjoyment or disposition of the property right within the limits established by the law. Trademarks, which are a type of IP rights, are no exception to this general understanding of property.

However, as regulation can effectively reduce or destroy the use of private property and the concept of indirect expropriation in investment agreements

230 Agreement Between the United States of America and the Socialist Republic of Vietnam on Trade Relations, signed on 13 July 2000, http://www.ustr.gov/assets/World_Regions/Southeast_Asia_Pacific/Vietnam/asset_upload_file917_10731.pdf.
231 This specific theme is also explored in Chapters 1, 4, 5, and 6.
232 See e.g. *Methanex Corp. v. United States*, Final Award on Jurisdiction and Merits, 3 August 2005, 44 ILM (2006) 1345; *Chemtura Corp. (formerly Crompton Corp.) v. Government of Canada*, Award, 2 August 2010, available at http://italaw.com/documents/ChemturaAward.pdf; *Saluka v. Czech Republic*, UNCITRAL Rules Arbitration, PCA, Award, 17 March 2006. Similar arguments were raised by Argentina in the *Azurix* case, see *Azurix Corp. v. The Argentine Republic*, Award, 14 July 2006, ICSID Case ARB/01/12 ¶ 278.
233 See, e.g., Italian Constitution, Article 42, German Basic Law, Article 14.
234 S. Montt, *State Liability in Investment Treaty Arbitration – Global Constitutional and Administrative Law in the BIT Generation*, Oxford: Hart Publishing, 2009, p. 172.
235 See J.W. Singer, 'The Ownership Society and Takings of Property: Castles, Investments and Just Obligations', *Harvard Environmental L Rev.* 30, 2006, pp. 309ff.

is very broad, a detailed provision clarifying that tobacco control measures in conformity with the FCTC will not be considered as measures tantamount to expropriation would help arbitrators to issue consistent decisions.

Conclusions

This chapter has explored the linkage between tobacco control and investment treaty guarantees. Recent case studies show that investors can (and have) claim(ed) that tobacco control measures infringe their rights under BITs. In this context, an excessive protection of investor's rights may negatively affect tobacco control policies.

The existing customary canons of treaty interpretation may help interpreters to avoid conflicts of norms. As investment law is part of international law, the former must be consistent with the norms of the latter and be interpreted in accordance with the customary rules of treaty interpretation. Although examined in a separate manner, the legal canons of treaty interpretation are complementary and may be used cumulatively. First, according to the canon of literal interpretation, there is no manifest inconsistency between the two sets of norms. On the contrary, some recent BITs expressly mention the need to protect public health in their text.

Second, according to the canon of systemic interpretation, investment treaties should not be considered as self-contained regimes, but as an important component part of public international law. Accordingly, arbitrators should adopt a holistic approach, taking public health treaties and relevant customary law into account when they interpret relevant investment treaty provisions. When discussing the investment law-legality of any tobacco control measure, it may first be necessary to consider whether and why the value of public health would not necessarily be of greater importance than that of investment protection and should therefore be given priority when serious health risks arising from smoking have been widely reconfirmed.[236]

Third, commentators increasingly suggest that guarantees protecting private property should be interpreted purposively.[237] As Professor Alexander highlights, '. . . property . . . may be thought to serve two quite different functions. The first is an individual or personal function: securing a zone of freedom for the individual in the realm of economic activity. . . . The second function that might be recognized is social and public . . . it is to serve the public good.'[238] While the concept of equity requires that a property owner not be compelled by the state to bear a greater burden vis-à-vis society at

236 See T.-Y. Lin, 'Addressing the Issue of Trade in Services and Public Health in the Case of Tobacco', *JWIT* 7, 2006, p. 561.
237 G.S. Alexander, *The Global Debate Over Constitutional Property*, Chicago: University of Chicago Press, 2006.
238 G.S. Alexander, 'Constitutionalizing Property: Two Experiences, Two Dilemmas', in J. McLean (ed.), *Property and the Constitution*, Oxford: Hart, 1999, p. 89.

large, the *telos* of property encapsulates both private rights and the public interest in property guarantees.

Finally, given the recent rise of international disputes concerning tobacco control measures before international economic law *fora*, introducing specific clauses in investment treaties clarifying that tobacco control measures in conformity with international standards are not to be considered as a form of expropriation would be a feasible option. While due consideration to public health may be considered an implicit requirement of any economic activity, contemporary public health includes not only classical elements such as the prevention of infectious diseases, but also less traditional components such as tobacco control. Through accurate treaty clauses, the host state may ensure that foreign investors are made aware of the selected level of public health protection. The use of *ad hoc* clauses would preventatively settle potential conflicts of interests between the host state and the investor. In addition, such clauses might constitute a useful compass for the arbitrators in eventual investment treaty disputes.

6 The environmental health spillovers of foreign direct investment in international investment arbitration

Introduction

Environmental health is an increasing concern of both industrialized and developing countries. As environmental hazards determined by processes of economic globalization seriously threaten health, the question is how to reconcile the need to promote environmental health with the need of economic development. This chapter addresses the question as to whether an enhanced investment protection hampers the host state's duty to pursue environmental health objectives. At the substantive level, investment treaties provide an extensive protection to investor rights in order to encourage FDI. Therefore, a potential tension exists when a state adopts environmental regulation interfering with foreign investments, as regulatory measures may be deemed to interfere with the economic value of the foreign investment. In parallel, there is the risk of host states adopting disguised protectionist measures. At the procedural level, investment treaties offer investors direct access to an international arbitral tribunal. Thus, foreign investors can (and have) directly challenge(d) national measures aimed at protecting environmental health and seek (sought) compensation for the impact on their business of such regulation.

A number of questions arise in this context. What is the role of science in investment disputes? Which standard of review should arbitral tribunals adopt to assess scientific evidence? Should arbitral tribunals accord deference to the acceptable levels of risks chosen by the relevant authorities of the host state? This chapter addresses these questions exploring the conflict areas between investment treaty governance and environmental health through an analysis of the recent arbitral jurisprudence. In this respect, this survey shows that the regime established according to investment treaties may not strike an appropriate balance between the different interests concerned.

This chapter proceeds as follows: first, it scrutinizes the conceptual and normative scope of environmental health; second, it explores and critically assesses the relevant case law; third, it puts forward the need to map the interactions between investor rights and environmental health protection; fourth, it analyzes environmental impact assessment as a tool of dispute prevention; fifth, it explores the role of science in international investment law and arbitration and the standard of review that is adopted in public health disputes. The chapter concludes with a critical assessment of the explored legal framework and case law.

The conceptual and normative scope of environmental health

Environmental health is a working definition which bridges the gap between environmental law and public health and encompasses both substantive and procedural components. At the substantive level, environmental health embraces all the aspects of environmental protection which are related to human health, including but not limited to air quality, food safety, hazardous materials management, land use planning, safe drinking water, and waste management. All these elements contribute to the determination of a healthy environment. At the procedural level, environmental health refers to the assessment, control and prevention of those environmental factors that can potentially affect environmental health.[1] States have the right/duty to adopt instruments to prevent the massive degradation of the habitat; as in the environmental field most activities that cause harm to the environment are caused by the private sector, therefore states have the right/duty to regulate the activities of private parties that may have environmental health spillovers.

There are two main reasons as to why the issue of environmental protection can be approached and dealt with from a public health perspective. First, environmental factors are increasingly responsible for ill-health in many parts of the world.[2] Second, while this chapter does not contest the intrinsic value of the environment,[3] it focuses on the anthropocentric dimension of environmental protection because such a perspective confers a degree of cogency and definition to environmental concerns. While the recognition of a distinct human right to environment remains controversial,[4] there has been a

---

1 World Health Organization (WHO), draft definition developed at a WHO consultation in Sofia, Bulgaria, (1993) available at http://www.health.gov/environment/Definitionsof EnvHealth/ehdef2.htm.
2 Y. von Schirnding, W. Onzivu and A.O. Adede, 'International Environmental Law and Global Public Health', *Bull. WHO* 80, 2002, p. 970.
3 C. Redgwell, 'Life, the Universe and Everything: A Critique of Anthropocentric Rights', in A. Boyle and M. Anderson (eds), *Human Rights Approaches to Environmental Protection*, Oxford: Clarendon Press, 1996, chapter 4.
4 There are three types, or generations, of human rights, each type having a different level of acceptance in the international community. The first generation includes civil and political rights contained in Articles 3 to 21 of the Universal Declaration of Human Rights (UDHR) and the International Covenant on Civil and Political Rights (ICCPR). The second generation includes social economic and cultural rights contained in Articles 22 to 27 of the UDHR and the International Covenant on Economic, Social and Cultural Rights (ICESCR). The third generation rights is a contested concept: while some deem the third generation or solidarity rights as the most recently recognized category of human rights, others contest their legal status as human rights.

growing recognition in public health law that the protection of the environment is a condition for the full enjoyment of health.

Conceptualizing environmental health as a component of public health determines a paradigm shift that allows the translation of environmental concerns into the language of the state's concerns to protect public health. Public health is, in turn, a fluid concept which reflects the concern of states to protect their populations. As one of the three constitutive elements of the state is its population – in addition to its territory and its organization[5] – it is clear that the preservation of its population is an essential function of the state. Without such protection, the very existence of the state would be endangered. Protecting public health is thus a primary duty of states which arises from constitutional and statutory law, as well as from the fundamental 'social contract' upon which most governments rest.[6] At the international level, several international law instruments have recognized the states' duty to protect public health and a number of environmental standards have been set clarifying the content of this duty. Consequently, one may argue that the right/duty of the state to protect its environmental health is a non-contested concept. As in the environmental field most activities that cause harm to the environment are caused by the private sector, states have the right/duty to adopt instruments to ensure that private parties do not engage in conduct that is conducive to the massive degradation of the habitat.

At the normative level, the linkage between environmental goods and health was originally – albeit implicitly – articulated by the founding document of international environmental law, the Stockholm Declaration on the Human Environment,[7] which recognized 'the fundamental right to freedom, equality and adequate conditions of life, in an environment of quality that permits a life of dignity and well-being'.[8] In addition, the Declaration clearly spelled out the linkage between a clean environment and human health, requiring states to take steps to prevent the pollution of the environment by substances which affect human health.[9] While this instrument has a mere hortatory value, it has paved the way for subsequent legal instruments.[10] For instance, the Aarhus Convention recognizes 'that adequate protection of the environment is essential to human well-being and the enjoyment of basic human rights, including the right to life itself'.[11]

---

5 See Montevideo Convention on the Rights and Duties of States, signed on 23 December 1933, Article 1.

6 D. Fidler, 'Challenges to Humanity's Health: The Contributions of International Environmental Law to National and Global Public Health', *Environmental Law Reporter* 31, 2001, pp. 10048–78.

7 Stockholm Declaration on the Human Environment 16 June 1972 UN Doc A/Conf 48/14/ rev. 1, 11 ILM 1416 (1972).

8 Stockholm Declaration, Principle 1.

9 Stockholm Declaration, Principle 7.

10 See e.g. San Salvador Protocol to the ACHR, Article 11.

11 United Nations Economic Commission for Europe, Aarhus Convention on Access to Information, Public Participation in Decision Making and Access to Justice in

Even the *General Comment No. 14* on the right to the highest attainable standard of health acknowledges the linkage between health and the environment, affirming that '. . . the drafting history and the express wording of Article 12.2 acknowledge that the right to health embraces a wide range of socio-economic factors that promote conditions in which people can lead a healthy life, and extends to the underlying determinants of health such as food and nutrition, housing, access to safe and potable water and adequate sanitation, safe and healthy working conditions and *a healthy environment.*' [Emphasis added][12]

In international human rights case law courts have increasingly recognized that 'environmental factors are to be taken into account in the interpretation of traditional human rights'.[13] In particular, courts have held that certain kinds of environmental impairment with severe harmful consequences for individuals or even the failure of public authorities to provide information about serious environmental risks to which individuals are exposed, may constitute a violation of other human rights.[14] For instance, in the *López Ostra* case,[15] the ECtHR found a serious case of environmental damage and accompanying health problems to be a violation of Article 8 of the Convention on the protection of private and family life. In *Guerra v. Italy*, as Italian authorities had been too slow in closing down a fertilizer plant that caused toxic emissions, the ECtHR found that the state omission amounted to a violation of Article 8 of the Convention.[16] Similarly, in *Fadeyeva v. Russia*,[17] concerning the pollution caused by an iron smelter of a private company, the Court found that the state had violated its positive obligations to prevent such harm and found a violation of Article 8. Despite the margin of appreciation

Environmental Matters, signed on 25 June 1998 and entered into force on 30 October 2001. 2161 UNTS 447, preambular paragraph 6.

12 *General Comment No. 14*, ¶ 4. UN Committee on Economic, Social and Cultural Rights, *General Comment No. 14*, adopted at the Committee's twenty-second session, 25 April–12 May 2000 (E/C.12/2000/4).

13 T. Meron, *The Humanization of International Law*, Leiden: Martinus Nijhoff Publishers, 2006, p. 451. See also K. MacDonald, 'A Right to a Healthful Environment – Humans and Habitats: Re-thinking Rights in an Age of Climate Change', *European Energy and Environmental Law Review*, 2008, p. 220.

14 M. Pallemaerts, 'Introduction: Human Rights and Environmental Protection', in M. Déjeant-Pons and M. Pallemaerts, *Human Rights and the Environment*, Strasbourg: Council of Europe Publishing, 2002, p. 15.

15 *López Ostra v. Spain*, (Application no. 16798/90) judgment of 9 December 1994, Publications of the ECtHR, Series A, No. 303-C. While the Court acknowledged that states have a margin of appreciation in the adoption of environmental policies, it concluded that in the case at hand there was a violation of Article 8. The competent Spanish authorities had funded, licensed and later failed to close down a plant which treated wastes from leather tanneries in a way that negatively affected the right to a private life of the neighbourhood.

16 *Guerra and Others v. Italy*, (116/1996/735/932) judgment of 19 February 1998, ECtHR, Reports of Judgments and Decision 1998-I, No 64.

17 *Fadeyeva v. Russia* (Application no 55723) Judgment of 30 November 2005.

granted to states in environmental matters, the interference had been of such a severe nature that it violated Article 8.[18]

While deeming environmental health as a public concern emphasizes the social contract between the state and its population, conceptualizing it as a human right stresses the individual dimension of health. While the focus of this book is on public health, it is assumed that the two conceptualizations – the right to health and public health – are not irreconcilable theories, but rather two sides of the same coin.

Environmental provisions in investment treaties

Investment treaties have addressed environmental health issues only in recent decades, but specific provisions pertaining to the environment have now become a constant feature.[19] A number of preambles of BITs contain reference to the environment.

For instance, the preamble of the NAFTA commits the Parties to attain trade and investment goals in a manner consistent with environmental protection and conservation, preserving the flexibility to safeguard the public welfare and promote sustainable development.[20] The Energy Charter Treaty's (ECT) preamble 'recogniz[es] the increasingly urgent need for measures to protect the environment'.[21] In the preambular paragraph of the 2002 EFTA Singapore Agreement the parties reaffirm 'their commitment to the principles set out in the UN Charter and the Universal Declaration of Human Rights'.[22] The preamble of the 2004 U.S. Model BIT recognizes, *inter alia*, 'the importance of providing effective means of asserting claims and enforcing rights with respect to investment under national law as well as through international arbitration' and expresses the parties' desire 'to achieve these objectives *in a manner consistent with the protection of health, safety and the environment . . .*' (emphasis added).

While it is generally held that preambles do not contain binding obligations *per se*,[23] they are influential in the interpretation of treaties, as

18 Ibidem, ¶ 134.
19 According to a recent study, 'No investment treaty concluded between 1958 and 1985 contained any reference to the environment, and fewer than 10 per cent of treaties concluded in any given year from 1985 to 2001 contained this feature. References to environmental concerns in such treaties have increased sharply since 2002. The share of newly concluded IIAs with explicit environmental references exceeded 50 per cent for the first time in 2005 and reached 89 per cent in 2008'. K. Gordon and J. Pohl, 'Environmental Concerns in International Investment Agreements: The "New Era" Has Commenced, But Harmonization Remains Far Off', *Columbia FDI Perspectives* 44, 15 August 2011.
20 NAFTA, preamble.
21 Energy Charter Treaty, 17 December 1994, 2080 UNTS 95, preamble.
22 Agreement Between the EFTA States and Singapore, signed on 26 June 2002 entered into force on 1 January 2003, available at http://secretariat.efta.int.
23 See, for instance, *Victor Pey Casado et Fondation "President Allende" contre Republique du Chili*, ICSID Case No ARB/98/2, Arbitral Award, 8 May 2008, at ¶ 348.

they explain the treaty purpose and underlying philosophy, and establish a dialogue between the treaty drafters and the adjudicators.[24] Article 31 of the VCLT, which is deemed to reflect a customary norm of treaty interpretation, recognizes that the context of a treaty comprises, *inter alia*, its preamble.[25] Although the late Professor Wälde argued that 'segregating' environmental concerns in preambles or merely imposing 'obligations de moyens' may amount to 'pseudo-action'[26] as the first is not binding and the latter merely imposes due diligence, it is also true these are important preliminary steps to infuse investment treaties with public health or environmental considerations. This approach, while not creating new obligations for the parties to an agreement, recognizes the potential for investment to affect environmental health. Recognizing this link is an important step in avoiding downward pressure on environmental health protection in the process of investment liberalization.

Besides preambles, a number of BITs include specific provisions relating to health and the environment. NAFTA Article 1114, entitled Environ-mental Measures, *inter alia*, states that: 'Nothing in this Chapter shall be construed to prevent a Party from adopting, maintaining or enforcing any measure otherwise consistent with this Chapter that it considers appropriate to ensure that investment activity in its territory is undertaken in a manner sensitive to environmental concerns.' The second paragraph of the same provision also states that 'The Parties recognize that it is inappropriate to encourage investment by relaxing domestic health, safety and environmental measures. [. . .]'

At a more general level, Article 104 of NAFTA, in relation to Environmental and Conservation Agreements, gives priority to these treaties over the provisions in other parts of NAFTA, 'provided that where a Party has a choice among equally effective and reasonably available means of complying with such obligations, the Party chooses the alternative that is the least inconsistent with the other provisions of this agreement'.[27] Therefore, if the environmental measures are mandatory under one of the listed MEAs, they will be permissible under NAFTA. If they are not mandatory, but merely designed to implement one of the listed agreements, they will need to be as consistent with NAFTA as possible.[28] It is worth recalling that NAFTA was complemented by a side

---

24 K. Roach, 'The Uses and Audiences of Preambles in Legislation', *McGill L J* 47, 2001, p. 129.

25 VCLT, Article 31.2.

26 T. Wälde, 'Sustainable Development and the 1994 Energy Charter Treaty: Between Pseudo-Action and the Management of Environmental Investment Risk', in F. Weiss, E. Denters and P. De Wart (eds), *International Economic Law With a Human Face*, The Hague: Kluwer, 1998, p. 244.

27 NAFTA Article 104.1.

28 J. Freedman, 'Implications of the NAFTA Investment Chapter for Environ-mental Regulation', in A. Kiss, D. Shelton and K. Ishibashi (eds), *Economic Globalization*

agreement, the North American Agreement on Environmental Cooperation (NAAEC) which is directed at fostering environmental cooperation amongst the Parties.[29]

Recent international investment treaties have become more sophisticated in content and express more clearly the public interest involved in health protection.[30] For instance, article 2 of the 1995 BIT between Russia and Hungary states 'this Agreement shall not preclude the application of either Contracting Party of measures, necessary for the maintenance of defence, national security and public order, protection of the environment, morality and public health'.[31] Other treaties provide for more articulated clauses. The Trans-Pacific Strategic Economic Partnership Agreement between Brunei Darussalam, Chile, Singapore and New Zealand (hereinafter Trans-Pacific SEP),[32] besides establishing mechanisms to raise labour and environment standards across the Trans-Pacific SEP countries, also sets out a range of general exceptions to its obligations for trade in goods and services. The Agreement expressly incorporates Article XX of GATT and its interpretative notes with regard to trade in goods and Article XIV of GATS with regard to trade in services.[33] These exceptions include measures necessary to protect human, animal or plant life or health, conservation of living and non-living exhaustible natural resources, public morals and so on and so forth.

Both U.S. and Canadian Model BITs expressly include a 'Non-precluded measures clause'.[34] The U.S. Model BIT provides that 'Nothing in this Treaty shall be construed to prevent a Party from adopting, maintaining, or enforcing any measure otherwise consistent with this Treaty that it considers appropriate to ensure that investment activity in its territory is undertaken in a manner sensitive to environmental concerns.'[35] The Canada 2003 Model FIPA states: 'subject to the requirement that such measures are not applied in a manner that would constitute arbitrary or unjustifiable discrimination between investments or between investors, or a disguised restriction on

and Compliance with International Environmental Agreements, The Hague: Kluwer Law International, 2003, p. 90.

29 The North American Agreement on Environmental Cooperation (NAAEC), the parallel side agreement to NAFTA, came into force on 1 January 1994. 32 ILM 1480 (1993).

30 UNCTAD, *WIR 2006 – FDI from Developing and Transition Economies: Implications for Development*, Geneva: UNCTAD, 2006.

31 1995 BIT between Russia and Hungary.

32 The Trans-Pacific Strategic Economic Partnership Agreement between Brunei Darussalam, Chile, Singapore and New Zealand was signed in Wellington on 18 July 2005 and entered into force on 1 May 2006. The text of the Agreement is available at http://www.mfat.govt. nz/downloads/trade-agreement/transpacific/main-agreement.pdf.

33 Trans-Pacific SEP, Chapter 19, Article 19.1.

34 W. Burke White and A. von Staden, 'Investment Protection in Extraordinary Times: The Interpretation and Application of Non-Precluded Measures Provisions in Bilateral Investment Treaties', *Vanderbilt J. Transnational Law* 48, 2008, p. 307.

35 U.S. Model BIT, Article 12(2).

international trade or investment, nothing in this agreement shall be construed to prevent a Party from adopting or enforcing measures necessary (a) to protect human, animal or plant life of health . . . or (c) for the conservation of living or non-living exhaustible resources'.[36] Similarly, the ECT requires states to regulate the environmental and safety aspects of the exploration and development of their energy resources.[37]

In some BITs, reservations exclude certain industries, such as health services, from the protective scope of the investment treaty. This would be compatible with the existing state obligations under the GATS Agreement which provide flexibility for states to decide what sectors may be subject to liberalization.[38] Ad hoc provisions of several recent U.S. Free Trade Agreements clarify that 'Except in rare circumstances, non-discriminatory regulatory actions by a Party that are designed and applied to protect legitimate public welfare objectives, such as public health, safety and the environment, do not constitute indirect expropriation.'[39]

However, from a public health perspective, introducing public health considerations as an exception to investment or trade rules admittedly is at odds with the alleged importance of public health. Exceptions are traditionally interpreted in a restrictive way. This concern is grounded in the jurisprudence adopted by NAFTA panels. *De facto*, a flexibility clause operates in very limited cases, where the risk to public health is so grave that the host state has no other chance than to adopt a given regulatory measure. Still, the implementation and functioning of such a clause very much depends on the specific circumstances of the case, the arguments presented by the parties and the composition of the arbitral tribunal. The functioning of NAFTA Article 1114(2), that is limited to environmental concerns, and does not cover health concerns, has not proven to be optimal. Authors have stressed that the investment treaty clauses referring to environmental protection include 'purely hortatory' language with unenforceable character.[40] For instance, the breach of NAFTA Article 1114(1) would give rise to no more than consultations among parties, while 'it may be questioned whether [Article 1114(2)] provides any meaningful relief for environmental regulations, or whether it is

---

36 Canada Model BIT, Article 11.

37 ECT, Article 18(3).

38 The impact of FDI on national health sectors is an emerging area of interest. See R.D. Smith, 'Foreign Direct Investment and Trade in Health Services: A Review of the Literature', *Social Science & Medicine* 59, 2004, pp. 2313–23. See also *Melvin J. Howard, Centurion Health Corporation & Howard Family Trust v. Government of Canada*, Order for the Termination of the Proceedings and Award on Costs, 2 August 2010.

39 U.S.–Chile Free Trade Agreement, Chapter 10, Annex 10-D, Article 4 (b). The U.S.–Chile FTA entered into force on 1 January 2004. The text of the agreement is available at http://www.ustr.gov.

40 See J. Kelsey, 'International Economic Agreements and Environmental Justice'. in K. Bosselmann and B.J. Richardson (eds). *Environmental Justice and Market Mechanisms*, London: Kluwer Law International, 1999, p. 168.

tautological, protecting only measures that are in any event "consistent with this chapter"'.[41]

Arbitrating disputes with environmental health elements

As the number of disputes with environmental health elements continues to increase, it is important to reflect on the method for identifying and characterizing such disputes. In a preliminary way, as Professor Sands astutely highlights, no two parties will agree that a dispute is essentially 'environmental'.[42] For instance, in *Chevron v. Ecuador*,[43] while Ecuador deemed the dispute to be an abuse of process so to frustrate the outcome of a national environmental dispute, the investor deemed that Ecuador had breached the fair and equitable treatment. The arbitral tribunal found that the claimants did not commit an abuse of process.[44] Similarly, in the pending *Renco* case, a U.S. corporation has filed an investor-state arbitration against the Peruvian government after the latter revoked the operating licence for the La Oroya smelter operated by Renco.[45] On the other hand, the Peruvian government alleges that a subsidiary of the company failed to comply with an environmental clean up programme.[46] The argument between the parties over the alleged environmental character of the dispute is a commonality in this kind of investment dispute. Therefore, it is more appropriate to talk about 'disputes which have an environmental component', rather than to characterize a dispute as 'environmental'. Indeed, the mere definition of a dispute as an 'environmental dispute' may have implications for a case.[47] This neutral approach is based on the consideration that 'environmental claims are rarely, if ever, raised in isolation of other international legal arguments'.[48]

In general terms, investment disputes with environmental health elements are characterized by the need to balance the legitimate interests of a state to

---

41 J. Freedman, 'Implications of the NAFTA Investment Chapter for Environmental Regulation', in A. Kiss, D. Shelton and K. Ishibashi (eds). *Economic Globalization and Compliance with International Environmental Agreements*, The Hague: Kluwer Law International, 2003, p. 94.

42 P. Sands, 'Litigating Environmental Disputes: Courts, Tribunals and the Progressive Development of International Environmental Law', in T. Ndiaye and R. Wolfrum (eds), *Law of the Sea, Environmental Law and Settlement of Disputes – Liber Amicorum Judge Thomas Mensah*, Leiden/Boston: Martinus Nijhoff Publishers, 2007, p. 315.

43 *Chevron Corp. and Texaco Petroleum Company v. The Republic of Ecuador*, Partial Award on Merits on 30 March 2010, ¶ 9.

44 Ibidem, ¶ 3.

45 *The Renco Group Inc. v. the Republic of Peru*, Claimant's Notice of Intent to Commence Arbitration under United States–Peru Trade Promotion Agreement, 29 December 2010, available at http://dev.aida-americas.org/sites/default/files/refDocuments/Notice%20of% 20Intent%20RencoGroup%20V%20Peru_NOI.pdf.

46 Sands, 'Litigating Environmental Disputes', p. 319.

47 Ibidem, p. 315. For the sake of brevity, however, I shall refer to environmental disputes.

protect and/or restore its environmental health and the legitimate interests of foreign investors to protect their property rights. Several issues arise in this context. While environmental concerns have been somehow integrated in investment treaties, environmental clauses remain rather vague and sometimes even subordinate environmental measures to consistency with investment treaty provisions.[49] The very fact that the balancing process occurs in the context of investor-state arbitration could lead to the procedure being deemed biased in favour of the investors. Finally, environmental health disputes invariably raise competing scientific claims. The arbitral tribunals are called upon to adjudicate on different scientific views presented in an equally compelling manner.[50] The question then becomes: How should adjudicators approach inconclusive data and diverging scientific opinions without adjudicating on scientific truths?

Turning our attention to the emerging environmental health case law, it is becoming clear that there is no such thing as a typical 'environmental dispute'. In a preliminary way, environmental cases operate *across the board*, arising in relation to investment in mineral exploitation, waste treatment, water management and numerous other sectors. Investors may claim that certain forms of environmental regulation constitute an indirect expropriation or regulatory taking, and that compensation has to be paid. If a direct expropriation has occurred, claims may concern the amount of compensation. Other claims may concern the violation of the fair and equitable treatment or discrimination. Although the specific claims are hereby singled out for analysis, it is worth highlighting that they are often linked together and their respective arguments may overlap.

Indirect expropriation

Several investment treaty arbitrations have dealt with the question as to whether regulation allegedly aimed to protect environmental health may be deemed to be an indirect expropriation. As there is no single notion of regulatory expropriation in customary international law and definitions vary in the context of different investment treaties, arbitral tribunals have not adopted a consistent approach to the issue. In this context, two main doctrines have emerged regarding how to determine whether a governmental measure

---

49 See S. Baughen, 'Expropriation and Environmental Regulation: The Lessons of NAFTA Chapter Eleven', *Journal of Environmental Law* 18, 2006, p. 222.
50 In principle, the complexity of scientific and technical data underlying legal disputes does not seem to have been an impediment to the exercise of jurisdiction. For instance, the ICJ, in the *Case Concerning Continental Shelf (Libya v. Malta)* which involved a large amount of geological data and diverging scientific arguments, held that 'the Court is unable to accept the position that in order to decide this case, it must first make a determination upon a disagreement between scientists. . .' *Continental Shelf (Libya v. Malta)*, [1985] ICJ 36, at 41.

constitutes an indirect expropriation: the *sole effects* doctrine and the *police powers* doctrine.[51] The *sole effects doctrine* requires that, when making this determination, reference be made only to the effect of the measure on the property allegedly expropriated. On the other hand, the *police powers doctrine* focuses on the purpose of the given regulatory measure. Neither doctrine has prevailed against the other in investment arbitrations and authors are divided on this issue.[52] While the sole effects approach is seen as favouring investor interests, the police powers theory is viewed as favouring states' rights to regulate.

The sole effects doctrine in environmental disputes

The sole effects doctrine gives more weight to the effects of the regulatory measure on the investor than to the regulatory purpose of a given measure. The underlying assumption of this doctrine is that regulatory measures are generally adopted for the public good and may impose some burdens on private property. However, if the burden imposed on certain properties is overwhelmingly or almost completely to deprive them of any economic benefit, the owner is entitled to compensation. Such approach does not preclude the adoption of environmental regulations, but attempts to distribute the costs in a more equitable manner, with the whole society rather than the sole foreign investor assuming the burden of the regulatory change.[53] Several cases lend support to such a doctrine.[54]

The *Metalclad* case, which is considered to be emblematic of the sole effects doctrine, involved a successful claim for expropriation against the Mexican government by a U.S.-based hazardous waste treatment facility.[55] In

---

51 B. Mostafa, 'The Sole Effects Doctrine, Police Powers and Indirect Expropriation Under International Law', *Australian ILJ* 15, 2008.

52 The literature on regulatory expropriation is extensive. See e.g., A. Newcombe, 'The Boundaries of Regulatory Expropriation in International Law', *ICSID Review-FILJ* 20, 2005, p. 1; C. Lévesque, 'Les fondements de la distinction entre l'expropriation et la réglementation en droit international', *R.G.D.* 33, 2003, p. 39; Y. Nouvel, 'Les mesures équivalent à une expropriation dans la pratique récente des tribunaux arbitraux', *RGDIP* 106, 2002, p. 79. Classical contributions include, e.g., J.H. Herz, 'Expropriation of Foreign Property', *AJIL* 35, 1941, p. 243; S. Friedman, *Expropriation in International Law*, London: Stevens & Sons Limited, 1953; B.A. Wortley, *Expropriation in Public International Law*, Cambridge: Cambridge University Press, 1959; G.C. Christie, 'What Constitutes a Taking of Property Under International Law', *BYIL* 33, 1962, p. 307; B.H. Weston, '"Constructive Takings" Under International Law: A Modest Foray Into the Problem of Creeping Expropriation', *Vanderbilt JIL* 16, 1975, p. 103; R. Higgins, 'The Taking of Property by the State: Recent Developments in International Law', *Rec. des Cours* 176, 1982, p. 259.

53 Higgins, 'The Taking of Property by the State: Recent Developments in International Law', p. 277.

54 See e.g. *Consortium RFCC v. Kingdom of Morocco*, ICSID Case No. ARB/00/6, Final Award 22 December 2003, 20 *ICSID Rev.-FILJ* (2005) ¶ 69; *Middle East Shipping v. Egypt*, Award, 12 April 2002, 7 *ICSID Reports* (2005), 178, at ¶ 107.

55 *Metalclad Corporation v. The United Mexican States*, Award 30 August 2000, Case No. ARB(AF)/97/1, 40 ILM 36.

1993, the Mexican Federal government authorized Metalclad to operate a hazardous waste treatment station in the State of San Luis Potosí. However, the company was denied a municipal construction permit because of the complex hydrology of the region. Studies indicated that the site's soils were unstable and toxic waste could infiltrate the subsoil and carry contamination. As the construction project was completed in 1995 without the proper municipal permit, the company was prevented from opening and operating the site due to continued local opposition and public demonstrations. After the municipal government denied Metalclad's request for a permit, the governor of San Luis Potosí declared the site part of a special ecological zone for the preservation of the area's unique biological diversity. Metalclad sued the government of Mexico under NAFTA Chapter 11, alleging indirect expropriation. The arbitral tribunal held that by permitting or tolerating the conduct of the municipal province in relation to Metalclad notwithstanding the fact that the project was fully approved and endorsed by the federal government, Mexico took a measure tantamount to expropriation in violation of NAFTA Article 1110(1).[56]

The tribunal adopted an extensive interpretation of indirect expropriation, holding that 'Expropriation under NAFTA includes not only open, deliberate and acknowledged takings of property, such as outright seizure or formal or obligatory transfer of title in favour of the host State, but also covert or incidental interference with the use of property which has the effect of depriving the owner, in whole or significant part, of the use or reasonably-to-be expected economic benefit of property even if not necessarily to the obvious benefit of the host state.'[57]

The subsequent *Tecmed* case reaffirmed the sole effects doctrine which had been adopted in *Metalclad*.[58] Tecmed, a Spanish company, filed a suit against the Government of the United Mexican States, arguing that Mexico's denial of a licence renewal for the operation of a hazardous waste landfill amounted *inter alia* to an indirect expropriation of the foreign investor's property. In turn, the respondent alleged that the denial of licence renewal was a legitimate regulatory measure issued in compliance with the state's police power in order to protect environmental health. As such, it would not amount to an expropriation under international law.[59] The tribunal primarily examined the effects of the regulatory measure on the property as the fundamental criterion for the decision as to whether indirect expropriation had taken place. As the effect of denying the licence was irreversible and the economic value of the assets was irremediably destroyed, the tribunal found *de facto* indirect expropriation of the investment. The tribunal stated that regulatory

---

56 Ibidem, ¶ 104.
57 Ibidem, ¶ 103 (emphasis added).
58 *Tecnicas Medioambientales Tecmed S.A. v. the United Mexican States*, Case No.ARB(AF)/00/2, Award, 29 May 2003, (2004) 43 ILM 133.
59 Ibidem, ¶ 125.

administrative actions are not *per se* excluded from the scope of the expropriatory measures even if they are beneficial to society as a whole. Also, the tribunal held that although states have the right to protect the environment, the proportionality between public and private interests should be taken into account.[60]

The adoption of the sole effects doctrine may end up 'threatening to place prohibitive costs on rational environmental management' and giving foreign investors 'much greater proprietary rights than domestic investors, thereby distorting economic competition'.[61] Both the Metalclad and Tecmed tribunals paid limited attention to the environmental health goals of the national measures; in both cases, however, the host state's claim that the goal of the adopted measures was public health protection could be further articulated.[62] If states more clearly articulated their claims, it would be possible for arbitral tribunals to better balance the different interests at stake.

The police powers doctrine in environmental disputes

According to the police powers doctrine, *bona fide* non-discriminatory regulation within the police powers of the state does not require compensation.[63] The police powers doctrine focuses on the inherent authority of a government to impose restrictions on private rights for the sake of public welfare, order, and security. The doctrine was derived from English common law principles mandating the limitation of private rights when needed for the preservation of the common good.[64] Analogous principles exist in civil law countries: indeed the legal principles used to sustain the police power of the state are the civil law concepts *sic utere tuo ut alterum non leadas* (use what is yours in a way that does not injure others) and *salus publica suprema lex esto* (public safety is the supreme law).[65]

Under international law, there is no comprehensive and categorical definition of what regulations fall within the police powers of states. The application of police power has traditionally implied the capacity of the state to promote the public health, morals, or safety, and the general well-being of

60 Ibidem, ¶ 157.
61 M.A. Munro, 'Expropriating Expropriation Law: The Implications of the Metalclad Decision on Canadian Expropriation Law and Environmental Land Use Regulation', *Asper Rev Int'l Bus. & Trade Law* 5, 2005, p. 75.
62 R. Suda, 'The Effect of Bilateral Investment Treaties on Human Rights Enforcement and Realization', in O. De Schutter (ed.), *Transnational Corporations and Human Rights*, Oxford: Hart Publishing, 2006, p. 140.
63 See A. Newcombe, 'The Boundaries of Regulatory Expropriation in International Law', *ICSID Review-FILJ* 20, 2005, p. 2.
64 J.E. Galva, C. Atchison, and S. Levey, 'Public Health Strategy and the Police Powers of the State', *Public Health Reports* 120, 2005, pp. 20–27.
65 See G. Reynolds and D. Kopel, 'The Evolving Police Power: Some Observations for a New Century', *Hastings Constitutional Law Quarterly* 27, 2000, pp. 511–37.

the community by enacting and enforcing laws for the promotion of the general welfare and regulating private rights in the public interest.[66] A common element of the measures is that property rights are restricted in order to prevent harm or nuisance caused by their use.[67]

While some authors deem this theory as a justification of state action which would otherwise amount to a deprivation that can be compensated or appropriation of property,[68] others deem it as a necessary corollary of property. For instance, Montt argues that such measures constitute an 'internal limit of property', as 'property rights are conferred . . . by the legal system under the explicit or implicit condition of not causing harm to third parties'.[69] As Howard Mann and Konrad von Moltke note: 'Under the traditional international law concept of the exercise of police powers, when a state acted in a non-discriminatory manner to protect public goods such as its environment, the health of its people or other public welfare interests, such actions were understood to fall outside the scope of what was meant by expropriation . . . Such acts were simply not covered by the concept of expropriation, were not a taking of property, and no compensation was payable as a matter of international law'.[70] In fact, not every state measure with a public purpose falls within the police powers of the state. One needs to distinguish between the exercise of police powers and other regulations that may constitute indirect expropriations and therefore require compensation. The introduction of the police powers doctrine in investment treaty arbitration has been successful in a number of cases.[71]

66   Galva, Atchison, and Levey, 'Public Health Strategy and the Police Powers of the State', p. 20.

67   For a seminar study, see E. Freund, *The Police Power: Public Policy and Constitutional Rights*, Chicago: Callahan, 1904.

68   Newcombe, 'The Boundaries of Regulatory Expropriation in International Law', p. 21; B. Choudhuri, 'Recapturing Public Power: Is Investment Arbitration's Engagement of the Public Interest Contributing to the Democratic Deficit?', *Vanderbilt J. Transn'l L.* 2008, 41, p. 794 (deeming police powers as an 'exception').

69   S. Montt, *State Liability in Investment Treaty Arbitration – Global Constitutional and Administrative Law in the BIT Generation*, Oxford: Hart Publishing, 2009, pp. 192–3.

70   H. Mann and K. Von Moltke, Protecting Investor Rights and the Public Good: Assessing NAFTA's Chapter 11, (2003) p. 16, *available at* http://www.iisd.org/trade/ILSDWorkshop/pdf/background_en.pdf.

71   *Sedco, Inc. v. National Iranian Oil Co.*, 10 Iran–U.S. C.T.R. 180, 25 ILM 629 (1986); *Too v. Greater Modesto*, (1989) 23 Iran–U.S. C.T.R. 378 (holding that '. . . A State is not responsible for loss of property or for other economic disadvantage resulting from bona fide general taxation or any other action that is commonly accepted as within the police power of States, provided it is not discriminatory and is not designed to cause the alien to abandon the property to the State or to sell it at a distress price . . .'). See also *Saluka Investments BV v. Czech Republic*, UNCITRAL Partial Award, ¶ 262 (2006) ('In the opinion of the Tribunal, the principle that a State does not commit an expropriation and is thus not liable to pay compensation to a dispossessed alien investor when it adopts general regulations that are "commonly accepted as within the police power of States" forms part of customary international law today.').

In *S.D. Myers v. Canada*, the tribunal rejected the claim that the ban on the export of PCB constituted an expropriation because the ban was temporary and there was no appropriation or transfer of benefits to the host state. The tribunal affirmed that 'regulatory conduct by public authorities is unlikely to be the subject of legitimate complaint under Article 1110 of NAFTA, although the tribunal does not rule out that possibility'.[72] Somehow, this case theoretically distinguished between legitimate regulation and indirect expropriation and put emphasis on the fact that there was no appropriation and the property was not taken from the owner. Although not expressly adopting the police powers doctrine, this case implicitly acknowledged a certain 'margin of appreciation' of the host state.

Instead, in the *Methanex* case,[73] the arbitral tribunal expressly referred to the police powers doctrine. Methanex, a Canadian investor, initiated arbitration against the United States of America, claiming compensation resulting from losses caused by the ban on the use of a gasoline additive. As scientific evidence showed that MTBE (methyl tertiary-butyl ether) contaminated groundwater and was difficult and expensive to clean up, the State of California enacted legislation to prevent the commercialization and use of MTBE. Methanex submitted that the Californian regulation was tantamount to expropriation within Article 1110 as the US measures would not be meant to serve a public purpose, rather they were enacted to seize the company's market share to favour the domestic ethanol industry. Since no compensation was paid, Methanex argued that this violated due process of law and the minimum standard of treatment.

The tribunal decided that there was no expropriation:

> . . . as a matter of general international law, a *non-discriminatory* regulation for a *public purpose*, which is enacted in accordance with *due process* and, which affects, inter alios, a foreign investor or investment is not deemed expropriatory and compensable unless *specific commitments* had been given by the regulating government to the then putative foreign investor contemplating investment that the government would refrain from such regulation. [italics added][74]

Having ascertained the non-discriminatory character of the measure and its public purpose,[75] the tribunal concluded that the Californian ban 'was motivated by the honest belief, held in good faith and on reasonable scientific grounds, that the MTBE contaminated groundwater was difficult and

---

72 *Myers v. Canada*, Partial Award, 13 November 2000, ¶ 281.
73 *Methanex Corporation v. United States of America*, Award, 3 August 2005, http://www.state.gov/documents/organization/51052.pdf.
74 Ibidem, Part IV – Chapter D – p. 4.
75 Ibidem, Part III, chapter A, ¶ 102(2).

expensive to clean up'.[76] The award did not suggest that the ban was scientifically correct, nor did it take a position on scientific truths. Nonetheless, the reasoning highlights that governments may regulate risks: in this context, emphasis will be put on *due process*. Since no specific commitments were ever given to Methanex, the tribunal held that the ban did not breach the legitimate expectations of Methanex.[77] Methanex had no reasonable expectation, as an investor, that it would be allowed to sell a product that was discovered to cause significant risk to environmental health. Furthermore, as the tribunal pointed out, Methanex invested in a state where environmental and health regulations commonly prohibited or restricted the use of some chemical compounds for environmental health reasons. The tribunal concluded that 'the California ban was made for a public purpose, was non-discriminatory, and was accomplished by due process, [. . .] [thus] from the standpoint of international law, it was a lawful regulation and not an expropriation'.[78]

More recently, a similar approach was adopted in the *Chemtura* case which concerned the question of whether the Government of Canada should pay compensation to a United States agricultural pesticide manufacturer for its ban of an agro-chemical called lindane. As Canada's Pest Management Regulatory Agency (PMRA) banned lindane on the basis of the chemical's health and environmental effects,[79] Chemtura – formerly known as Crompton – initiated arbitral proceedings, claiming *inter alia* that the measure amounted to indirect expropriation and requesting the reinstatement of all registrations relating to its lindane products and/or the damages resulting from Canada's alleged breaches.[80] According to Chemtura, the regulation was not based on a rigorous scientific risk assessment[81] and provoked a discriminatory effect requiring the use of substitute Canadian products in lieu of lindane.

The tribunal noted that 'it [wa]s not its task to determine whether certain uses of lindane [we]re dangerous . . . the rule of a Chapter 11 Tribunal is not to second-guess the correctness of the science-based decision-making of highly specialized national regulatory agencies'.[82] The tribunal added, however, that 'it c[ould] not ignore the fact that lindane has raised increasingly serious concerns both in other countries and at the international level since the 1970s'.[83] As a large number of countries had already banned lindane, and lindane is in the list of chemicals designated for elimination under the Stockholm Convention on Persistent Organic Pollutants,[84] in the tribunal's

76 Ibidem.
77 Ibidem, Part IV – Chapter D – p. 5.
78 Ibidem, IV – D – ¶ 15.
79 *Chemtura v. Canada*, Award, 2 August 2010, ¶ 29.
80 *Crompton Corp. v. Government of Canada*, Notice of Arbitration, 10 February 2005, ¶¶ 45–7.
81 Ibidem, ¶ 35.
82 *Chemtura Corp. v. Government of Canada*, Award, ¶ 134.
83 Ibidem, ¶ 135.
84 Ibidem, ¶¶ 135–6.

view, 'the evidence of the record [di]d not show bad faith or disingenuous conduct on the part of Canada' but 'it show[ed] that the Special review was undertaken by the PMRA in pursuance of its mandate and as a result of Canada's *international obligations*'.[85]

With regard to the allegation of expropriation, the tribunal held that, since the sales from lindane products were a relatively small part of the overall sales of Chemtura, '. . . the interference of the Respondent with the Claimant's investment c[ould] not be deemed "substantial"'[86] and that '. . . in any event . . . the measures challenged by the claimant constituted a valid exercise of the Respondent's police powers. The PMRA took measures within its mandate, in a non-discriminatory manner, motivated by the increasing awareness of the dangers presented by lindane for human health and the environment. A measure adopted under such circumstances is a valid exercise of the State's police powers and, as a result, does not constitute an expropriation'.[87] Thus, the tribunal found that no expropriation had occurred.[88]

Ascertaining discrimination in environmental disputes

A crucial element in investment disputes with environmental elements is the ascertainment of non-discrimination.[89] The key question is whether foreign investments 'are being regulated because the activity in question presents certain risks to the environment, or whether they are being regulated because they are foreign invest[ments]'.[90]

Nowadays it is undoubtedly difficult to spot openly discriminatory *language* in environmental or social regulations, although these characteristics have appeared in investment law and arbitration. For instance, Chile adopted openly discriminatory environmental regulation which imposed particular environmental requirements on foreign-invested firms which were not required of other firms.[91] The *Gallo* case concerned regulation which prevented the creation of a man-made lake on a former open-pit mine site and its use as a landfill for municipal waste[92] and in its title included reference to the mine.[93]

---

85 Ibidem, ¶ 138 [emphasis added].

86 Ibidem, ¶ 263.

87 Ibidem, ¶ 266.

88 Ibidem, ¶ 267.

89 The non-discrimination principle is typically reflected in the investment treaty provisions of the national treatment (NT) and the most-favoured-nation (MFN) treatment. See F. Ortino, 'Non-Discriminatory Treatment in Investment Disputes', in P.-M. Dupuy, F. Francioni and E.-U. Petersmann (eds), *Human Rights in International Investment Law and Arbitration*, Oxford: Oxford University Press, 2009, pp. 344–66.

90 See Mann and von Moltke, Protecting Investor Rights and the Public Good, p. 25.

91 K. Von Moltke, *Discrimination and Non-Discrimination in Foreign Direct Investment Mining Issues*, Paris: OECD, 2002, p. 16.

92 *Vito Gallo v. Government of Canada*, Investor's Memorial Public Version, 1 March 2010, ¶ 1.

93 *Vito Gallo v. Government of Canada*, Procedural Order No 1, 4 June 2008, ¶¶ 37–8.

Canada argued that the enacted legislation was due to the hydro-geological conditions of the mine.[94] As the case was dismissed on procedural ground, no ruling was made on the substantive issues.[95] In an analogous pending case concerning various measures taken by the Ontario Government and local authorities affecting the investor's proposal to convert agricultural lands into an aggregate quarry, the investor is alleging that the measures were targeting only lands owned by the company.[96] Reportedly, the Minister who issued the relevant measures stated he acted in the public interest 'due to the potential harm from the quarry to groundwater that feeds wells, wetlands and streams.'[97]

The discriminatory *effect* of a given regulatory measure is more difficult to assess. The use of apparently neutral criteria may affect a particular group of people. For instance, in the *Ethyl* case, Ethyl relied on trade law jurisprudence to argue that even equally formal treatment may result in less favourable treatment for a foreigner, and that the term 'no less favourable' calls for effective equality in treatment.[98] As Canada had banned import of MMT, Ethyl argued that such a measure discriminated investors that imported MMT vis-à-vis domestic manufacturers of MMT or competitive products.[99] In its Statement of Defence, Canada stated that '[t]he public health and environmental impacts of long-term, lower dose exposure to . . . MMT are unknown' and argued that 'the Act was enacted for the maintenance of health and for the protection of the environment'.[100] Wälde and Kolo argued that Canada could have invoked the precautionary principle to justify its ban.[101] As the case was settled, no ruling on this argument was made.[102]

In the subsequent *Myers* case, a U.S. company, specialized in the remediation of polychlorinated biphenol (PCB) waste, alleged that Canada had violated NAFTA Chapter 11 by enacting an export ban on PCB waste. The ban denied the claimant the opportunity to undertake the PCB remediation business importing PCB from Canada to its remediation facility in the United

---

94 *Vito G Gallo v. Government of Canada*, Statement of Defence, 15 September 2008, ¶ 138.
95 L.E. Peterson, 'Canada Prevails in NAFTA Arbitration Over Thwarted Garbage Disposal Project', *IAR*, 27 September 2011.
96 *St Marys VCNA, LLC v. Government of Canada*, Notice of Intent to Submit a Claim to Arbitration under Section B of Chapter 11 of the NAFTA, 13 May 2011, at ¶ 10, available at http://www.international.gc.ca/trade-agreements-accords-commerciaux/assets/pdfs/St_Marys_VCNA_LLC_vs_Govt_of_Canada-Notice_of_Intent.pdf.
97 R. Benzie, 'Cement Company Seeks $275M in Compensation over Scuttled Quarry', *The Star*, 10 August 2011.
98 *Ethyl Corporation v. Canada*, Notice of Arbitration under the Arbitration Rules of the UNCITRAL and the NAFTA, 14 April 1997, ¶¶ 15–17.
99 *Ethyl Corporation v. Canada*, Statement of Claim, 2 October 1997, ¶¶ 33–6.
100 *Ethyl Corporation v. Canada*, Statement of Defence, 27 November 1997, ¶ 30 and ¶ 95.
101 T. Wälde and A. Kolo, 'Environmental Regulation, Investment Protection and "Regulatory Taking" in International Law', *ICLQ* 50, 2001, p. 834.
102 Canada settled the claim, repealing the ban on MMT and reportedly paying Ethyl US$19.3 million. For commentary, see R. Moloo and J. Jacinto, 'Environmental and Health Regulation: Assessing Liability Under Investment Treaties', *Berkeley JIL* 29, 2011, p. 130.

States. The claimant argued that the ban had been applied in a discriminatory manner, in effect favouring Canadian operators who were not involved in transborder activities. The tribunal found *inter alia* that Canada had violated the National Treatment provision. The tribunal extensively discussed the Canadian Minister for Environment's explicit instructions to reserve domestic waste processing industries for Canadians.[103] The evidence before the tribunal suggested that the ban arose out of economic protectionism, and had a *discriminatory intent* and *effect*. Very little attention was paid to the Basel Convention on the Control of Transboundary Movements of Hazardous Wastes and their Disposal (Basel Convention).[104] Indeed, Canada argued that even if the export ban favoured domestic industry, as a signatory to the Basel Convention, the state was legitimately entitled, and in fact required, to ensure the availability of adequate in-country disposal facilities for PCB. However, the arbitral panel found impermissible discrimination against the claimant, since the export ban favoured Canadian companies over foreign companies.[105]

Instead, in discrimination cases, it is argued that a two-pronged test might be used.[106] If discrimination is found in the first instance, adjudicators should enquire as to whether such discrimination might be justified by a legitimate objective. In the assessment of the likeness of circumstances, attention should be paid to the specific characteristics of each project. For instance, in the *Gallo* case, Canada argued that the enacted legislation was due to the hydrogeological conditions of the mine, as data was insufficient to demonstrate that the hydraulic containment system would work effectively and no drinking water would be contaminated.[107] As the case was dismissed on procedural ground,[108] it is not possible to know how the arbitral tribunal would have weighted the arguments presented by the parties – the alleged discrimination

---

103 *S.D. Myers Inc. v. Government of Canada*, Award, 13 November 2000, 40 ILM 6, 1408–92, ¶ 183.

104 Basel Convention on the Control of Transboundary Movements of Hazardous Wastes and their Disposal (Basel Convention), 22 March 1989, 28 ILM 656 (1989).

105 This approach adopted by the arbitral panel considerably differs from that adopted by the ECJ in the *Belgian Waste Disposal* case. In 1992 the ECJ ruled that Belgian legislation limiting the free movement of waste did not violate the provision on free movement of goods. The legislation prohibited the disposal in Wallonia of waste originating from another state, in breach of several directives related to transboundary movement of waste. However, the Court deemed that the Belgian legislation was justified on environmental grounds. The Court rejected the Commission's argument that the legislation discriminated between waste produced in Wallonia and waste produced elsewhere. On the contrary, it adopted the principle that environmental damage should be prevented: therefore waste should be disposed of as close as possible to the place where it is produced. See Case C-2/90, *EC Commission v. Belgium* [1993] 1 CMLR 365.

106 See F. Gonzales Rojas, 'The Notion of Discrimination in Article 1102 NAFTA', Jean Monnet Working Paper 05/05 (2005).

107 *Vito G Gallo v. Government of Canada*, Statement of Defence, 15 September 2008, ¶ 138.

108 L.E. Peterson, 'Canada Prevails in NAFTA Arbitration Over Thwarted Garbage Disposal Project', *IAR*, 27 September 2011.

and the alleged justification of the same to determine whether there was discrimination and if this was the case, whether this was justified by the circumstances of the case.

As Higgins put it, 'discrimination does not necessarily require that everyone be treated identically. There may be reasons, good reasons, for differentiations being made.[109] Even *prima facie* discriminatory measures may be justified, because of public health concerns. Any distinct treatment of a foreign investor based on its foreign status may be unjustifiable, except where legitimate reason for differential treatment exists. For instance, in 1894 Brazilian authorities facing an outbreak of cholera destroyed watermelons and dismissed claims for compensation. The U.S. State Department, in response to compensation requests of American producers, concluded that the measures were justified under the circumstances and declined to espouse the claim.[110] In *Kemikalieinspektionen v. Toolex Alpha AB*, the ECJ stated that the prohibition on industrial use of trichloroethylene contravened article 28 of the EC Treaty but was justified under Article 30 as being necessary for the protection of human health and/or the environment. While the chemical was not a known carcinogen, the Court stated that '[t]aking account of the latest medical research on the subject, and also the difficulty of establishing the threshold above which exposure to trichloroethylene poses a serious health risk to humans [. . .] there is no evidence in this case to justify a conclusion by the court that national legislation such as that at issue in the case in the main proceedings goes beyond what is necessary to achieve the objective in view'.[111]

An investment arbitration claim presenting similar issues was filed in 2003 when the United States decided to close the U.S.–Canadian border to beef and cattle after a case of mad cow disease was discovered in Canada.[112] A group of Canadian cattlemen brought a NAFTA Chapter 11 suit alleging that the U.S. discriminated against Canadian operators, because it allowed U.S. cattlemen who owned Canadian cattle to keep it, while stopping Canadian cattle (of Canadian operators) at the border. Thus, Canadian cattlemen requested damages for losses incurred during the border closure. The case was dismissed on jurisdictional grounds, but it is important to point out that similar cases may arise in future and that doctrinal reflection is of the utmost importance.

One may wonder whether the legitimate objectives can justify disproportionate measures. Arbitral tribunals are divided on this issue. For instance, in the *Myers* case, the arbitral tribunal assumed that Canada had a legitimate right to advance its Basel Convention obligations, but it stated that 'where a party has a choice among equally effective and reasonably available alternatives for complying . . . with a Basel Convention obligation, it is obliged to choose the alternative that is . . . least inconsistent . . . with the

109 R. Higgins, 'Ethics and International Law', *Leiden JIL* 23, 2010, pp. 277–89.
110 See J.B. Moore, 'Brazilian Watermelons', *Digest of International Law* 6, 1894, p. 751.
111 ECJ, *Kemikalieinspektionen v. Toolex Alpha AB* [2000] ECR I-5681, ¶ 45.
112 *Canadian Cattlemen for Fair Trade v. United States*, Award on Jurisdiction, 28 January 2008.

NAFTA'.[113] In other words, 'where a state can achieve its chosen level of environmental protection through a variety of equally effective and reasonable means, it is obliged to adopt the alternative that is most consistent with open trade'.[114] In the *Methanex* case, Methanex argued that the state had less drastic alternatives for preventing the contamination of water supplies than a ban on MTBE, for instance, enforcing existing rules on leaking underground storage tanks.[115] The argument was dismissed by the arbitral tribunal which deemed the state measures legitimate in the light of public concern on water contamination.[116]

While authors have pointed out that proportionality may constitute a useful guidance in assessing the legitimacy of certain regulatory measures,[117] problems arise with regard to the individuation of 'least-investment restrictive measures'. Not only does this terminology not belong to investment treaty language, but it seems uncritically borrowed from international trade law. Whether such a transplant is possible and desirable may be questioned. *First*, while there is a strong political and economic case for the application of the MFN standard to trade – as tariff discrimination would cause trade distortion contrary to the principle of comparative advantage – it is not clear that such a strong economic and political case is automatically transportable to the investment context.[118] *Second*, it may be pointed out that 'the transition from like products to like investments entails a dramatic change in scope'.[119] Unlike with trade in goods, barriers to entry and operation of foreign investors do not typically take the form of border taxes, whose effects are easily quantifiable and understood. Investment measures will normally comprise regulatory options open to the host state. Thus the scope of operation of the MFN standard in the investment arena is potentially much broader than that in trade for goods. *Third*, as WTO adjudicative bodies have adopted a very careful approach to introducing and evaluating non-trade concerns in trade disputes, the model may present drawbacks.[120]

---

113 *Myers* award, ¶ 215.
114 Ibidem, ¶ 221.
115 *Methanex* award, Part II, Chapter D, ¶ 24.
116 *Methanex* award, Part III, Chapter B ¶ 9.
117 J. Krommendijk and J. Morijn, '"Proportional" by What Measure(s)? Balancing Investor Interests and Human Rights by Way of Applying the Proportionality Principle in Investor-State Arbitration', in Dupuy, Francioni and Petersmann (eds), *Human Rights in International Investment Law and Arbitration*, Oxford: Oxford University Press, 2009, pp. 422–52.
118 J. Kurtz, 'The MFN Standard and Foreign Investment – An Uneasy Fit?', *JWIT* 5, 2004, pp. 861–86.
119 'One sign of this change is that investments increasingly replace the concept of "like" with that of "like circumstances", recognizing the wider range of factors that need to be taken into account in relation to investments.' Von Moltke, *Discrimination and Non Discrimination*, p. 23.
120 See P. Mavroidis, 'No-Outsourcing of Law? WTO Law as Practised by WTO Courts', *AJIL* 102, 2008, p. 421.

The fair and equitable treatment standard in environmental disputes

Arbitral tribunals have stressed the importance of procedural safeguards to ensure that private interests and public goods are properly balanced. An increasing emphasis is placed on administrative due process issues. In this context, the fair and equitable standard has become a key issue in disputes with environmental elements. In NAFTA Chapter 11, the requirement is phrased as follows: 'Each Party shall accord to investments of investors of another Party treatment in accordance with international law, including fair and equitable treatment and full protection and security'. Although the wording of this standard is ambiguous and allows different interpretations, it provides a basic standard of protection that an investor may invoke, which is detached from the law of the host country.[121] Because of its elasticity, the FET clause fills the gaps which are left by more specific standards in order to obtain the level of investor protection intended by the treaties.[122]

While historically, the FET standard was considered to be breached when the state conduct was of an egregious and shocking nature,[123] it has been applied in recent cases to conduct taken in good faith, when investors' expectations were frustrated by state action.[124] For instance, in *Metalclad*, the tribunal held that Mexico violated the FET standard, because the company was led to believe that the federal and state permits it secured allowed for the construction and operation of the landfill. Thus, the tribunal held that Mexico failed to provide 'a transparent and predictable framework for Metalclad's business planning and investment'[125] and that the Mexican government had deprived Metalclad of its reasonable expectations. Although the Supreme Court of British Columbia held that the NAFTA panel erred when it imported the transparency provisions of NAFTA Chapter 18 into Chapter 11,[126] from a systemic perspective, authors have pointed out the importance of regulatory transparency and good faith in the conduct of the state.[127] Accordingly, the

---

121 See UNCTAD, *Investment, Trade and International Policy Agreements – WIR 1996*, New York and Geneva: UNCTAD, 1996, p. 182.
122 R Dolzer, 'Fair and Equitable Treatment: A Key Standard in Investment Treaties', *International Lawyer* 39, 2005, pp. 87–106.
123 *Neer v. United Mexican States*, Award, 4 RIAA 60 (1960).
124 A. Cosbey, H. Mann, L. Peterson and K. von Moltke, *Investment and Sustainable Development. A Guide to the Use and Potential of International Investment Agreements*, Winnipeg: IISD, 2004, pp. 11–12.
125 *Metalclad Corporation v. The United Mexican States*, ¶ 99.
126 See *The United Mexican States v. Metalclad Corporation*, Supreme Court of British Columbia, 2001 BCSC 664, available at http://www.courts.gov.bc.ca/jdb-txt/SC/01/06/2001 BCSC0664.htm.
127 T. Weiler, 'Good Faith and Regulatory Transparency: The Story of Metalclad v Mexico' in T. Weiler (ed), *International Investment Law and Arbitration: Leading Cases from ICSID, NAFTA, Bilateral Treaties and Customary International Law*, London: Cameron May, 2005, pp. 701–45.

state must respect specific representations made by its officials to investors, who have reasonably relied upon them in good faith.

In the *Tecmed* case, the Arbitral Tribunal found a breach of the FET standard as it deemed the licence to be denied on socio-political considerations, and not on compelling reasons of public interest.[128] The tribunal noted that the community pressure was not so serious as to result in social crisis or public unrest.[129] Moreover, the tribunal pointed out that the Mexican authorities had acted in an ambiguous way and should have expressed their willingness to close the landfill more clearly.[130] Again, in the pending *Abengoa* case, Mexico is responding to similar claims concerning the rejection of a construction permit renewal.[131] Local opposition against a toxic waste treatment facility was fuelled with fears that the operation of the facility would generate an increase in pollution and health problems in the area.[132]

In the *Chemtura* case, the tribunal found that the review of lindane was not conducted in a manner that reached the threshold to violate the FET: '[A]s a sophisticated registrant experienced in a highly regulated industry, the Claimant could not reasonably ignore the PMRA's practices and the importance of the evaluation of exposure risks within such practices'.[133] More importantly, the tribunal affirmed that 'scientific divergence . . . cannot in and of itself serve as a basis for a finding of breach of Article 1105 of NAFTA'.[134]

A similar case arose when Dow AgroSciences LLC (DAS), a subsidiary of the US Dow Chemical Company, served a Notice of Intent to submit a claim to arbitration under NAFTA Chapter Eleven against the Government of Canada.[135] DAS complained that a lawn pesticide, dichlorophenoxyacetic acid (2,4-D) was banned in the province of Quebec because of political reasons rather than scientific criteria. In support of such a statement, the company cited an internal communication of the Quebec government stating that the substance could not be banned on 'scientific criteria' but rather on the precautionary approach.[136] DAS claimed *inter alia* breaches of the FET provision of NAFTA Chapter 11.[137] The case was recently settled; the parties agreed that the measures adopted by Quebec were to be maintained; the claimant irrevocably and permanently withdrew its Notice of Arbitration and

---

128 *Tecmed* Award, ¶ 132.
129 Ibidem, ¶ 133.
130 Ibidem, ¶ 164.
131 *Abengoa S.A. and COFIDES, S.A. v. United Mexican States*, ICSID Case No. ARB(AF)/09/2.
132 F. Cabrera Diaz, 'Spanish Firms Launch ICSID Dispute Against Mexico Over Stalled Toxic Waste Disposal Project', *ITN*, 12 January 2010.
133 *Chemtura* Award, ¶ 149.
134 Ibidem, ¶ 154.
135 *Dow AgroSciences LLC v. the Government of Canada*, Notice of Intent to Submit a Claim to Arbitration under Chapter Eleven of the NAFTA, 25 August 2008.
136 Ibidem, ¶ 7.
137 Ibidem.

waived all claims for costs.[138] Canada's Minister of International Trade stated that such agreement 'affirm[ed] the right of governments to regulate the use of pesticides'.[139] However, the parties 'acknowledged that . . . products containing 2,4-D do not pose an unacceptable risk to human health or the environment, provided that the instructions on the label are followed.'[140] Thus, one may wonder whether such a statement could unduly limit the possibility for Canada to adopt more stringent regulation in the future.

Reconciling environmental health and investor rights

After having scrutinized the interplay between environmental health considerations and investor rights in investment treaty law and arbitration, this section enucleates some legal tools that might prevent or help settling disputes with environmental health elements. First, Environmental Impact Assessments as a useful method of dispute avoidance are scrutinized.[141] Second, the role of science in investor-state arbitration is examined. Third, the standard of review adopted in investor-state arbitrations is addressed. Lastly, some final remarks will conclude the chapter.

Environmental Impact Assessment

Environmental Impact Assessment (EIA) is an instrument of environmental governance that ensures that the environmental implications of decisions are taken into account before the decisions are made.[142] Although EIA provides a 'procedural framework for decision making' and 'does not regulate the substance of the decision',[143] the procedural-substantive dichotomy is more apparent than real, as EIA influences the outcome of the decision-making process.[144] As EIA aims to integrate environmental considerations in economic activities, it may be an instrument of dispute prevention.[145] However, recent investment treaty disputes with environmental health

---

138 *Settlement Agreement between Dow AgroSciences LLC and Her Majesty the Queen in Right of Canada*, 25 May 2011, available at http://www.international.gc.ca/trade-agreements-accords-commerciaux/assets/pdfs/DowAgroSciences_Settlement-eng.pdf .

139 'Canada and Dow Chemical Settle Claim over Pesticide Ban', *ITN*, 12 July 2011.

140 Ibidem, ¶ 3.a.

141 See F. Francioni, 'Dispute Avoidance in International Environmental Law', in A. Kiss, D. Shelton and K. Ishibashi (eds), *Economic Globalization and Compliance with International Environmental Agreements,* The Hague: Kluwer Law International, 2003, pp. 229–43.

142 The WHO does not recommend the use of a separate health impact assessment, but the inclusion of health consideration within the existing EIA tool. A Gilpin, *Environmental Impact Assessment: Cutting Edge for the Twenty First Century*, Cambridge: Cambridge University Press, 1995, p. 87.

143 J. Holder, *Environmental Assessment – The Regulation of Decision Making*, Oxford: Oxford University Press, 2004, chapter 1.

144 Ibidem.

145 Francioni, 'Dispute Avoidance in International Environmental Law', p. 235.

elements have questioned the way of conducting EIAs. This section critically assesses these recent investment disputes, and questions whether EIA can facilitate the integration of environmental health considerations into economic activities.[146]

In *Maffezini v. Spain*,[147] an Argentine investor *inter alia* complained that the Spanish authorities had misinformed him about the costs of the project, and pressured the company to make the investment before the EIA process was finalized and before its implications were known. Therefore, according to the claimant, the Spanish authorities would have been responsible for the additional costs resulting from the EIA. The arbitral tribunal dismissed the claims concerning the EIA: 'the environmental impact assessment procedure is basic for adequate protection of the environment and the application of appropriate environmental measures. This is true not only under Spanish and EEC Law, but also increasingly so under international law.'[148] In sum, the tribunal had the perception that 'the investor . . . tried to minimize this requirement so as to avoid additional costs or technical difficulties'.[149] By contrast, the tribunal held that Spain had simply required compliance with its environmental laws in a manner consistent with its investment treaty commitments.[150]

In a pending NAFTA case, recently initiated against the Government of Canada, the Clayton family and their US corporation, Bilcon, objected to the manner in which an EIA has been undertaken.[151] The investors proposed to mine basalt in the coastal Canadian province of Nova Scotia and then ship it by tanker to their New Jersey site. The project attracted a large amount of public discussion in Nova Scotia, and was ultimately rejected following the EIA. In the Notice of Arbitration, the claimants acknowledged that an EIA was required for their project, but they claimed that the process was unusually protracted, discretionary, and politically motivated. Therefore, the claimants alleged discrimination and violation of the FET standard.

In its Statement of Defence,[152] Canada argued that the measures adopted by the local authorities did not breach the relevant provisions of NAFTA Chapter

---

146 See D. Collins, 'Environmental Impact Statements and Public Participation in International Investment Law', *Manchester JIEL* 7, 2010, p. 4 and V. Vadi, 'Environmental Impact Assessment in Investment Disputes', *Polish YIL* 30, 2010, pp. 169–205.
147 *Emilio Augusto Maffezini v. The Kingdom of Spain*, ICSID Case No ARB/97/7, Award of the Tribunal, 13 November 2000.
148 Ibidem, ¶ 67.
149 Ibidem, ¶ 70.
150 Ibidem, ¶ 71.
151 *William Ralph Clayton, William Richard Clayton, Douglas Clayton, Daniel Clayton and Bilcon of Delaware Inc. v. Government of Canada*, Notice of Arbitration, 26 May 2008.
152 *William Ralph Clayton, William Richard Clayton, Douglas Clayton, Daniel Clayton and Bilcon of Delaware Inc. v. Government of Canada*, (Clayton and Bilcon v. Canada) Statement of Defence of the Government of Canada, 4 May 2009, available at http://www.pca-cpa.org/upload/files/CanadaStatementDefence04May.PDF.

11 and pointed out that the location of the project, Digby Neck, was comprised in a biosphere reserve designated by UNESCO in 2001.[153] Canada also stated that the Environmental Impact Statement prepared by Bilcon was assessed by a panel composed of experts in oceanography, planning and environmental studies. After collecting all relevant information, soliciting public comment and holding public hearings,[154] the panel recommended the relevant authorities to reject the proposed project in its entirety due to 'the significant adverse environmental effects that [it] would cause to the physical, biological and human environment on Digby Neck . . ., including on the "core community values" of the affected communities'.[155] Both the Nova Scotia Minister of the Environment and the Government of Canada accepted the conclusions of the panel and rejected Bilcon's project.

In another pending case, a US company, Pac Rim Cayman LLC, commenced international arbitration proceedings against the Republic of El Salvador under the U.S.–Central America Free Trade Agreement (CAFTA).[156] According to the claimant, which planned to explore and develop its 'El Dorado' gold mine in El Salvador, El Salvador breached international and national standards as it did not issue extraction permits within its own mandated time frames and pursuant to the terms of applicable laws.[157] Thus, the company requested compensation for damages.[158] The case has not been decided yet.

As seen above, EIAs have come to the forefront of legal debate in investment disputes. In abstract terms, detecting the environmental consequences of the project before it is implemented, and ensuring that planned activities are compatible with sound environmental management may prevent the risks of environmental damage and ensure the reconciliation of private and public interests. However, the above-examined disputes show that EIA needs to respect international standards of transparency and fairness. While legislative changes may be seen as a normal business risk, this does not exempt states from a general duty of good faith and transparency. In conclusion, the fact that to date EIA procedures have not prevented investment treaty disputes does not mean that they may not do so in the future. They clearly have such potential if they follow adequate procedural standards.

153 Ibidem, ¶ 10.
154 Ibidem, ¶¶ 60–64.
155 Ibidem, ¶ 66.
156 *Pac Rim Cayman LLC v. Republic of El Salvador*, Notice of Intent to Submit a Claim to Arbitration Under Chapter Ten of the Central America–United States–Dominican Republic Free Trade Agreement, 9 December 2008, available at http://www.minec.gob.sv/index.php?option=com_phocadownload&view=category&id=26:otros-documentos&Itemid=63.
157 In particular, the company alleges CAFTA violations of Article 10.3 (national treatment), Article 10.4 (most-favoured-nation treatment), Article 10.5 (minimum standard of treatment) and article 10.7 (expropriation).
158 Ibidem, ¶ 38.

The role of science in international investment law and arbitration

As 'the presence and integrity of scientific support is a principal touchstone for determining the legitimacy of many national regulatory efforts aimed at ensuring environmental integrity or safeguarding public health',[159] the role of science in international law and adjudication has attracted increasing attention in current legal discourse.[160] Nonetheless, very few contributions have addressed the role of science in international investment arbitration.[161] This section addresses this gap in legal literature and discusses the role of science in international investment arbitration. Given the only-recent rise of investor-state arbitrations and the fact that most BITs do not address issues such as scientific evidence, risk assessment etc., this field of inquiry still presents embryonic features and this section can only provide a preliminary assessment.

A significant element which arbitrators have taken into account when evaluating the legitimacy of a given regulatory measure is the existence of international standards, or *scientific consensus*,[162] affirmed in instruments adopted by international bodies. If the adopted measures are based on international standards, it is easier for the host state to argue that the adopted measures were based on sound scientific criteria. For instance, the *Chemtura* tribunal stated that it '[could] not ignore the fact that lindane has raised increasingly serious concerns both in other countries and at the international level since the 1970s'.[163] The tribunal also established that the respondent had 'amply established the existence of [environmental and health] concerns' by referring to a number of countries banning or restricting the use of lindane and relevant international legal instruments.[164] Similarly in *Maffezini*, the requirement of an EIA was deemed to be legitimate in light of current international standards.

However, experts may well disagree on scientific issues and thus science may be inconclusive.[165] Science does not provide definitive answers as 'the scientific

---

159 D.A. Wirth, 'The Role of Science in the Uruguay Round and NAFTA Trade Disciplines', *Cornell ILJ* 27, 1994, pp. 817–18.
160 See e.g. J. Peel, *Science and Risk Regulation in International Law*, Cambridge: Cambridge University Press, 2010; C. Foster, *Science and the Precautionary Principle in International Court and Tribunals*, Cambridge: Cambridge University Press, 2011.
161 See M. Orellana, 'Science, Risk and Uncertainty: Public Health Measures and Investment Disciplines', in P. Kahn and T. Wälde (eds), *New Aspects of International Investment Law*, Leiden/Boston: Martinus Nijhoff and Hague Academy of International Law, 2007, pp. 671–789; T. Weiler, 'The Treatment of SPS Measures Under NAFTA Chapter 11: Preliminary Answers to an Open-Ended Question', *Boston College International and Comparative Law Review* 26, 2003, p. 229.
162 S. Smyth, W.A. Kerr and P.W.B. Phillips, 'Recent Trends in the Scientific Basis of Sanitary and Phytosanitary Trade Rules and Their Potential Impact on Investment', *JWIT* 12, 2011, p. 13.
163 *Chemtura* award, ¶ 135.
164 Ibidem, ¶ 133.
165 Orellana, 'Science, Risk and Uncertainty', p. 680.

method is based on challenging accepted wisdom'[166] and scientific findings are subject to constant revision. Scientific consensus becomes more and more elusive moving from core knowledge to frontier areas of research and new discoveries.[167] As Orellana puts it, 'such frontier areas are characterized by persistent uncertainty and diverging interpretations . . .'[168] Finally, scientific debate may be mixed with and influenced by social and political considerations.[169]

If a case presents scientific uncertainty and a plurality of scientific opinions, arbitrators may put emphasis on the scientific method and on due process, particularly with regard to transparency and public participation. For instance, the *Chemtura* tribunal affirmed that 'scientific divergence . . . cannot in and of itself serve as a basis for a finding of breach of Article 1105 of NAFTA'.[170] Accordingly, adjudicators should consider whether policy makers have adopted reasonable scientific method and due process in their risk assessment. Their enquiry would focus on whether regulations have been adopted in a transparent manner and whether they are subject to domestic remedies and/or judicial review. Similarly in the *Methanex* case, the tribunal concluded that the report prepared by the University of California (on which the adopted measures relied) reflected 'a serious, objective and scientific approach to a complex problem',[171] focusing on procedural aspects. The tribunal held that the Report 'was subjected at the time to public hearings, testimony and peer-review; and its emergence as a serious scientific work *from such an open and informed debate* is the best evidence that it was not the product of a political sham'.[172]

In case of scientific uncertainty, questions remain as to what extent scientific questions that are not fully researched, or where only preliminary scientific evidence exists, can be taken into account. Questions remain as to whether states can rely on minority scientific opinions or have to adhere to mainstream science; or whether the precautionary principle can be invoked in a situation of scientific uncertainty surrounding the effectiveness of a policy option aimed at tackling scientifically certain health risks.[173]

It is worth recalling that a number of states have adopted a precautionary approach to public health issues, intervening and protecting the public from exposure to harm where scientific investigation discovered plausible public health risks. According to such an approach, decision makers may need to

---

166 Smyth, Kerr and Phillips, 'Recent Trends in the Scientific Basis of Sanitary and Phytosanitary Trade Rules', p. 12.
167 Orellana, 'Science, Risk and Uncertainty', p. 682.
168 Ibidem.
169 Ibidem, p. 681.
170 *Chemtura* award, ¶ 154.
171 *Methanex* award, Part III, Ch. A, ¶ 101.
172 Ibidem, emphasis added.
173 In this sense, see EFTA Court, Case E-16/10, *Philip Morris Norway v. Staten v/Helse- org omsorgsdepartementet*, 12 September 2011, available at http://www.eftacourt.int/images/uploads/16_10_Judgment_EN.pdf.

prevent harm before it occurs.[174] As Principle 15 of the Rio Declaration states, 'In order to protect the environment, the precautionary approach shall be widely applied by States according to their capabilities. Where there are threats of serious or irreversible damage, lack of full scientific certainty shall not be used as a reason for postponing cost-effective measures to prevent environmental degradation.'[175]

However, the legal status of the approach is uncertain. Some deem the precautionary approach as a norm of customary international law or a general principle of law.[176] More carefully (and perhaps more accurately) the Seabed Disputes Chamber of the International Tribunal for the Law of the Sea has observed that: '[t]he precautionary approach has been incorporated into a growing number of international treaties and other instruments, many of which reflect the formulation of Principle 15 of the Rio Declaration. In the view of the Chamber, this has initiated a trend towards making this approach part of customary international law.'[177] Other international courts and tribunals have adopted a different stance.[178] For instance while the WTO Appellate Body has acknowledged that 'responsible, representative governments commonly act from perspectives of prudence and precaution',[179] it did not pronounce on the legal status of the precautionary approach under international law.[180]

The standard of review

In the clash of cultures between investment protection and the pursuit of public health objectives by the host state, the standard of review plays a

---

174 The literature on the precautionary principle is extensive. See, e.g., L. Marini, *Il principio di precauzione nel diritto internazionale e comunitario*, Padova: CEDAM, 2004; J. Zander, *The Application of the Precautionary Principle in Practice – Comparative Dimensions*, Cambridge: Cambridge University Press, 2010; Peel, *Science and Risk Regulation in International Law*; Foster, *Science and the Precautionary Principle in International Court and Tribunals*.

175 United Nations Conference on Environment and Development: Rio Declaration on Environment and Development, adopted at Rio de Janeiro, 14 June 1992, 31 ILM 874 (1992).

176 See, e.g., O. McIntyre and T. Mosedale, 'The Precautionary Principle as a Norm of Customary International Law', *Journal of Environmental Law* 9, 1997, p. 221.

177 Seabed Disputes Chamber of the International Tribunal for the Law of the Sea, Advisory Opinion, Responsibilities and Obligations of States Sponsoring Persons and Entities with Respect to Activities in the Area, Case No. 17, 1 February 2011, available at http://www.itlos.org/start2_en.html (accessed on 7 March 2011), ¶ 135.

178 For an excellent analysis of the approaches adopted by the panels and the Appellate Body of the World Trade Organization, see L. Gruszczynski, *Regulating Health and Environmental Risks Under WTO Law: A Critical Analysis of the SPS Agreement*, Oxford: Oxford University Press, 2010.

179 Appellate Body Report, *U.S. – Continued Suspension of Obligations in the EC-Hormones Dispute*, WT/DS320/AB/R, 16 October 2008, at ¶ 124.

180 Appellate Body Report, *European Communities – Measures Concerning Meat and Meat Products (Hormones)*, WT/DS26/AB/R, 16 January 1998, ¶ 123.

fundamental role because the degree of deference given by arbitral tribunals in reviewing a given decision of the relevant authorities influences the outcome of the proceedings. Most (if not all) BITs do not explicitly define which is the standard of review to be adopted by arbitral tribunals. Thus, defining the appropriate standard of review has been left to adjudicators. Can arbitrators second-guess the regulatory choices of the relevant authorities? Should they adopt a purely deferential standard of review so that the regulatory autonomy of the state is completely unbound?

With regard to public health-related disputes, authors have suggested the adoption of a 'qualified deference'.[181] Like other international adjudicative bodies,[182] arbitral tribunals are not to undertake a *de novo* review of the evidence once brought before the national authorities, merely repeating the fact-finding conducted by the latter. It is not appropriate for arbitral tribunals to decide on the validity of the scientific findings underlying public health measures.[183] For instance, the *Chemtura* tribunal noted at the outset that 'it [was] not its task to determine whether certain uses of lindane are dangerous' and that 'the rule of a Chapter 11 Tribunal is not to second-guess the correctness of the science-based decision-making of highly specialized national regulatory agencies'.[184]

On the other hand, arbitral tribunals, as other international tribunals, should not be deterred to scrutinize the given national measures and their compliance with the host state investment law obligations. Thus, arbitral tribunals are not to pay a total deference before national measures, simply accepting the determinations of the relevant national authorities as final. Rather, they must objectively assess whether the competent authorities complied with their international investment law obligations in making their determinations. The *Chemtura* tribunal stated that the review 'must be conducted *in concreto*,[185] . . . [taking] into account all the circumstances, including the fact that certain agencies manage highly specialized domains involving scientific and public policy determinations'.[186]

The arbitral tribunal has an obligation to consider the evidence presented to it and to make factual findings on the basis of that evidence. The arbitral tribunal will evaluate the relevance and probative force of the

---

181 Orellana, 'Science, Risk and Uncertainty', p. 723.

182 See, e.g, DSU, Article 11.

183 For instance, in *EC – Measures Affecting Asbestos and Asbestos Containing Products*, the WTO panel pointed out that 'in relation to the scientific information submitted by the parties and the experts, . . . it is not its function to settle a scientific debate, not being composed of experts in the field of the possible human health risks posed by asbestos. Consequently, *the Panel does not intend to set itself up as an arbiter of the opinions expressed by the scientific community.*' [emphasis added]. *European Communities – Measures Affecting Asbestos and Asbestos Containing Products*, Panel Report, Doc. WT/DS135/R, 18 September 2000, ¶ 8.181.

184 *Chemtura* award, ¶ 134.

185 Ibidem, ¶ 98.

186 Ibidem, ¶ 123.

evidence, and interpret relevant national law for the purpose of determining whether the host country has met its obligations under the BIT.[187] For instance, the *Chemtura* tribunal noted that it '[could] not ignore the fact that lindane has raised increasingly serious concerns both in other countries and at the international level since the 1970s'[188] on the basis of the evidence provided by the defendant. The tribunal deemed that the respondent had 'amply established the existence of [environmental and health] concerns' by referring to a number of countries banning or restricting the use of lindane and international legal instruments further signalling international concern about the human health and environmental effects of the chemical.[189] Questions remain as to the possibility for the arbitral tribunal of appointing neutral experts and/or to seek information from relevant international organizations.

Thus, it will be important for the states to show that their regulations are aimed at achieving legitimate public goals and follow due process of law. As an arbitral tribunal held, '[. . .] "public interest" requires some genuine interest of the public. If mere reference to "public interest" can magically put such interest in existence and therefore satisfy this requirement, then this requirement would be rendered meaningless since the Tribunal can imagine no situation where this requirement would not have been met.'[190] Similarly Wälde and Kolo point out that acts of protectionism or mistreatment of foreign investors are often 'camouflaged in the much more palatable clothes of sacred environmental causes' and caution against 'not so holy alliances between protectionist interest and environmental idealism'.[191] In this sense, as Wälde and Kolo put it, 'such controls can be seen as a desirable constraint over the domestic political process' as 'investor-State litigation rights are a step towards good governance in international economic relations'.[192]

Arguably, the *margin of appreciation doctrine*, which was developed by the ECtHR, could assist the arbitrators to secure some latitude for the host state to define and adopt public health policies.[193] According to the margin of appreciation doctrine, states maintain a space for manoeuvre in fulfilling their international law obligations due to their social, cultural and historic

---

187 PCIJ, *German Interests in Polish Upper Silesia*, (Ger. v. Pol.) [1926], PCIJ Rep., Series A, No. 7, p. 19.

188 *Chemtura* award, ¶ 135.

189 Ibidem.

190 *ADC Affiliate Limited and ADC & ADMC Management Limited v. Republic of Hungary*, ICSID Case ARB/03/16, Award 2 October 2006, ¶ 432.

191 T. Wälde and A. Kolo, 'Environmental Regulation, Investment Protection and "Regulatory Taking" in International Law', *ICLQ* 50, 2001, p. 820.

192 Ibidem, p. 846.

193 M. Orellana, 'The Role of Science in Investment Arbitrations Concerning Public Health and the Environment', *YIEL* 17, 2006, p. 54.

features.[194] Such doctrine grants qualified deference to governmental regulations adopted on the basis of scientific evidence and reduces the risk of arbitral tribunals second guessing democratic authorities.[195] The margin of appreciation doctrine would apply specifically to the risk management, where value judgments and other public considerations apply. Notwithstanding its theoretical merits, the margin of appreciation doctrine was dismissed by the *Chemtura* tribunal which held that the standard of review is not 'an abstract assessment circumscribed by a legal doctrine about the margin of appreciation of specialized regulatory agencies', but rather 'must be conducted *in concreto*'.[196]

Conclusions

This chapter has examined the particular intersection between international environmental law, public health and international investment law. Environmental health is a theoretical tool which highlights the linkage between the environment and public health. The regulatory competence of states to protect environmental health, which has traditionally been part of state sovereignty, has somehow been reinforced by a web of MEAs which have reaffirmed the states' duty to protect environmental health. Several investment treaties acknowledge such competence through co-ordination clauses and declaratory statements in their preambles.

The mutual supportiveness between economic development and environmental considerations was aptly expressed in the *Iron-Rhine Arbitration* in which the arbitral tribunal stated that 'Environmental law and the law on development stand not as alternatives but as mutually reinforcing integral concepts . . .'.[197] In this regard, the principle of sustainable development[198] requires states to focus on the protection of human well-being in the management of natural resources, also taking into account intergenerational equity and environmental concerns.[199]

However, conflicts may arise between investment treaty guarantees and national regulations aimed at protecting environmental health. Foreign investors, who have direct access to international arbitral tribunals, may claim that such regulations amount to investment treaty breaches. Authors have cautioned that investment treaty law and arbitration risk becoming an

---

194 E. Benvenisti, 'Margin of Appreciation, Consensus and Universal Standards', *NYU JIL & Politics* 31, 1999, p. 843; Y. Shany, 'Towards a General Margin of Appreciation Doctrine in International Law?' *EJIL* 16, 2005, p. 907.
195 Orellana, 'Science, Risk and Uncertainty', p. 675.
196 Ibidem.
197 PCA, *Iron Rhine (Ijzeren Rijn) Railway* (Belgium v. Netherlands), arbitral award, 24 May 2005.
198 ICJ, *Case Concerning the Gabcikovo-Nagymaros Project* (Hungary v. Slovakia) (1997) ¶ 140.
199 S. Smith, 'Ecologically Sustainable Development: Integrating Economics, Ecology and Law', *Willamette Law Review* 31, 1995, pp. 263–4.

example of 'asymmetrical scale politics' where 'local institutions and actors [are] being given responsibility without power, while international institutions and actors [are] gaining power without responsibility'.[200]

This chapter has shown the possible areas of conflict between environmental health concerns and investors' property rights and has scrutinized the legal tools that may help the reconciliation of these different values and goals within investment treaty law and arbitration. In particular, this chapter has focused on Environmental Impact Assessment as a mechanism of dispute prevention and the role of science in investor-state arbitration. Other legal mechanisms that may help reconciling the different interests at stake will be dealt with in the next chapter.

---

200 V.H.W. Wang, 'Investor Protection or Environmental Protection? "Green Development" Under CAFTA', *Colum. J. Envtl. L.* 32, 2007 (internal citations omitted).

Part III

Reconciling public health and investor rights in international investment law

Introductory note

The tension between international investment law and public health law, and the growing tide of investor-state arbitrations including public health elements bring to the fore a number of questions regarding the relationship between these domains of international law.[1] Is international law a unitarian system? Does international investment law and arbitration provide enough consideration to public health objectives? What are the boundaries of investor rights? Is investment treaty arbitration a suitable forum for settling such disputes? In sum, the two fundamental dilemmas are, respectively, whether investment law is clinically isolated from public international law and whether investor-state arbitration is an adequate forum for discussing health-related issues.

The third part of the book addresses these questions offering a theoretical paradigm to reconcile public health and investor rights within investment treaty law and arbitration. At the substantive level, investment law and public health law are components of international law. Thus, when the two sub-systems collide a balance needs to be struck between investor rights and public health.[2] It is argued that interpretation allows for such a synthesis and that, although other fora may be better equipped to deal with the normative pluralism which characterizes contemporary international law, investor state arbitration is not a self-contained regime, nor should it be.

1 M. Hirsch, 'Interactions between Investment and Non-Investment Obligations in International Investment Law', *TDM* 3, 2006, p. 3.
2 T. Altangerel, 'The Principle of Balance: Balancing Economic, Environmental and Social Factors in International Economic Law', *Manchester JIEL* 1, 2004, pp. 4–19.

7 Reconciling conflicting interests

Introduction

International investment law and public health law interact and overlap in a variety of ways. This relationship may determine positive synergies.[1] For instance, while economic growth spurred by FDI may have a positive impact on public health, public health favours economic activities. However, investment governance can limit the regulatory autonomy and the capacity of states to impose obligations on transnational corporations.[2] If a state adopts public health regulation which a foreign company deemed in violation of relevant investment provisions, adjudicators will have to establish which norm prevails and then whether such incompatibility may play a role with regard to the possible remedies.[3] In certain cases, apparent conflicts may be solved through treaty interpretation and the reconciliation of norms.

As seen above, international investment tribunals have not adopted a systematic and coherent approach to this issue. The confidentiality of the proceedings, the existence of divergent opinions among scholars and the diversity of legal regimes to be applied have contributed to this fragmented landscape. As the existing body of arbitral awards shows a lack of coherence, this chapter explores the legal toolkit that may help the practitioner and the interpreter to reconcile different international obligations.

The chapter proceeds as follows. First, this chapter addresses the questions as to whether international investment law is a subset of international law and, whether in turn, it is contributing to the development of international law. Second, the law which is applicable in investment treaty arbitrations will be examined. Third, the issues of balancing and reconciliation of norms will be scrutinized. Fourth, this chapter focuses on interpretation as a tool for

1 M. Hirsch, 'Interactions between Investment and Non-Investment Obligations in International Investment Law', *TDM* 3, 2006, p. 5.
2 R. Suda, 'The Effect of Bilateral Investment Treaties on Human Rights Enforcement and Realization', *NYU School of Law Global Law Working Paper n. 01/05*, 2005, p. 53.
3 Ibidem, p. 6.

reconciling the different interests at stake. The chapter concludes with some final remarks.

Unity versus fragmentation

The relationship between international law and international investment law has taken on a greater significance with the extraordinary flourishing of investment treaties in recent years.[4] Although in a formal sense, investment treaties differ little from other international treaties, the legal regimes they create are often at variance with the assumptions underlying the traditional sovereign state model. Investment provisions create a privileged regime within the boundaries of the state which may appear to be self-contained under many respects. Also, investment treaty arbitration constitutes a major departure from customary international law.

Adopting a unitary approach, this book supports the argument that international law, albeit decentralized, is not an anarchic amalgam of different norms, but has a structure similar to a system.[5] The notion of legal system or legal order was famously articulated by Santi Romano;[6] according to his doctrine, the legal system was not only a set of norms, but it was the unit comprising these rules and a specific social constituency. As international law governs the relations of a social body, namely the international community, international law is a legal system. Because distinct sets of rules of international law are not applied to distinct social entities, 'they cannot give rise to different independent legal systems'.[7]

The thesis of the unity between international law and international investment law is supported by several arguments. *First*, from a historical perspective, contemporary international investment law has its roots in the development of customs concerning the treatment of aliens and state responsibility, which is one of the oldest branches of international law. Notwithstanding the existence of an 'investment law culture',[8] investment

---

4 See P.-M. Dupuy, 'Unification Rather than Fragmentation of International Law? The Case of International Investment Law and Human Rights', in P.-M. Dupuy, F. Francioni and E.-U. Petersmann (eds), *Human Rights in International Investment Law and Arbitration*, Oxford: Oxford University Press, 2009. With regard to the more general debate on the unity or fragmentation of international law, see e.g. P.-M. Dupuy, 'A Doctrinal Debate in the Globalization Era: on the "Fragmentation" of International Law', *EJLS* 1, 2007, pp. 1–19; B. Simma and D. Pulkowski, 'Of Planets and the Universe: Self Contained Regimes in International Law', *EJIL* 17, 2006, pp. 483–529; B. Simma, 'Self-Contained Regimes?', *Netherlands YBIL* 16, 1985, pp. 11–136.

5 See J. Pauwelyn, *Conflict of Norms in Public International Law*, Cambridge: Cambridge University Press, 2003, p. 9.

6 S. Romano, *L'ordinamento giuridico*, 2nd edn., Firenze: Sansoni, 1946.

7 O. Casanovas, *Unity and Pluralism in Public International Law*, The Hague: Martinus Nijhoff Publishers, 2001, p. 67.

8 Every legal system develops its own culture and related lexicon deriving from the system's implementation. See D. Steger, 'The Culture of the WTO: Why it Needs to Change', *JIEL* 10, 2007, p. 483.

treaties are international treaties by their own nature. Investor-state arbitration is a creature of international law, with public law elements. The authority of the arbitral tribunal does not merely depend on the will of the parties, but on an international treaty. Where there is no such treaty, there is no jurisdiction: the foreign investor has to invoke the diplomatic protection of the home state or recur to local or regional remedies.

Second, in many circumstances, international law is the law applicable to investment disputes according to a given arbitral clause or relevant treaty provision. Even in those cases where the applicable law is the law of the host state, it is worth recalling that national legal systems are permeated by international law, be they monist or dualist systems.[9] Thus, when arbitrators apply national provisions that reflect international law norms, the boundaries between the international and the national planes become blurred.

Third, it may be observed that there is osmosis and reciprocal conceptual fluidity between international law and international investment law as the contained system also contributes to the development of the container system. Indeed, investment treaty arbitration plays an active role in the development of the substantive and procedural content of international law.[10] The contributions of this process include the emergence of investor's direct claims before international arbitral tribunals, the clarification of rules relating to treaty interpretation and the same interpretation of treaty and customary norms relating to the protection of aliens. This has been acknowledged by the ICJ, which has noted that 'the role of diplomatic protection has somewhat faded, as in practice, recourse is only made to such court in rare cases where treaty régimes do not exist or have proved inoperative'.[11] The increasing obsolescence of diplomatic protection – or its residual nature – with regard to foreign investors was not conceivable fifty years ago, when the first BIT was concluded between Germany and Pakistan.[12] Arguably, these developments have implications for some of the assumptions on which international law has traditionally been based.

Fourth, international treaty provisions cannot be interpreted in *a vacuum*. On the contrary, according to Article 31.3.c of the VCLT any relevant rule of international law applicable in the relationship between the parties should be taken into account, together with the context. Indeed, arbitrators have referred

---

9 Dupuy, 'Unification Rather than Fragmentation of International Law?', p. 59.
10 See generally S. Schill, *The Multilateralization of International Investment Law*, Cambridge: Cambridge University Press, 2009.
11 ICJ, *Ahmadou Sadio Diallo (Republic of Guinea v. Democratic Republic of the Congo) (Preliminary Objections)* Judgment, 24 May 2007 <http://www.icj-cij.org>.
12 The 1959 Germany–Pakistan BIT is the first known BIT. The first BIT that provided for investor-state arbitration with unqualified state consent was the Chad–Italy BIT (1969) and the first arbitration that upheld the validity of a unilateral arbitration clause was *SPP v. Egypt. Southern Pacific Properties (Middle East) Limited v. Egypt* (Decision on Jurisdiction), 27 November 1985, ICSID Rep 112.

to international law norms and cases in their reasoning.[13] To say that there is *continuity* between international law and international investment law does not imply a sort of *pre-established harmony* between the system and its sub-system.[14] Rather, the appropriate equilibrium needs to be found both by policy makers and interpreters. This chapter is devoted to the search of such coherence, and focuses on two main themes: the applicable law and treaty interpretation.

The applicable law

With regard to the applicable law, given the fundamental principle of party autonomy in international arbitration, the arbitrators' inquiry is primarily guided by the determination of whether the parties themselves have chosen the law governing their dispute.[15] It is only in the absence of such choice that the arbitrators must determine the law that will apply to the dispute. Several BITs contain a composite choice of law clauses, typically including treaty rules, host state law and customary international law.[16] For instance, the U.S. Model BIT (2004) provides that in certain cases, 'the tribunal shall decide the issues in dispute in accordance with this Treaty and applicable rules of international law'.[17] Similarly, Article 1131 of the NAFTA states that '[a] tribunal established under this Section shall decide the issues in dispute in accordance with this Agreement and applicable rules of international law'.[18]

For cases brought before the ICSID, the ICSID Convention provides that a tribunal will apply the law selected by the parties or, in the absence of such a choice, the law of the host country and such principles of international law as are applicable.[19] The latter clause has determined intense debate among scholars. Some authors take the view that international law is limited to a supplementary and corrective role. It is supplementary in that it fills the *lacunae* of the host country's law; it is corrective in that it applies if the host law violates international law. However, other authors have argued that international law would always apply, as either national law is consistent with it, or if it is not, then the former is superseded by the latter.[20]

---

13 V. Vadi, 'Critical Comparisons: The Role of Comparative Law in Investment Treaty Arbitration', *Denver J. of Int'l L. & Policy* 39, 2010, pp. 67–100.
14 These terms belong to the philosophical discourse. See G. Leibniz, *Discourse on Metaphysics* XIV (1686) reprinted, Montana: Kessinger Publishing, 2007.
15 R. Bishop, J. Crawford and M. Reisman, *Foreign Investment Disputes*, The Hague: Kluwer Law International, 2005, p. 13.
16 Y. Banifatemi, 'The Law Applicable in Investment Treaty Arbitration', in K. Yannaca Small (ed.), *Arbitration Under International Investment Agreements: A Guide to the Key Issues*, Oxford: Oxford University Press, 2010, p. 191.
17 U.S. Model BIT (2004), Article 30(1).
18 NAFTA, Article 1131(1).
19 ICSID Convention, Article 42.
20 Bishop, Crawford and Reisman, Foreign Investment Disputes, p. 14.

Even in the absence of any reference to international law in the compromissory clause, there are other ways for an international arbitrator to refer to it.[21] *First,* when the constitution of the host state opts for monism granting primacy to public international law, the latter penetrates the law applicable to the contract. Even in states which adopt the dualist theory and require international law norms to be 'translated' into national ones, arbitrators do apply norms of international law, when they apply the national norms which convey them. As Professor Kreindler points out, '. . . even where the parties have not agreed, directly or indirectly, to the application of international law "rules" or "principles", international law may already be internally applicable as part of the domestic law chosen by the parties . . .'[22]

If international law is part of the applicable law, because of the compromissory clause or because of the treaty or the arbitral rules, the arbitrators would not exceed their mandate if they applied international law norms. If the parties make express reference to international law norms, the arbitral tribunal may deal with these claims, albeit *incidenter tantum.* It is not a question of direct application of non-investment norms *principaliter* by arbitral tribunals. Rather, it is a question of incidental evaluation of measures adopted by the host state in compliance with its international law obligations to determine whether such measures may be justified, even if *prima facie* they appear to be inconsistent with investment treaties.[23]

In any case, arbitrators are still bound to apply relevant peremptory norms of international law norms whether or not such approach is pleaded by the parties. The question is not whether to add new claims to those articulated by the parties, but to give due consideration to the applicable law.[24] As Jan Paulsson puts it, 'a tribunal in an investment dispute cannot content itself with inept pleadings, and simply uphold the least implausible of the two. Furthermore, as the PCIJ put it in *Brazilian Loans*, an international tribunal is "deemed itself to know what [international law] is". . .'[25] Transnational

21 Dupuy, 'Unification Rather than Fragmentation of International Law?', p. 25.
22 R.H. Kreindler, 'The Law Applicable to International Investment Disputes', in N. Horn (ed.), *Arbitrating Foreign Investment Disputes*, The Hague: Kluwer Law International, 2004, pp. 413–14.
23 For an analogous view in the WTO context, see F. Francioni, 'WTO Law in Context: The Integration of International Human Rights and Environmental Law in the Dispute Settlement Process', in G. Sacerdoti, A. Yanovich and J. Bohanes (eds), *The WTO at Ten*, Cambridge: Cambridge University Press, 2006, p. 139.
24 The applicable law and the principle of *nec ultra petita* are two different issues. The applicable law concerns the body of law that is applicable to the dispute. The principle of *nec ultra petita* concerns the arguments raised by the parties but does not infringe or supersede the mandatory rules eventually applicable to the dispute. See, for instance, G. Cordero Moss, 'Is The Arbitral Tribunal Bound by the Parties' Factual and Legal Pleadings?', *Stockholm International Arbitration Review* 3, 2006, p. 13.
25 J. Paulsson, 'International Arbitration and the Generation of Legal Norms: Treaty Arbitration and International Law', ICCA Congress Series, The Hague: Kluwer Law, 2006, pp. 888–9.

public policy (or *ordre public international*) would always be applicable.[26] The English House of Lords in 1853 described *public policy* as 'that principle of law which holds that no subject can lawfully do that which has a tendency to be injurious to the public or against public good'.[27] *Transnational public policy* refers to those principles that receive an international consensus as to universal standards and accepted norms that must always apply.[28] The concept of 'transnational public policy', or 'truly international public policy', is said to comprise fundamental rules of natural law; principles of universal justice possessing an absolute value or absolute truth[29] covering fundamental laws with a higher status than the ordinary rules of international law (*jus cogens*).[30]

Jus cogens is defined by Article 53 of the VCLT as 'a norm accepted and recognized by the international community of states as a whole as a norm from which no derogation is permitted and which can be modified only by a subsequent norm of general international law having the same character'.[31] While this provision sets a legal framework on how peremptory norms work, it does not specify which norms constitute *jus cogens*.[32] However, the fact that the notion of peremptory norms is elusive should not lead us to conclude that *jus cogens* has no ascertainable basis.[33] Although there is no simple criterion by which to identify a general rule of international law as having the character of *jus cogens*, the concept of *jus cogens* is positive law.[34] Generally accepted examples are the prohibition of the use of force, the prohibition of slavery, torture, systemic racial discrimination, piracy, and genocide.[35] Given the legal uncertainty surrounding the term, it is up to international

---

26 A. Orakhelashvili, *Peremptory Norms in International Law*, Oxford: Oxford University Press, 2006, p. 492; Dupuy, 'Unification Rather than Fragmentation of International Law?', p. 25.

27 *Egerton v. Brownlow* (1853) 4 HLC 1.

28 A. Sheppard, 'Public Policy and the Enforcement of Arbitral Awards: Should There Be a Global Standard?', *TDM* 1, 2004, p. 1.

29 P. Meyer, *Droit International Privé*, Paris: Montchrestien, 1994, p. 140.

30 P. Lalive, 'Ordre public transnational (ou réellement international) et arbitrage international', *Revue de l'Arbitrage*, 1986, pp. 329–73.

31 VCLT, Article 53.

32 VCLT, Article 53.

33 For some sceptical views, see M.W. Janis, 'Jus Cogens: An Artful Not a Scientific Reality', *Conn. JIL* 3, 1987–1988, p. 370; A. D'Amato, 'It's a Bird, It's a Plane, It's Jus Cogens!', *Conn. JIL* 6, 1990–1991, p. 2 ('a critic may object that *jus cogens* has no substantive content; . . . the sheer ephemerality of *jus cogens* is an asset, enabling any writer to christen any ordinary norm of his or her choice as a new *jus cogens* norm, thereby in one stroke investing it with magical power'); M. Koskenniemi, 'International Law in Europe: Between Tradition and Renewal', *EJIL* 16, 2005, p. 113 (*jus cogens* and obligations *erga omnes* 'have no clear reference in this world but . . . [i]nstead of meaning, they invoke a nostalgia for having such a meaning . . .').

34 P.-M. Dupuy, 'Some Reflections on Contemporary International Law and the Appeal to Universal Values: A Response to Martti Koskenniemi', *EJIL* 16, 2005, p. 136.

35 See E.J. Criddle and E. Fox-Decent, 'A Fiduciary Theory of Jus Cogens', *Yale JIL* 34, 2008, p. 331.

adjudicating bodies to decipher the complex tapestry of international law in determining its meaning. Although *jus cogens* does not include every aspect of public health at the moment, it may expand to include these juridical objects in the future, because of its dynamic aspect.[36]

How have international tribunals dealt with *jus cogens*? Authors have criticized the approach adopted by the ICJ in the *Gabcikovo-Nagymaros* case, where the Court stated that since none of the parties invoked *jus cogens* norms of environmental law, it would not examine the effects and scope of Article 64 of the VCLT.[37] As Orakhelashvili points out, such a restrictive approach did not address the question as to whether certain environmental norms have a peremptory character.[38] Thus, it is suggested that the Court should have adjudicated on the issue *'motu proprio* since it involved the question of objective invalidity' of a treaty.[39] In this regard, it is worth highlighting that the ICJ has been extremely cautious regarding *jus cogens* rules.[40] In the *Military and Paramilitary Activities in Nicaragua* case, the ICJ limited itself to noting that the parties considered that the principle of the prohibition of the use of force was a *jus cogens* norm.[41] In its Advisory Opinion concerning the *Legality of the Threat of or Use of Nuclear Weapons*, the court considered it to be unnecessary to pronounce on the character of *jus cogens* of principles of international humanitarian law.[42] More recently, the ICJ held that the peremptory character of a norm may not provide a basis for the jurisdiction of the Court, which is always grounded in the consent of the parties.[43]

Instead, *jus cogens* has been forcefully asserted in a series of international arbitrations. For instance, in the *Maria Luz* arbitration, the Czar of Russia, sitting as the sole arbitrator, declared that Japan 'had not breached the general rules of the Law of the Nations' in freeing the slaves carried on the Peruvian vessel *Maria Luz* and denying the subsequent demands for indemnity of the Peruvian citizens.[44] In the *Aminoil* case, the international arbitral tribunal maintained the existence of *jus cogens*, albeit excluding that the invoked norm had peremptory character. In particular, the arbitral tribunal stated that permanent sovereignty over natural resources did not prohibit the possibility

36 New peremptory norms may arise and may modify the existing norms. See VCLT, Articles 64 and 53.
37 *Gabcikovo-Nagymaros*, ICJ Reports 1998, 76.
38 Orakhelashvili, *Peremptory Norms in International Law*, p. 498.
39 Ibidem, 498.
40 A. Bianchi, 'Human Rights and the Magic of Jus Cogens', *EJIL* 19, 2008, p. 502.
41 *Military and Paramilitary Activities in and against Nicaragua (Nicaragua v. United States of America)* Merits, Judgment, *ICJ Reports 1986*, ¶ 190.
42 *Legality of the Threat or Use of Nuclear Weapons*, Advisory Opinion, *ICJ Reports 1996* ¶ 83.
43 *Armed Activities on the Territory of the Congo* (New Application 2002) (Dem. Rep. Congo v. Rwanda) Jurisdiction and Admissibility [2006] ICJ Rep. 1, ¶ 64.
44 *Maria Luz* Arbitration, award rendered by the Czar of Russia, 17–19 May 1875, quoted by Lalive, 'Ordre public transnational (ou réellement international) et arbitrage international', p. 49.

of states to subscribe to stabilization clauses.[45] Adopting a more subtle solution, in the *Texaco* case, the arbitral tribunal did not deny the *jus cogens* nature of permanent sovereignty, but stated that the contested contract between the host state and the foreign investor was the exercise of sovereignty over natural resources.[46]

Similarly, in an ICC arbitration, Mr. Lagergreen acting as a sole arbitrator affirmed that 'it cannot be contested that there exists a general principle of law recognized by civilized nations that contracts which seriously violate *bonos mores* or international public policy are invalid . . .'.[47] In the ICSID case *World Duty Free Company Limited v. The Republic of Kenya*,[48] the arbitral tribunal stated that 'in light of domestic laws and international conventions relating to corruption, and in light of decisions taken in the matter by courts and international tribunals, this tribunal is convinced that bribery is contrary to the international public policy of most, if not all states. Thus, claims based on contracts of corruption or on contracts obtained by corruption cannot be upheld by this Arbitral Tribunal.'[49] Adopting a similar view, the ICSID Tribunal in the *Methanex* case asserted that 'as a matter of *international constitutional law*, a tribunal has an independent duty to apply imperative principles of law of *jus cogens* and not to give effect to the parties' choice of laws which are inconsistent with such principles.'[50]

In other cases, as Professor Martin Hunter points out, notwithstanding arbitrators 'would claim that they have never applied transnational public policy principles in formulating their awards', they have applied public policy principles, in particular with regard to environmental goods.[51] Indeed, it has been highlighted that 'public policy is a flexible and dynamic concept to be used as a corrective mechanism. It can also be a tool to balance complex and often conflicting goals such as protection of the environment while assuring the rights of foreign investors.'[52]

Therefore, authors have highlighted that 'any tribunal owes an obligation to the international community to apply international public policy' and that 'the faithful application of public order would acquit a tribunal of its obligations to the parties to apply the law chosen by them through compromise or otherwise, but nothing can acquit a tribunal of its mandate to apply public policy'.[53] In case public policy does not belong to the

45 See *Kuwait v. Aminoil*, ILR, vol 66, 587–8, ¶90.2.
46 *Texaco*, 53 ILR 482, ¶78.
47 ICC Award No 1110 (1963), XXI YBCA 52 (1996), p. 336.
48 *World Duty Free v. Republic of Kenya*, ICSID Case No ARB/00/7, Award of 4 October 2006 at ¶ 157.
49 Ibidem.
50 *Methanex v. United States of America*, Award, Part IV, ch C, 11.
51 M. Hunter and G. Conde e Silva, 'Transnational Public Policy and its Application in Investment Arbitrations', *JWIT* 4, 2003, p. 372.
52 Ibidem, p. 374.
53 Orakhelashvili, *Peremptory Norms in International Law*, p. 493; R. Kreindler, 'Approaches to the Application of Transnational Public Policy by Arbitrators', *JWIT* 4, 2003, p. 244 ('the

applicable law, i.e. national law, authors suggest that arbitrators invoke human rights as part of the general principles of law.[54] The principal purpose of international public order is to maintain the integrity of the fundamental norms of international law. In this sense, public policy would concern a 'constitutional' aspect of public international law.[55] One cannot but agree on such an approach which would not amount to arbitral law making, but to the recognition that arbitrations do not take place in a *vacuum* rather they contribute to the development of international law and must be in conformity with its basic rules.

In the literature one of the recurrent arguments is that public policy is '. . . a very unruly horse, and when once you get astride it you never know where it will carry you'.[56] Some have cautioned that it 'can readily be made to serve hidden sectional interests, not apparent at first sight . . . leav[ing] everybody absolutely free to argue for or against the *jus cogens* character of any particular rule of international law'.[57] Others have even argued that peremptory norms represent a false universalism which refers to nothing factual except for the longing on the part of international lawyers that there be such a thing.[58]

While it can obviously be agreed upon that there is a need to prevent the misuse of peremptory norms and free decision making,[59] the difficulties in identifying norms of *jus cogens*, and the necessity to avoid abuses of such concept should not lead adjudicators to dismiss *jus cogens* tout court. *Jus cogens* is already integrated into positive law and constitutes 'an important structural element of international law as a legal system'.[60] Therefore, according to some authors, public policy would have a *positive* function, by stating the need to guarantee a minimum level of quality for international awards.[61] In conclusion, it seems correct to consider *jus cogens* as a legal concept, to be considered applicable by relevant judges and arbitrators.[62]

arbitrator need(s) not to apply the agreed or determined governing law if doing so would cause him to violate international public policy'); J.D.M. Lew, L.A. Mistelis and S.M. Kröll, *Comparative International Commercial Arbitration*, The Hague: Kluwer Law International, 2003, pp. 93–4 ('To the extent that human rights protection constitutes a core part of international or national public policy, human rights aspects must be considered by the tribunal').

54 Ibidem, p. 94.
55 Orakhelashvili, *Peremptory Norms in International Law*, p. 1.
56 *Richardson v. Mellish* (1824) 2 Bing. 228; [1824–34] All ER Rep. 258.
57 G. Schwarzenberger, 'International *Jus Cogens*?', *Tex L Rev* 43, 1964–1965, p. 477 [internal citations omitted].
58 M. Koskenniemi, 'International Law in Europe: Between Tradition and Renewal', *EJIL* 16, 2005, p. 122.
59 A. Verdross, 'Jus Dispositivum and Jus Cogens in International Law', *AJIL* 60, 1966, p. 62.
60 O. Casanovas, *Unity and Pluralism in Public International Law*, p. 77.
61 See M. Rubino-Sammartano, *International Arbitration Law and Practice*, The Hague: Kluwer Law International, 2001, p. 507; H. Arfazadeh, *Ordre public et arbitrage international à l'épreuve de la mondialisation*, Bruxelles: Bruylant, 2005, p. 178.
62 In his separate opinion to the ruling on jurisdiction in the case *Armed Activities in the Territory of the Congo between the Democratic Republic of the Congo and Rwanda*, Judge Dugard

Public policy

International law permeates investment treaty arbitration also with regard to the enforceability of arbitral awards. Arbitral tribunals have an obligation to the parties to render an enforceable award.[63] If an arbitral award breaches norms of international law, its enforcement can be denied by national courts on public policy grounds.[64] In this context, the 1958 New York Convention on the Recognition and Enforcement of Foreign Arbitral Awards[65] expressly provides for a limited judicial review on the merits of an award for public policy reasons.[66] Similarly, the UNCITRAL Model Law[67] provides that the court shall refuse recognition or enforcement of an award if it finds that the award is in conflict with the public policy of this state.[68] As the Model Law has formed the basis for international arbitration laws adopted by many countries throughout the world, violation of public policy is held as a ground for annulment in numerous countries. Indeed, some commentators deem public policy as the ultimate and necessary limit to the autonomy of international arbitration.[69] Judicial control would persist to the extent of the awards' conformity with transnational public policy. This constitutes the traditional or *negative* role of public policy which acts as a limit to the recognition of arbitral awards.[70]

With regard to investment arbitration, ICSID awards are considered truly delocalized. Indeed, the ICSID Convention excludes any attack on the award in the national courts, and ICSID awards are deemed to be final and self-executing.[71] As the ICSID Convention provides an internal system of

affirmed: 'norms of jus cogens advance both principles and policy . . . they must inevitably play a dominant role in the process of judicial choice'. *Armed Activities on the Territory of the Congo (Dem. Rep. Congo v. Rwanda)* Judgment, Jurisdiction and Admissibility [2006] ICJ Rep. 1. Separate Opinion of Judge *ad hoc* Dugard, ¶ 10.

63 See, for instance article 35 ICC Arbitration Rules: '. . . the Arbitral Tribunal shall act in the spirit of these rules and shall make every effort to make sure that the Award is enforceable at law'.

64 The grounds for setting aside arbitral awards are set out in the *lex loci arbitri* or the law of the seat which establishes the link between an arbitration procedure and a certain legal order. See T. Giovannini, 'The Making and Enforcement of the Arbitral Award: What Are the Grounds On Which Awards Are Most Often Set Aside?', *Business Lawyer International* 1, 2001, p. 115.

65 New York Convention on the Recognition and Enforcement of Foreign Arbitral Awards, 10 June 1958, 330 UNTS 38.

66 New York Convention, Article V.2.

67 United Nations Commission on International Trade Law (UNCITRAL) Model Law on International Commercial Arbitration, UN documents A/40/17 Annex 1 and A/61/17, Annex I, adopted on 21 June 1985 and amended on 7 July 2006. The Model Law is designed to assist states in reforming and modernizing their laws on arbitral procedure.

68 UNCITRAL Model Law on International Commercial Arbitration, Article 36 (1)(b)(ii).

69 H. Arfazadeh, 'In the Shadow of the Unruly Horse: International Arbitration and the Public Policy Exception', *American Review of International Arbitration* 13, 2002, pp. 1–10.

70 See Rubino-Sammartano, *International Arbitration Law and Practice*, p. 504.

71 Article 54(1) of the ICSID Convention requires Contracting States to enforce an ICSID award 'as if it were a final judgment of a court in that State'.

remedies,[72] and, notably, an internal annulment mechanism, it excludes appeals or any other remedies at the national level.[73] In its quest for finality and enforceability of its awards, the Convention has created an autonomous regime for recognition and execution which excludes the applicability of relevant national arbitration laws. Crucially, public policy is not a ground for annulment of the arbitral award under the ICSID Convention. As Schreuer highlights, 'The finality of awards would also exclude any examination of their compliance with international public policy or international law in general'.[74]

However, this does not mean that arbitrators should not respect international law and public policy. The arbitral tribunal must observe international law under Article 42 of the ICSID Convention.[75] Giardina rightly points out that the fact that ICSID awards are recognized and enforced as binding on all states parties to the relevant agreements requires their necessary compliance with international law. Thus, respect of public international law would be an *implicit requisite* of ICSID awards.[76]

Also, national courts have shown some resistance to the detachment of ICSID awards from every form of judicial supervision, and have elaborated a distinction between enforcement and execution. Thus, while ICSID rules would cover enforcement, the law governing execution would be national law. Also, issues of international *ordre public* appeared in several cases.[77] Furthermore, arbitral awards under the so-called ICSID Additional Facility, as well as those rendered under commercial arbitration rules (e.g. UNCITRAL, ICC etc.) may be reviewed in local courts. Consequently, a growing national jurisprudence is emerging, albeit not all these cases are in the public domain.

The enforceability of arbitral awards constitutes a pillar of investment treaty arbitration as the system relies on the finality of arbitral awards and legal certainty. Furthermore, according to Article 27 of the VCLT, a state cannot rely on its national law to justify non-compliance with its treaty obligations.[78] Yet, public policy is not a mere national concept as the existence of a proper international public order common to all nations is widely recognized. The international community as a whole requires arbitral justice to respect the general interests protected by transnational public policy.[79] Thus, there would

---

72 The ICSID Convention provides for the following remedies: interpretation of the award (Article 50), rectification of the award (Article 51), and annulment of the award (Article 52).
73 ICSID Convention, Article 53(1).
74 C. Schreuer, *The ICSID Convention: A Commentary*, Cambridge: Cambridge University Press, 2001, p. 1129.
75 Ibidem.
76 A. Giardina, 'International Investment Arbitration: Recent Developments as to the Applicable Law and Unilateral Recourse', *Law and Practice of International Courts and Tribunals* 5, 2007, pp. 29–39.
77 See E. Baldwin, M. Kantor and M. Nolan, 'Limits to Enforcement of ICSID Awards', *J Intl Arb* 23, 2006, p. 8.
78 *Certain German Interests in Polish Upper Silesia*, PCIJ Series A/B, No. 46, 167.
79 C. Seraglini, *Lois de police et justice arbitrale internationale*, Paris: Dalloz, 2001, p. 533.

be a difference between public order as such, and *ordre public vraiment international* of the international community of states.[80] In this sense, if an award was contrary to peremptory norms of public international law, the relevant authorities would be obliged not to execute it, because of *ordre public vraiment international*.[81]

With regard to public health, some of its contents already present a *jus cogens* status. For instance, in a recent case, a U.S. court recognized that the experimentation of pharmaceuticals on African children, by a U.S. corporation with the support of the host state, without prior informed consent, amounted to violation of customary rules of international law:[82] 'the judgment concluded that human experiments under such conditions are contrary to the principles of the law of the nations as they result from usages established among civilized peoples, from the laws of humanity, and from the dictates of public conscience'.[83] Non-consensual medical experimentation may amount to torture, whose prohibition is part of *jus cogens*.[84]

Some public health norms are treaty norms, but have the potential to become customary norms. The codification of the right to health in the ICESCR represents a high achievement of the international community, and may contribute to the consolidation of the relevant norm in customary international law. Other public health norms have already achieved customary law status. For instance norms relating to quarantine express universally shared awareness that in order to prevent the spread of infectious diseases certain illnesses require a cool-off period. States have the duty to prevent the spread of epidemics and health emergencies. These norms are meant to protect the society as a whole and represent *lois de police* par excellence.

Because the well-being of entire populations could be endangered by tobacco consumption, environmental health risks and the lack of access to medicines, it may be argued that it is the duty of the state to regulate these different but similar phenomena in order to protect public health and the common weal. If an international award did not recognize the legitimacy of such objectives, such an award could not possibly be executed at the national

---

80 Orakhelashvili, *Peremptory Norms in International Law*, p. 27.

81 According to some, the rules of *jus cogens* are those which constitute the 'international public order', using these terms as synonyms: 'International *jus cogens* and international public policy are synonyms, conveying the idea of rules of international law which may not be changed by consent between individual subjects of international law'. See Schwarzenberger, 'International *Jus Cogens?*', p. 455. Others distinguish between the two concepts: for instance, according to Virally, the notions of *jus cogens* and *ordre public* are 'notions voisines'. See M. Virally, 'Réflexions sure le "jus cogens"', *Annuaire Français de droit international*, 1966, p. 7.

82 *Rabi Abdullahi v. Pfizer*, U.S. Court of Appeals for the Second Circuit, 30 January 2009, <http://caselaw.lp.findlaw.com/data2/circs/2nd/054863p.pdf>.

83 The Court acknowledged that 'the evolution of the prohibition [on non consensual medical experimentation] began with the war crimes trials at Nuremberg. . .'. Ibidem, p. 25.

84 *Siderman de Blake v. Republic of Argentina*, 965 f.2d 699, 715 (9th Cir 1992).

level. If a contracting state failed to abide by and comply with the award rendered, the state of the foreign investor could decide to bring an international claim on behalf of the investor before the International Court of Justice. However, this would be a discretionary move, according to the traditional rules of diplomatic protection. Also, the International Court of Justice would have to consider whether the duty to prevent the spread of pandemics belongs to international public order and whether the measures at stake respond to that objective.

Again, it is worth noting that not every public health issue deserves the same level of deference. While it is generally recognized that states may adopt high standards of public health protection, not every public health objective may present the same level of urgency and cogency. For instance, the prevention of the spread of lethal pandemics of international reach may present imperative character, also in consideration of specific intervention by the organs of the United Nations. For instance, both the General Assembly and the Security Council assumed a clear-cut position on certain pandemics.[85] Even when the regulatory measures pursue a public policy objective of imperative character, issues concerning their appropriateness and reasonableness may arise.

In general terms, in order to avoid subsequent challenges, the arbitrators should take public policy considerations into account in the course of the arbitral proceedings. Not only does public policy protect the compelling public interests of single states, but it also protects the fundamental interests of the international community at large. Above all, public policy compels arbitrators to integrate these diverse and often conflicting interests into one coherent conception of international justice.

Conflict and reconciliation of norms in investor–state arbitration

Traditionally conflict has been perceived in a negative fashion, as a struggle for definite dominance. However, as Professor Slaughter contends, conflict may be seen as 'the motor of positive change'[86] and 'if law successfully manages conflicts, then repeated conflicts should actually strengthen the legal order'.[87] The potential for conflict of norms is inherent in every legal system. As such, it should not be conceived as a sort of pathology or an anomaly in the law, but as a characteristic of the system.[88] Not only does international law not constitute an exception to this, but it offers fertile ground for overlapping norms and conflicting obligations.

85 UN Security Council Resolution 1308, adopted unanimously on 17 July 2000; UNGA Declaration of Commitment on HIV/AIDS, A/RES/S-26/2, 2 August 2001.
86 A.M. Slaughter, *A New World Order*, Princeton and Oxford: Princeton University Press, 2004, p. 209.
87 Ibidem.
88 Pauwelyn, *Conflict of Norms in Public International Law*, p. 12.

The act of reconciling conflicts or of perceiving them as compatible entails a complex interpretative process. When the domestic law is the law applicable to the dispute, arbitrators will have to apply the relevant norms which may belong to the constitutional order of the host state. Apart from the compulsory application of transnational public policy norms, internal norms are generally structured in a precise hierarchical order. Thus, the task of the arbitrators will be facilitated by this structured harmony among national normative sources. On the other hand, if international law is the applicable law, a subsequent question which arises is whether norms belonging to different international law subsystems are truly comparable.[89]

According to some authors, the difference in nature between public health law and investor protections would mean that they operate on different levels and are thus not amenable to balancing.[90] Therefore, only human rights courts should be empowered to adjudicate on highly sensitive issues involving fundamental human rights. One may wonder, however, whether a holistic approach might be preferred. Not only would such an approach bring coherence to international law, but it would also favour the 'humanization' of the same.[91] Considering international public law as a 'universe of inter-connected islands' may have a positive impact on economic globalization, spurring and bringing together economic and social development.[92]

While it is not possible to contest the importance of protecting aliens in international law, it is important to keep in mind that investor rights are not absolute but may be limited for legitimate reasons. The investment model may emphasize the rights of the investors but the latter do not only have rights, but also duties.[93] This is particularly true with regard to public health. While it is clear that arbitrators cannot adjudicate eventual violations by the host state of public health law as this would be outside their mandate; they should not simply dismiss or ignore public health-related arguments. The elements of public health law which belong to *jus cogens* can be deemed to be a component of the applicable law. The other elements of public health will be relevant as a matter of treaty interpretation.

In case of conflict in the implementation of the state responsibilities concerning public health and investor rights, the arbitrators will be called to balance these rights, through a procedure similar to that established and

89 C. Valcke, 'Comparative Law as Comparative Jurisprudence – The Comparability of Legal Systems', *AJCL* 52, 2004, p. 713.
90 Orellana, 'Science, Risk and Uncertainty', p. 720.
91 T. Meron, *The Humanization of International Law*, The Hague: Martinus Nijhoff, 2006.
92 J. Pauwelyn, 'Bridging Fragmentation and Unity, International Law as a Universe of Inter-Connected Islands', *Michigan JIL* 25, 2004, p. 903.
93 See, for instance, Article 29.2 of the UDHR, stating that 'In the exercise of his rights and freedoms, everyone shall be subject only to such limitations as are determined by law solely for the purpose of securing due recognition and respect for the rights and freedoms of others and of meeting the just requirements of morality, public order and the general welfare in a democratic society.'

consolidated by human rights bodies and national constitutional courts. The attempt to prove the compatibility of two norms has been defined as the 'reconciliation' of norms.[94] It is important to consider that 'in many instances, what may seem like a conflict will not be a conflict but only a divergence which can be streamlined by means of [. . .] treaty interpretation'.[95] Pursuant to the process of treaty interpretation and other legal techniques, many apparent conflicts can be resolved or even prevented.

Inherent normative conflicts, which arise when a norm constitutes in itself breach of another norm, albeit theoretically conceivable, will rarely, if ever, appear in practice.[96] Instead, conflicts in the applicable law have often arisen in the context of investor-state arbitration, when compliance with one norm entailed non-compliance with the other.[97] Indeed, it may be argued that conflicts in the application of norms arise because conflict prevention and management of apparent conflicts have not been attempted or have failed. Thus, both apparent conflicts and conflicts in the applicable law deserve scrutiny.

Interpretation

Customary norms of treaty interpretation, as set out in Articles 31, 32 and 33 of the VCLT, guide parties and arbitrators to interpret the text of the treaties. Not only are these rules expressly incorporated in some investment treaties,[98] but contemporary arbitral jurisprudence is replete with references to Article 31–33 of the VCLT.[99] These norms include the principle of good faith in interpreting treaty provisions and provide that the intentions of the parties are revealed through the ordinary meaning of the terms of the treaty, in their context, and in light of its object and purpose.[100]

Pursuant to Article 31(3)(c) of the VCLT, the treaty interpreter shall take into account 'any relevant rules of international law applicable in the relations between the parties'. As stated by Sinclair, pursuant to Article 31(3)(c), '[e]very treaty provision must be read not only in its own context, but in the wider context of general international law, whether conventional or customary'.[101] Therefore, this provision properly expresses the principle of *systemic* integration within the international legal system, indicating that treaty regimes are

---

94 S.A. Sadat-Akhavi, *Methods of Resolving Conflicts between Treaties*, Leiden: Martinus Nijhoff Publishers, 2003, p. 33. As the author puts it, 'Two norms are reconcilable when there is at least one way of complying with all their requirements'.
95 Pauwelyn, *Conflict of Norms in Public International Law*, p. 6.
96 Ibidem, p. 275.
97 W. Jenks, 'The Conflict of Law-Making Treaties', *BYIL* 30, 1953, p. 426. See also E. Vranes, 'The Definition of Norm Conflict in International Law and Legal Theory', *EJIL* 17, 2006, p. 395.
98 See e.g. AUSFTA Article 21.9.2.
99 See, e.g., *Noble Ventures v. Romania*, Award, 12 October 2005, ¶ 50.
100 VCLT, Article 31.
101 I. Sinclair, *The Vienna Convention on the Law of Treaties*, Manchester: Manchester University Press, 1984, p. 139.

themselves creatures of international law.[102] As Koskenniemi explains, 'legal interpretation and thus legal reasoning builds systemic relationships between rules and principles. Far from being merely an "academic" aspect of the legal craft, systemic thinking penetrates all legal reasoning, including the practice of law application by judges and administrators'.[103]

Article 31(3)(c) also allows space for dynamic or *evolutionary* treaty interpretation. As the content of international law changes and develops continuously, any approach to interpretation must find a means of dealing with this dynamism. As the ICJ recognized, an adjudicator's interpretation cannot remain unaffected by subsequent developments of law.[104] Such a technique was used by the WTO Appellate Body when it interpreted the term 'exhaustible natural resources' in Article XX(g) of the GATT 1994.[105] Similarly, the ECtHR has repeatedly affirmed that the ECHR is 'a living tree which must be interpreted in the light of present-day conditions' in a dynamic and evolutive fashion.[106]

Judicial borrowing in investment treaty arbitration

Arbitral tribunals have increasingly used *judicial borrowing* in investor-state arbitration, making reference to the case law and standards belonging to different systems. *Judicial borrowing* is a dynamic process that may lead to a sort of judicial globalization[107] or the development of a 'common law of international adjudication'.[108] Professor Slaughter, who first identified the twin issues of global community of courts and global jurisprudence, defines judicial globalization as 'the [. . .] conceptual shift [. . .] from two systems – international and domestic – to one; from international and national judges to judges applying international law, national law or a mixture of both'.[109] Also, she highlights the development of the doctrine of *judicial comity*, a set of principles guiding courts in giving deference to foreign courts 'as a matter of respect owed by judges to judges, rather than of the more general respect owed

---

102 C. McLachlan, 'The Principle of Systematic Integration and Article 31(3)(c) of the Vienna Convention', *ICLQ* 54, 2005, p. 280.

103 United Nations, International Law Commission 'Fragmentation of International Law: Difficulties arising from the Diversification and Expansion of International Law, Report of the Study Group on the International Law Finalized by Martti Koskenniemi' UN Doc A/CN.4/L.682, 13 April 2006, at ¶ 35.

104 ICJ Advisory Opinion of 21 June 1971, *Legal Consequences for States of the Continued Presence of South Africa in Namibia (South-West Africa) Notwithstanding Security Council Resolution 276 (1970)*, ICJ Reports 1971, 31.

105 WTO Appellate Body Report, *U.S.-Shrimp*, ¶ 130.

106 *Tyrer v. United Kingdom*, 25 April 1978, Rec. A 26.

107 A.-M. Slaughter, 'Judicial Globalization', *Virginia JIL* 40, 1999–2000, pp. 1103–24.

108 C. Brown, *A Common Law of International Adjudication*, Oxford: Oxford University Press, 2007, p. 53.

109 A.-M. Slaughter, 'A Global Community of Courts', *Harvard JIL* 44, 2003, p. 193.

by one nation to another'.[110] Judicial borrowing is particularly useful to cope with systemic lacunae of a given legal system. As a comparatist scholar once put it, 'transplanting is, in fact, the most fertile source of development' as the insertion of an alien ruling into another system may cause it to operate in a fresh way.[111]

With regard to investment arbitration, the judicial borrowing method may be particularly useful in interpreting and clarifying public health concepts. In general terms, Montt has highlighted that comparative law benchmarks can help adjudicators in interpreting and applying broad- and open-ended investment treaty provisions.[112] More specifically, as the previous chapters have shown, cross-fertilization and judicial dialogue have created an important body of global jurisprudence which specifically concerns public health in its various aspects.[113] As Slaughter highlights 'increasing cross fertilization of ideas and precedents among constitutional judges around the world is gradually giving rise to increasingly visible international consensus on various issues – a consensus that, in turn, carries its own compelling weight'.[114]

However, two questions arise in this connection. First, can arbitrators rely on the case law and literature of other international organizations? Second, can arbitrators rely on national precedents and legal scholarship? These questions will be addressed in the following subsections.

The use of precedents of other international courts and tribunals in investment treaty arbitration

Although there is no doctrine of precedent in international law,[115] judicial decisions can be used as a subsidiary means for the determination of the rules of international law.[116] Indeed, investment treaty tribunals have often referred to the decisions of other international courts for guidance, including but not limited to ICJ decisions, and WTO case law.[117] The case for drawing

---

110 A.-M. Slaughter, *A New World Order*, Princeton and Oxford: Princeton University Press, 2004, p. 67.

111 A. Watson, *Legal Transplants – An Approach to Comparative Law*, 2nd edn., Athens/London: University of Georgia Press, 1994, p. 95.

112 S. Montt, *State Liability in Investment Treaty Arbitration – Global Constitutional and Administrative Law in the BIT Generation*, Oxfrod: Hart Publishing, 2009, p. 166.

113 When judges do cite foreign decisions as persuasive authority and they follow similar reasoning, cross-fertilization evolves in something deeper resembling an emerging global jurisprudence. See C. McCrudden, 'Judicial Comparativism and Human Rights', in E. Örükü and D. Nelken (eds), *Comparative Law: A Handbook*, Oxford: Hart Publishing, 2007, pp. 371–98.

114 Slaughter, *A New World Order*, p. 78.

115 See, for instance, Article 53(1) of the ICSID Convention ('The award shall be binding on the parties . . .').

116 ICJ Statute, Article 38(1).

117 See C. Schreuer, 'Conversations Across Cases – Is There a Doctrine of Precedent in Investment Arbitration?', *TDM* 5, 2008.

from these different bodies of law is evident. On the one hand, authors have noted that 'international courts essentially do share the same functions' by settling international disputes in accordance with law and ensuring the proper administration of justice.[118] On the other hand, certain international treaties present an articulated regime that the investment treaties presuppose.

Indeed, several WTO Agreements provide standards regarding the regulatory treatment of foreign investors.[119] Most notably, the TRIPS Agreement provides for intellectual property guarantees that are restated or enhanced in investment treaties. In such cases, the argument for integrating WTO standards within investment law can become compelling if there is a *renvoi matériel* or incorporation of such standards in the text of the investment treaty. Other authors support such an approach, as it would impede the dilution of multilateral norms while providing predictability.[120] As Hsu points out, such borrowing would 'offer direction in substantive interpretation of treaty language' as arbitral panels would be 'able to draw upon the expertise of WTO dispute panels and the Appellate Body in the development of legal concepts and principles' albeit maintaining the possibility to contract away such jurisprudence by setting their own interpretation.[121]

However, on a cautionary note, it is important to highlight that distinctions exist between the different systems of norms. Textual differences need to be taken into account, as interpretation cannot be used to transpose obligations from one field to another, or to create new obligations. Such line of reasoning undoubtedly involves the dilatation of the treaty terms beyond the purpose of the treaty makers, clearly determining margins of uncertainty. Correctly, some arbitral tribunals have followed the literal treaty terms viz. expansive jurisdictional trends. For instance, in the *Methanex* case, when the claimant sought to show that it was a producer 'in like circumstances' as compared with U.S. domestic producers, by arguing that Methanex produced 'like products' and relying on related WTO jurisprudence, the tribunal declined to rely on such jurisprudence, because Chapter 11 did not contain the term of art 'like product' which is relevant in the interpretation of GATT Article III.[122] In addition, investment law does not incorporate a necessity standard in its disciplines, and in cases of breach, its remedies include compensation, not cessation.

---

118 C. Brown, 'The Use of Precedents of Other International Courts and Tribunals in Investment Treaty Arbitration', *TDM* 5, 2008, pp. 1–4.
119 C. Pfaff, 'Alternative Approaches to Foreign Investment Protection', *TDM* 3, 2006, pp. 1–16.
120 L. Hsu, 'Applicability of WTO Law in Regional Trade Agreements: Identifying the Links', in L. Bartels and F. Ortino (eds), *Regional Trade Agreements and the WTO Legal System*, Oxford: Oxford University Press, 2006, p. 551.
121 Ibidem.
122 *Methanex* case, Final Award, Part IV, Ch B, ¶¶ 23–38.

As other international organizations also play an active role in international standard setting, especially with regard to public health, consideration of other treaty regimes is conceptually possible. For instance, in the *Biloune* case,[123] the investor argued that the government of Ghana had breached both the investment treaty and human rights obligations, and in the *Euro-Tunnel* case the claimant argued that the obligations of the United Kingdom and France should be read in conjunction with the ECHR and its First Protocol.[124] Also *amicus curiae* may recall non-investment provisions in their briefs. Finally, human rights obligations have also been invoked in the determination of remedies phase.[125]

However, arbitral tribunals have generally adopted a cautious approach to the issue.[126] While the *Tecmed* tribunal relied on the proportionality test which has been formulated by the ECHR,[127] the arbitral tribunal in *Biloune* held that it lacked jurisdiction to address violations of human rights treaties as an independent cause of action.[128] Arbitral tribunals are forums of limited jurisdiction, empowered to hear claims on treaty violations. Similarly, the *Siemens* tribunal rejected the application of the margin of appreciation doctrine in investment arbitration, holding that 'Article 1 of the First Protocol to the European Convention on Human Rights permits a margin of appreciation not found in customary international law or the Treaty'.[129]

International judicial borrowing, that is, borrowing analytical elements from the decisions of other international fora in the interpretation of international law is compatible with the unity of public international law and promotes its coherence. The previous chapters show the potential complementarity between investment law and public health, and the need to interpret and apply public health law and international investment law not separately, but in a holistic fashion. Judicial dialogue already takes place. More substantially, public health law and environmental law may provide interpretative guidance to arbitral tribunals hearing disputes with public health elements.

---

123 *Biloune and Marine Drive Complex Ltd v. Ghana Investments Centre and the Government of Ghana*, Award, (1993) 95 ILR 183.

124 *Channel Tunnel Group v. Governments of the United Kingdom and France* (Partial Award) 2007, ¶¶ 107–10.

125 See e.g. *Compañía del Desarollo de Santa Elena v. Republic of Costa Rica*, ICSID Case No. ARB/96/1, Final Award of 17 February 2000, 15(1) *ICSID Review-FILJ* (2000), 169–204.

126 M. Hirsch, 'Conflicting Obligations in International Investment Law: Investment Tribunals' Perspective', in T. Broude and Y. Shany (eds), *The Shifting Allocation of Authority in International Law – Essays in Honour of Professor Ruth Lapidoth*, Oxford: Hart Publishing, 2008, pp. 323–43.

127 *Tecmed* Award, ¶ 122.

128 *Biloune v. Ghana*, Award, 213.

129 *Siemens v. the Argentine Republic*, Award, 6 February 2007, available at http://italaw.com/documents/Siemens-Argentina-Award.pdf, ¶ 354.

The problem with judicial borrowing is that it is a very powerful instrument which must be handled properly. The major risk consists in adopting an ideology of free decision making and creating anarchy. It is often assumed that comparative law is a neutral process, but this is not always the case.[130] For instance, the selection of the comparators is a crucial element; the outcome of any given case may differ depending on which material is selected for comparison. In the case selection there may be a certain bias as making reference to human rights case law instead of looking at WTO jurisprudence makes a difference in the context of a specific case.[131] Furthermore, while investors have made reference to Article 20 of the TRIPS Agreement while alleging the violation of their trademark, it is worth recalling that if one uses the TRIPS Agreement as hermeneutic comparator, he or she needs to take into account the agreement as a whole, including the set of objectives and principles in Articles 7 and 8. As other authors have pointed out, 'the dissimilar architecture of treaties, including objectives, obligations, defenses and remedies advises against attempts of outright transposition of rules, methodologies or solutions . . .'[132]

The use of precedents of national courts in investor-state arbitration

With regard to the issue of whether or not national case law is applicable to the dispute, a distinction needs to be made.[133] If the applicable law is that of the host state, reference to its jurisprudence in order to clarify relevant provisions may be made *ipso jure*. Questions arise with regard to reference to jurisprudence of other national courts.[134] Some authors have pointed out that the issue of regulatory expropriation and other similar issues identified in investor-state dispute settlement, initially emerged as 'constitutional issues in national law', and have only recently acquired international relevance.[135] Therefore, according to Wälde and Kolo, the constitutional character of the debate on regulatory taking in U.S. jurisprudence would make it 'particularly apposite to serve as a laboratory – but also as a relative precedent – for the interpretative challenges' in international dispute settlement, and 'comparative constitutional law seems to provide the most suitable analogy and

130 V. Vadi, 'Critical Comparisons: The Role of Comparative Law in Investor State Arbitration', *Denver JIL & Policy*, 2010, p. 84.
131 See R. Hirsch, 'The Question of Case Selection in Comparative Constitutional Law', *AJCL* 53, 2005, p. 125.
132 Orellana, 'Science, Risk and Uncertainty', p. 788.
133 Vadi, 'Critical Comparisons', pp. 67–100.
134 For a seminal study on the importance of comparative law in international law and arbitration see H. Lauterpacht, *Private Law Sources and Analogies of International Law with Special Reference to International Arbitration*, London: Longmans, Green and co, 1927.
135 Wälde & Kolo, 'Environmental Regulation, Investment Protection and "Regulatory Taking" in International Law', p. 821.

precedent'.[136] Furthermore, not only can comparative public law 'serve as a critical tool in analyzing and in further developing international investment law' but it 'ultimately may help to strengthen the often contested legitimacy of investor-state dispute resolution'.[137]

However, borrowing national cases is a problematic issue. Indeed, one of the main features of investment arbitration is its detachment or separation from national courts and their potential biases. From an international law perspective, investment treaties institutionalize a limited set of obligations voluntarily consented to by sovereign states. Also, it may be practically impossible to take the wide variety of national jurisprudence into account. Ideally, a tribunal should make a thorough survey of comparative law, making use of the scholarly work that has been done on the issue. But this does not happen in practice. Usually only the laws of a small number of countries are cited. Furthermore, criteria for comparisons are not objective standards. For instance, some authors have criticized reference to U.S. jurisprudence because this would be tantamount to rewriting other countries' constitutional experience.[138] Drawing on a particular constitutional experience of a country risks re-politicizing investment disputes, against more neutral international canons.[139] Finally, one may question whether this amounts to an extraterritorial application of law.

In conclusion, as an eminent comparative law scholar has pointed out, 'the conscious and limited use of national legal traditions is advantageous in that it enriches international law with useful source materials, analogies and techniques'.[140] However, more than a century ago, Oppenheim warned that 'the science of international law must be careful in the appreciation of such municipal case law'.[141] If the applicable law is the law of the host state, of course reference may be made to the administrative law and jurisprudence of the host state. Where the applicable law is international law, reference to national cases becomes a more sensitive issue which has to be decided by the arbitrators. In any case, if national 'precedents' as well as international ones may be taken into account for the persuasiveness of their *ratio decidendi*, they are not binding on international arbitrators unless they constitute evidence of state practice and *opinio juris* of customary norms or are expressions of general principles of law.

136 Ibidem, p. 822.
137 S. Schill, 'Preface', in S. Schill (ed.), *International Investment Law and Comparative Public Law*, Oxford: Oxford University Press, 2010, p. ix.
138 D. Schneiderman, 'Constitution or Model Treaty? Struggling Over the Interpretative Authority of NAFTA', in S. Choudry (ed.), *The Migration of Constitutional Ideas*, Cambridge: Cambridge University Press, 2006, pp. 294–315.
139 D. Kennedy, 'New Approaches to Comparative Law: Comparativism and International Governance', 2 *Utah Law Review*, 1997, p. 545.
140 L.V. Prott, *The Latent Power of Culture and the International Judge*, Abingdon: Professional Books, 1979.
141 L. Oppenheim, 'The Science of International Law: Its Tasks and Methods', *AJIL* 2, 1908, p. 336.

Treatment in accordance with international law

Fair and Equitable Treatment (henceforth FET) has been described as the 'alpha and omega of investor-state arbitration'.[142] Although the wording of this standard is ambiguous, and it may allow different interpretations, it is generally considered that the aim of this clause is to provide a basic and absolute standard, detached from the host country's law, which an investor may invoke.[143] More importantly, the FET standard offers the possibility of introducing international law in the context of the arbitral proceedings.

According to NAFTA Article 1105, 'Each party shall accord to investments of investors of another Party *treatment in accordance with international law*, including fair and equitable treatment and full protection and security' (emphasis added). Investors and NAFTA parties have considerably questioned what body of law *international law* refers to in that provision. Early arbitral decisions demonstrate that NAFTA tribunals did not regard Article 1105 as restricted to customary international law. Investors have often referred in this respect to Article 38 of the ICJ Statute, which provides that the Court, whose function it is to decide in accordance with international law, shall apply international conventions, international customs, general principles of law and – as a subsidiary means for the determination of rules of law – judicial decisions and teachings of publicists. For instance, in *Pope & Talbot*, the investor asserted that international law requirements of Article 1105 included all the sources of international law found in Article 38 of the ICJ Statute.[144] Furthermore, in the *SD Myers* arbitration,[145] one of the arbitrators concurred, but, unlike the majority, contended that: 'The interpretation of Article 1105 must [. . .] also take into account the letter or spirit of widely though not universally accepted international agreements like those in the WTO system [. . .]. This line of argument [. . .] gives reasonable value to all the words of Article 1105 of NAFTA. It invites interpreters of Article 1105 to look to the "state of the art" in international trade agreements to determine the content of the minimum international standard, rather than relying on personal subjective notions [. . .]'[146]

The NAFTA parties, on the other hand, have argued that the phrase must be interpreted restrictively as meaning *customary* international law only, often referring to the narrow standard set in the 1920s *Neer* award.[147] With regard to treaty law, as the arbitral tribunal in the *Mondev* case pointed out, 'If there

142 C. Brower, 'Fair and Equitable Treatment under NAFTA Chapter 11', *ASIL Proceedings* 96, 2002, p. 9.
143 See UNCTAD, *WIR 1996 Investment, Trade and International Policy Agreements*, New York and Geneva: UNCTAD, 1996, p. 182.
144 *Pope & Talbot Inc v. Government of Canada*, Award on the Merits (Phase 2), 10 April 2001, 7 ICSID Rep 43 ¶ 107.
145 *SD Myers v. Canada*, Partial Award, 13 November 2000.
146 *SD Myers v. Canada*, Concurring Opinion by Dr B Schwartz, ¶¶ 234, 257–8.
147 *Neer v. United Mexican States*, Award, 4 RIAA 60 (1926).

had been an intention to incorporate by reference extraneous treaty standards in Article 1105 and to make Chapter 11 arbitration applicable to them, some clear indication of this would have been expected'.[148] Indeed, on 31 July 2001 the NAFTA Free Trade Commission followed this line of argument, adopting the *Notes of Interpretation of Certain Chapter 11 Provisions*. In the notes, the NAFTA parties state, *inter alia*, that 'the concepts of "fair and equitable treatment" and "full protection and security" do not require treatment in addition to or beyond that which is required by the customary international law minimum standard of treatment of aliens. [. . .]'[149] As the *Notes* were adopted when several cases under Article 1105 were pending, they caused concern among investors as well as a fierce debate among academics.[150]

However, commentators warn that the result reached in the NAFTA (and the subsequent CAFTA)[151] context should not be applied also to other treaties. According to these authors, looking beyond the idiosyncrasies of NAFTA and the subsequent CAFTA, the thousands of investment treaties currently in force around the world would remain unaffected by the *Notes*. In the absence of a clear indication to the contrary, the fair and equitable standard contained in BITs is an autonomous concept.[152] Furthermore, even with regard to NAFTA claims, subsequent NAFTA tribunals have held that the FET standard is an evolving concept.[153]

While historically the fair and equitable standard was considered to be breached when the state conduct was of an egregious and shocking nature,[154] recent trends in the case law suggest that the standard has evolved to include transparency, legitimate expectations and good faith.[155] In parallel, some scholars have posited that this standard ought to be relevant not only with regard to the state's conduct, but also with regard to the investors' behaviour in the conduct of business.[156] Accordingly, an investor may be deemed to have, *inter alia*, the duty to refrain from unconscionable conduct and the duty to conduct business in a reasonable manner under the FET standard.

---

148 *Mondev International Ltd v. United States of America*, Case No ARB(AF)/99/2, Final Award, at ¶ 121.
149 NAFTA Free Trade Commission, Notes of Interpretation of Certain Chapter 11 provisions, 31 July 2001, available at http://www.dfait-maeci.gc.ca/tna-nac/NAFTA_interpr-en.asp at ¶ 2.
150 See for instance, C. Brower II, 'Investor-State Disputes under NAFTA: The Empire Strikes Back', *Columbia Journal of Transnational Law* 40, 2001, p. 43.
151 See CAFTA Article 10.5
152 C. Schreuer, 'Fair and Equitable Treatment in Arbitral Practice', *JWIT* 6, 2005, pp. 357–86.
153 *Mondev v. United States*, Final Award, 11 October 2002, ¶ 119.
154 *Neer v. United Mexican States*, Award, 4 RIAA 60 (1960).
155 See R.H. Kreindler, 'Fair and Equitable Treatment – A Comparative International Law Approach', *TDM* 3, 2006, p. 7.
156 See P. Muchlinski, '"Caveat Investor?" The Relevance of the Conduct of the Investor Under the Fair and Equitable Treatment Standard', *ICLQ* 55, 2006, p. 535.

As multinational corporations have increasingly played an important role in the economic and social sphere, having the capacity to foster economic development, as well as to cause harm to public goods, in recent years the strict public–private divide in international law has been somewhat outdated[157] and expectations have arisen that investors respect the emerging principles of corporate social responsibility.[158] Instruments like the OECD Guidelines for Multinational Enterprises[159] and the UN Global Compact[160] provide for specific business standards; and the UN Framework for Business and Human Rights assumes that companies do have legal responsibilities.[161] Although these instruments have no binding character, they constitute part of a growing *opinio juris ac necessitatis* which may contribute to the emergence of customary law. Furthermore, according to Muchlinski, failure to meet these standards 'could act as a factor in determining whether the investor's complaint of unfair and inequitable treatment is properly made out'.[162]

Furthermore, the concept of 'equity' within the fair and equitable standard is a legal concept that is susceptible to interpretation and application by a tribunal without an authorization by the parties to go beyond the law. On the one hand, the thesis that the FET standard can be understood 'as an embodiment of the rule of law'[163] *sic et simpliciter* does not seem to accurately reflect the multifaceted content of the standard. On the other hand, it is correct to point out that the FET standard encapsulates 'an element of *non-dit* . . . which constitutes both its paradox and its fortune: a paradox because it is impossible to tie it to a definition: its fortune because only such a flexible concept can be adapted to such diversity of factual situations arising in the context of the international law of foreign investments'.[164] When the adjudicators need to bring this standard to life, they can refer to the concept of equity, 'understood

---

157 See P. Alston, 'The Not-a-Cat Syndrome: Can International Human Rights Regime Accommodate Non-State Actors?', in P. Alston (ed.), *Non-State Actors and Human Rights*, Oxford: Oxford University Press, 2005, pp. 3–33.

158 See V. Lowe, 'Corporations as International Actors and International Law Makers', *IYIL* 14, 2004, p. 30.

159 OECD Guidelines for Multinational Enterprises (2000) available at http://www.oecd.org. The Guidelines are recommendations addressed by governments to multinational enterprises operating in or from adhering countries.

160 UN Global Compact, available at http://www.globalcompact.org. The Global Compact constitutes a voluntary practical framework for companies that are committed to sustainability and responsible business practices.

161 UN Human Rights Council, *Protect, Respect and Remedy: A Framework for Business and Human Rights* – Report of the Special Representative of the Secretary General John Ruggie, on the issue of human rights and trans-national corporations and other business enterprises to the Human Rights Council, 7 April 2008, A/HRC/8/5.

162 Muchlinski, 'Caveat Investor?', p. 535.

163 S.W. Schill, 'Fair and Equitable Treatment Under Investment Treaties as an Embodiment of the Rule of Law', NYU Int'l Law & Justice Working Papers No 6/2006, p. 37.

164 I. Tudor, *The Fair and Equitable Treatment Standard in the International Law of Foreign Investment*, Oxford: Oxford University Press, 2008, p. 237.

as the search for the elementary respect of justice, inherent to the application of the rule of law (*equity infra legem*)'.[165] Therefore, it seems appropriate to point out that the relationship between the FET standard and a series of fundamental values can be established through the common reference to equity. In this sense, equity is 'an instrumental criterion of interpretation of the applicable law' or 'a method for infusing elements of reasonableness' in order to adapt such law to the specific circumstances of the case.[166]

Finally, it is worth mentioning that equity may become a *material* source of the law as a 'general principle of law' pursuant to Article 38.1(c) of the ICJ Statute.[167] Certain maxims of equity can be construed as 'general principles of law recognized by civilized nations'.[168] Similarly, in the *Norwegian Shipowners' Claims* case,[169] in the view of the tribunal, law and equity in an international context meant 'general principles of justice as distinguished from any particular system of jurisprudence or the municipal law of any state'.[170] This construction of equity as a material component of the category of general principles of law is also supported by the authoritative opinion of academic writers.[171] In conclusion, be it part of the customary FET treatment or an autonomous general principle of international law, equity *infra legem* may weave 'basic consideration of fairness and justice into the fabric of the law, so as to adjust the general and abstract rules of international law to the specificities of each individual case', and may have an integrating function in the sense of filling the gaps in the law.[172]

Conclusions

The recent flourishing of investment treaties poses a challenge for international lawyers, as it raises the question as to whether or not investment law is clinically isolated from public international law. The question is clearly linked to the debated topic as to whether public international law is a fragmented system or not. Adopting a unitary approach, this chapter advocates the importance of the unity of international law and of achieving coherence among the different sources of international law within investment treaty arbitration.

---

165 Dupuy, 'Unification Rather Than Fragmentation of International Law?', p. 52.
166 ICJ, *North Sea Continental Shelf Case, Germany v. Denmark and the Netherlands*, 20 February 1969 at ¶ 88.
167 F. Francioni, 'Equity in International Law', *Max Planck Encyclopedia of Public International Law*, Oxford: Oxford University Press, 2007 ¶ 1.
168 *The Diversion of Water from the Meuse* (Netherlands v. Belgium), (Individual Opinion by Mr. Hudson), PCIJ, 1937, Ser. A/B No 70, 76–8.
169 *Norwegian Shipowners' Claims Case* (Norway v. USA), (1922) 1 RIAA p. 307.
170 Ibidem, p. 331.
171 See C. De Visscher, 'Contribution à l'étude des sources de droit international', *Revue de droit international et législation comparée* 60, 1933 pp. 414ff; Lauterpacht, *Private Law Sources and Analogies of International Law*, ¶ 28.
172 Francioni, 'Equity in International Law', ¶ 26.

In this sense, investment treaty law and arbitration would not constitute a self-contained regime, but an integrated part of public international law. Not only is investment treaty arbitration a creature of international law, being established by international treaties, but international law is, in many cases, the applicable law to the proceedings. Many investment treaties, arbitral rules and contract clauses provide for the applicability of international law in the context of the proceedings. Customary rules of treaty interpretation further require contextual or systematic interpretation. By furthering the judicial dialogue among international courts and tribunals, the consideration of public health concerns has the potential for ultimately promoting the humanization of international law.

Where peremptory norms of international law matter in the context of an investment treaty arbitration, arbitrators have to take these fundamental norms into account. The award would not be rendered *ultra vires* because rules of *jus cogens* or peremptory rules of international law are binding upon all states and private actors. Arbitral awards violating such norms of higher status may be challenged on public policy grounds at the seat of arbitration. Consequently, a few international norms protecting public health can indirectly apply to private parties through the public order concept, which invalidates legal acts violating public policy.

Conclusions

Public health has always lain at the heart of state sovereignty, as the state has been traditionally conceived as guardian or trustee of the public good. In recent years, because of globalization and the increasing awareness of the fact that public health issues are of international concern, such a state prerogative has been reaffirmed by a series of international law instruments. This *corpus juris* has highlighted the human rights dimension of health and specified some of its contents. Nowadays, public health does not merely belong to the constitutional traditions of a number of states, but it constitutes an emerging field of public international law. While some international law instruments have affirmed the existence of an individual right to health, which would indirectly confirm and strengthen the state prerogative to protect public health, some components of public health law already belong to customary international law. Norms concerning quarantine measures or the prohibition of non-consensual medical experimentation belong to customary law, and some jurisprudence has deemed them to be norms of *jus cogens*.[1] It is possible to foresee that certain public health norms, that nowadays have a mere treaty law status, may gradually evolve into customary international law norms and even reach the status of peremptory norms. The categorization of the *core content* of the human right to health goes in this direction.

In parallel, international investment law has become one of the most developed and sophisticated fields of public international law. Unlike the situation that prevailed immediately after World War II, foreign investors are now protected primarily by international investment treaties, rather than by customary international law alone. International investment treaties have become charters of rights for foreign investors, establishing fundamental principles such as non-discrimination, fair and equitable treatment, and so on and so forth.[2] So far, investment treaties have protected investors' property rights and ensured foreign investors direct access to international arbitration.

---

1 See, *inter alia, Rabi Abdullahi v. Pfizer, Inc.* (2nd Cir. 30 January 2009).
2 See e.g., D. Schneiderman, *Constitutionalizing Economic Globalization – Investment Rules and Democracy's Promise*, Cambridge: Cambridge University Press, 2008.

The aim of this book has been to explore the interaction between public health law and international investment law. In abstract terms, the two fields of law may be seen as complementary because public health is fundamental to poverty reduction, human development and economic growth, and foreign direct investment is aimed at promoting development. In turn, basic levels of economic development are of fundamental importance to the realization of the fullest attainable standard of health. Therefore, there may be a positive synergy between public health law and the law of foreign investment.

However, conflicts of norms may arise. Foreign investments, as other economic activities, need to be regulated and, in some circumstances, problems may arise in relation to the manner of reconciling investor rights and public health. These subject matter areas of public international law have generally been deemed as separate areas of law. Only recently has there been an attempt to scrutinize the interplay between investors' rights and public health.[3] While the inter-relationship between public health and investor rights may be studied from a variety of different perspectives and institutional settings, this book has adopted an 'internal' approach with respect to international investment law and arbitration. The choice of this approach is not meant to imply that the institutional setting of international investment law is to be preferred to other approaches to reconcile the interests at stake.[4] Instead, looking at the linkage between public health and FDI from an inside view of international investment law allows a reflection on the emerging case law of investment treaty arbitration. Although investment treaty arbitration may not constitute the best forum ever in which disputes with public health elements can be settled, a rich case law has emerged in recent years. Therefore, an analysis and critical assessment of this emerging field of study was necessary.

While disputes in which public health elements arise may seem to be highly political conflicts, they may be reduced to legal debate. In a way, every international dispute is of political character because it is important to the host state.[5] In addition, a wrong done to the individual is a wrong

---

3 See P.-M. Dupuy, F. Francioni and E.-U. Petersmann (eds), *Human Rights in International Investment Law and Arbitration*, Oxford: Oxford University Press, 2009.

4 On the contrary, it is acknowledged that other fora, like the ICJ and regional human rights courts, represent useful alternatives.

5 For instance, in the *Tunis and Morocco Nationality Decrees* case, the French government enacted certain Nationality Decrees which conferred French Nationality on persons born in the French zone. Great Britain protested because the decrees conferred French nationality on British subjects who were thus made liable to French military service. Thus, the British government proposed to settle the dispute by arbitration. The French government, however, refused to admit that the dispute was of a legal nature but held that it concerned a vital interest of the state and its public powers (*puissance publique*). The Permanent Court of Arbitration was asked to give an Advisory Opinion on the matters and held that the matter was not of mere domestic jurisdiction but that reference to several international treaties had

done to his or her home state.[6] The merit of investment treaty arbitration consists in depoliticizing disputes by reducing them to contexts of a legal nature and providing an impartial forum for settling them. Opting out from investor-state arbitration would isolate the state from the current practice of the international community and might deter potential foreign investors from investing in that state. Isolationism would ultimately delay or even impede the peaceful settlement of international disputes in conformity with principles of justice and international law as required by the UN Charter.[7]

The Vienna Convention on the Law of Treaties (VCLT) establishes a framework which governs the interplay between different international law rules. In particular, it addresses three different relationships i.e.: 1) that between two or more treaties relating to the same subject matter; 2) that between a treaty and *jus cogens* norms; and 3) that between a treaty and other relevant rules of international law. The two latter relationships have been the focus of this book. With regard to the relationship between a treaty and *jus cogens* norms, Article 53 of the VCLT states that a treaty shall be void if at the time of its conclusion it conflicts with a peremptory norm of general international law. As mentioned above, an argument has been made that components of the right to health and the right to life have reached the status of *jus cogens* norms. If one accepts such argument, the necessary consequence would be the nullity of investment treaties that conflict with such a peremptory norm. However, the argument that investment treaties are incompatible *a priori* and *tout court* with elements of public health proves too much. Rather, it is the *interpretation* of investor rights as absolute rights which may be deemed incompatible with the core elements of public health. Therefore, as such interpretation would determine the incompatibility of the investment treaty with a *jus cogens* norm (if one accepts the hypothesis that access to medicines or other components of health already belong to *jus cogens*), it should be avoided.

With regard to the relationship between a treaty obligation and other international law sources, international law comes into play under any investment treaty pursuant to Article 31(3)(c) of the VCLT, which provides that the treaty interpreter shall take into account 'any relevant rules of international law applicable in the relations between the parties'. This is perhaps the most appropriate framework of analysis to scrutinize the interplay between public health law and investment law. Article 31(3)(c) emphasizes the 'unity of international law',[8] and may favour the emergence of the principle

to be made. PCIJ, *Nationality Decrees Issued in Tunis and Morocco (French Zone) on November 8th, 1921*, Advisory Opinion, [1922] PCIJ 3, 4 October 1922.

6 See H. Lauterpacht, *The Function of Law in the International Community*, Oxford: Clarendon Press, 1933, p. 160.
7 UN Charter, Article 1.
8 See P. Sands, 'Sustainable Development: Treaty, Custom and the Cross-Fertilization of International Law', in A. Boyle and D. Freestone (eds), *International Law and Sustainable Development – Past Achievements and Future Challenges*, Oxford: Oxford University Press, 1999, pp. 39–60.

of mutual supportiveness or integration between different treaty regimes.[9] International law serves as relevant context and colours the interpretation of the investment treaties. Therefore, investment treaties should not be considered as isolated from public international law but as an important component of the system. Accordingly, relevant public health law should be taken into account in investment treaty disputes.

Apart from the process of treaty interpretation, international law must apply in investment treaty arbitration if it is indicated in the text of the treaty as the applicable law. Furthermore, international law may be indirectly applicable when the law of the host state – be it a monist or dual system – incorporates it. Therefore, even if the applicable law is that of the host state, arbitrators need to take into account norms of public international law, which may have an integrative or even corrective role. Non-investment rules may prevail over investment obligations, even in cases before an arbitral tribunal, if they offer a valid defence against alleged breaches of investment guarantees. Because of their limited mandate, arbitrators cannot adjudicate on eventual violations of public health law, but can take public health law into account *incidenter tantum* when assessing whether state conduct violated investment treaty provisions. If some elements of public health law, i.e. access to essential medicines, are deemed to be peremptory norms, then they must be taken into account by arbitrators. From the peremptory character of these norms, it would follow that the enforceability of arbitral awards violating them could be refused on transnational public policy grounds.

This book contends that arbitrators may reconcile the conflicting legal claims of the parties in dispute and find the right balance.[10] As Judge Huber stated almost a century ago: 'International law, like law in general, has the object of assuring the coexistence of different interests which are worthy of legal protection'[11] and 'The conflicting interests . . . in connection with the question of indemnification of aliens, are, on the one hand, the interest of the state in the exercise of its authority in its own territory without interference or supervision by foreign states, and on the other hand, the interest of the state in seeing the rights of its nationals in a foreign country respected and effectively protected.'[12]

There is no single solution to the issue of reconciling public health and investor rights in international investment law. Every case is different and has

---

9 See, *inter alia*, M. Sanwal, 'Trends in Environmental Governance: The Emergence of a Mutual Supportiveness Approach to Achieve Sustainable Development', *Global Environmental Politics* 4, 2004, pp. 16–22.

10 See Lauterpacht, *The Function of Law in the International Community*, p. 119.

11 Arbitral Award Rendered in Conformity with the Special Agreement Concluded on January 23, 1925 between the United States and the Netherlands Relating to the Arbitration of Differences Respecting Sovereignty over the Island of Palmas (*Island of Palmas* Arbitration), 4 April 1928, AJIL 22, 1928, pp. 867–912.

12 *Affaire des biens britanniques au Maroc espagnol – Espagne v. Royaume Uni* (*British claims in the Spanish zone of Morocco*), Accord Anglo Espagnol du 29 Mai 1923, La Haye, 1er Mai 1925, 2 RIAA, 615–742.

to be decided according to its specificities. Whenever a state adopts public health regulations in conformity with international standards and in a non-discriminatory way, there is a strong presumption that such a measure does not amount to a breach of investment treaty guarantees but constitutes a mere control of use. On the other hand, whenever state measures are not justified by international standards and have a discriminatory effect on foreign investments, such measures can, but not necessarily, amount to a violation of relevant investment treaty provisions. In some circumstances, public health measures may appear as discriminatory. It is then up to the arbitrators to establish whether such measures are based on the nationality of the investor, or on an objective public health criterion. In any case, not every state regulation may be considered as justified just because the state affirms that it has been taken to protect public health. Furthermore, even justified policy goals may be excessive or disproportionate. Thus, the arbitral tribunals will have to balance the different *teloi* of public health law and investment law to reach a satisfactory reconciliation of these objectives.

The increasing relevance of public health in the international law discourse can have a positive influence on humanizing international economic relations. While the traditional goal of foreign investment has been linked to the flourishing of economic activities (from the investor perspective) and economic development (from the host state perspective), FDI has the potential to increase human well-being and peaceful relations among nations. It may raise standards of living and foster the creation of jobs and the transfer of technology. In parallel, it may also act as leverage to foster respect of human rights, including the right to health. However, if a conflict of norms arises between investment treaty law and other rules of public international law, arbitral tribunals should take the whole body of international law into account to settle the dispute 'in conformity with the principles of justice and international law'.[13]

---

13 See Article 1 of the UN Charter and the Preamble of the VCLT.

Selected bibliography

Books

Abbott, F.M., 'TRIPS and Human Rights: Preliminary Reflections', in F. Abbott, C. Breining-Kaufmann and T. Cottier (eds), *International Trade and Human Rights Foundations and Conceptual Issues*, Ann Arbor: University of Michigan Press, 2006.

Ackerman, B. and Golove, D., *Is NAFTA Constitutional?* Cambridge, MA: Harvard University Press, 1995.

Alexander, G.S., 'Constitutionalizing Property: Two Experiences, Two Dilemmas', in J. McLean (ed), *Property and the Constitution*, Oxford: Hart, 1999.

Alexander, G.S., *The Global Debate Over Constitutional Property*, Chicago: University of Chicago Press, 2006.

Alston, P., 'The Not-a-Cat Syndrome: Can International Human Rights Regime Accommodate Non-State Actors?', in P. Alston (ed.), *Non-State Actors and Human Rights*, Oxford: Oxford University Press, 2005.

Alvarez, J. and Sauvant, K.P., (eds), *The Evolving International Investment Regime – Expectations, Realities and Options*, Oxford: Oxford University Press, 2011.

Arfazadeh, H., *Ordre public et arbitrage international à l'épreuve de la mondialisation*, Bruxelles: Bruylant, 2005.

Aust, A., *Handbook of International Law*, 2nd edn., Cambridge: Cambridge University Press, 2010.

Banifatemi, Y., 'The Law Applicable in Investment Treaty Arbitration' in K. Yannaca Small (ed.), Arbitration Under International Investment Agreements: A Guide to the Key Issues, Oxford: Oxford University Press, 2010.

Belanger, M., 'Droit international de la santé et developpement', in A. Pellet and J.-M. Sorel (eds), *Le droit international du developpement social et culturel*, Paris: L'Hermès, 1997.

Bhagwati, J., *In Defense of Globalization*, Oxford: Oxford University Press, 2004.

Bilmore, I., 'The "Right to Health" According to the WHO', in T. Wagner and L. Carbone (eds), *Fifty Years after the Declaration – The United Nations' Record on Human Rights*, Lanham: University Press of America, 2001.

Binder, C., Kriebaum, U., Reinisch, A. and Wittich, S. (eds) *International Investment Law for the 21st Century*, Oxford: Oxford University Press, 2009.

Bishop, R., Crawford, J. and Reisman, M., *Foreign Investment Disputes*, The Hague: Kluwer Law International, 2005.

Blackaby, N., 'Investment Arbitration and Commercial Arbitration (or the Tale of the Dolphin and the Shark', in J. Lew and L. Mistelis, *Pervasive Problems in International Arbitration*, The Hague: Kluwer Law International, 2006.

Böckstiegel, K.-H., 'Arbitration of Foreign Investment Disputes – An Introduction', in A.J. Van Den Berg (ed.), *New Horizons in International Commercial Arbitration and Beyond*, The Hague: Kluwer Law International, 2005.

Boyle, A. and Freestone, D., 'Introduction', in A. Boyle and D. Freestone (eds), *International Law and Sustainable Development – Past Achievements and Future Challenges*, Oxford: Oxford University Press, 1999.

Brown, C., *A Common Law of International Adjudication*, Oxford: Oxford University Press, 2007.

Brownlie, I., *Principles of Public International Law*, 5th edn., Oxford: Oxford University Press, 1998.

Bull, H., *The Anarchical Society: A Study of Order in World Politics*, London: Macmillan, 1977.

Bürhing-Uhle, C., Kirchhoff, L. and Scherer, G., *Arbitration and Mediation in International Business*, The Hague: Kluwer, 1996.

Carroll, E. and Mackie, K., *International Mediation – The Art of Business Diplomacy*, The Hague: Kluwer, 2006.

Casanovas, O., *Unity and Pluralism in Public International Law*, The Hague: Martinus Nijhoff Publishers, 2001.

Chapman, A., 'Core Obligations Related to the Right to Health', in A. Chapman and S. Russell (eds), *Core Obligations: Building a Framework for Economic, Social and Cultural Rights*, Antwerp: Intersentia, 2002.

Chayes, A. and Chayes, A.H., *The New Sovereignty*, Cambridge, MA: Harvard University Press, 1995.

Cicero, M.T., *De Legibus* (52BC), Cicero *On the Republic, on the Laws*, (trans C Keyes), New York: Loeb, 1928.

Collier, J. and Lowe, V., *The Settlement of Disputes in International Law*, Oxford: Oxford University Press, 1999.

Comeaux, P. and Kinsella, N., *Protecting Foreign Investment under International Law*, New York: Oceana Publications, 1997.

Conforti, B., *Diritto internazionale*, Napoli: Editoriale Scientifica, 1997.

Correa, C., *Trade Related Aspects of Intellectual Property Rights. A Commentary on the TRIPS Agreement*, Oxford: Oxford University Press, 2007.

Cosbey, A., Mann, H., Peterson, L. and von Moltke, K., *Investment and Sustainable Development. A Guide to the Use and Potential of International Investment Agreements*, Winnipeg: IISD, 2004.

Cottier, T., Pauwelyn, J. and Bürgi Bonanomi, E. (eds), *Human Rights and International Trade*, Oxford: Oxford University Press, 2005.

Di Blase, A., 'Human-Right-Related Aspects in the Settlement of International Disputes on Intellectual Property Rights', in G. Venturini *et al.* (eds), *Liber Amicorum Fausto Pocar*, Milano: Giuffrè, 2009.

Drahos, P., *A Philosophy of Intellectual Property*, Dartmouth: Ashgate, 1996.

Drahos, P. and Braithwaite, J., *Information Feudalism – Who Owns the Knowledge Economy?* New York: The New Press, 2003.

Dupuy, P.-M., 'Human Rights and International Investment Law: A Case for Fragmentation or Unity of Public International Law?', in P.-M. Dupuy, F. Francioni and E.-U. Petersmann, *Human Rights in International Investment Law and Arbitration*, Oxford: Oxford University Press, 2009.

Dupuy, P.-M., 'Unification Rather than Fragmentation of International Law? The Case of International Investment Law and Human Rights', in P.-M. Dupuy, F. Francioni and E.-U. Petersmann (eds), *Human Rights in International Investment Law and Arbitration*, Oxford: Oxford University Press, 2009.

Dupuy, R.-J. (ed.), *The Right to Health as a Human Right*, Aalphen den Rijn: Sijthoff & Noordhoff, 1979.

Dupuy, P.-M., Francioni, F. and Petersmann, E.-U. (eds), *Human Rights in International Investment Law and Arbitration*, Oxford: Oxford University Press, 2009.

Dworkin, R., *Law's Empire*, Cambridge, MA: Harvard University Press, 1986.

Fisher, R. and Ury, W., *Getting to Yes: Negotiating Agreement Without Giving In*, New York: Penguin Books, 1983.

Foster, C., *Science and the Precautionary Principle in International Court and Tribunals*, Cambridge: Cambridge University Press, 2011.

Francioni, F., 'Dispute Avoidance in International Environmental Law', in A. Kiss, D. Shelton and K. Ishibashi (eds), *Economic Globalization and Compliance with International Environmental Agreements*, The Hague: Kluwer Law, 2003.

Francioni, F., 'WTO Law in Context: The Integration of International Human Rights and Environmental Law in the Dispute Settlement Process', in G. Sacerdoti, A. Yanovich and J. Bohanes (eds), *The WTO at Ten*, Cambridge: Cambridge University Press, 2006.

Francioni, F., 'Equity', in *Max Planck Encyclopaedia of Public International Law*, Oxford: Oxford University Press, 2007.

Francioni, F., 'Sviluppo sostenibile e principi di diritto internazionale dell'ambiente', in P. Fois, *Il principio dello sviluppo sostenibile nel diritto internazionale ed europeo dell'ambiente*, Napoli: Editoriale Scientifica, 2007.

Franck, S., 'Challenges Facing Investment Disputes: Reconsidering Dispute Resolution in International Investment Agreements', in K. Sauvant (ed.), *Appeals Mechanism in International Investment Disputes*, Oxford: Oxford University Press, 2008.

Freedman, J., 'Implications of the NAFTA Investment Chapter for Environmental Regulation', in A. Kiss, D. Shelton and K. Ishibashi (eds), *Economic Globalization and Compliance with International Environmental Agreements*, The Hague: Kluwer Law International, 2003.

Freund, E., *The Police Power: Public Policy and Constitutional Rights*, Chicago: Callahan, 1904.

Friedman, S., *Expropriation in International Law*, London: Stevens & Sons Limited, 1953.

Friedrichs, J., 'The Neomedieval Renaissance: Global Governance and International Law in the New Middle Ages', in I. Dekker (ed.), *Governance and International Legal Theory*, Utrecht: Martinus Nijhoff, 2004.

Gardiner, R., *Treaty Interpretation*, New York: Oxford University Press, 2008.

Gervais, D., 'The Changing Landscape of International Intellectual Property', in C. Heath and A. Kamperman Sanders (eds), *Intellectual Property and Free Trade Agreements*, Oxford and Portland: Hart Publishing, 2007.

Gervais, D., *The TRIPS Agreement: Drafting History and Analysis*, 3rd edn., London: Sweet & Maxwell, 2008.

Gibson, J., *Intellectual Property, Medicine and Health: Current Debates*, Farnham: Ashgate, 2009.

Gilpin, A., *Environmental Impact Assessment: Cutting Edge for the Twenty First Century*, Cambridge: Cambridge University Press, 1995.

Gostin, L.O., *Public Health Law: Power, Duty, Restraint*, Berkeley: University of California Press, 2000.

Gostin, L.O., *Public Health Law Power Duty Restraint* (2nd edn), Berkeley: University of California Press, 2008.

Gruszczynski, L., *Regulating Health and Environmental Risks Under WTO Law*, Oxford: Oxford University Press, 2010.

Guzman, A., *How International Law Works*, Oxford: Oxford University Press, 2008.

Hannikainen, L., *Peremptory Norms (Jus Cogens) in International Law*, Helsinki: Lakimiesliiton Kustannus, 1988.

Hart, H.L.A., *The Concept of Law*, Oxford: Clarendon Press, 1961.

Heath, C., 'The Most-Favoured Nation Treatment and Intellectual Property Rights', in C. Heath and A. Kamperman Sanders (eds), *Intellectual Property and Free Trade Agreements*, Oxford and Portland: Hart Publishing, 2007.

Helfer, L., and Austin, G.W., *Human Rights and Intellectual Property*, Cambridge: Cambridge University Press, 2011.

Henkin, L., *International Law: Politics and Values*, Dordrecht: Martinus Nijhoff Publishers, 1995.

Hestermeyer, H., *Human Rights and the WTO, The Case of Patents and Access to Medicines*, Oxford: Oxford University Press, 2007.

Higgins, R., *Problems and Process: International Law and How we Use it*, Oxford: Oxford University Press, 1994.

Hirsch, M., 'Conflicting Obligations in International Investment Law: Investment Tribunals' Perspective', in T. Broude and Y. Shany (eds), *The Shifting Allocation of Authority in International Law – Essays in Honour of Professor Ruth Lapidoth*, Oxford: Hart Publishing, 2008.

Hofmann, R., and Tams, C. (eds), *International Investment Law and General International Law*, Baden: Nomos, 2011.

Holder, J., *Environmental Assessment – The Regulation of Decision Making*, Oxford: Oxford University Press, 2004.

Hsu, L., 'Applicability of WTO Law in Regional Trade Agreements: Identifying the Links', in L. Bartels and F. Ortino, *Regional Trade Agreements and the WTO Legal System*, Oxford: Oxford University Press, 2006.

Hunt, P., *Reclaiming Social Rights*, Dartmouth: Aldershot, 1996.

Jackson, J., *The World Trading System*, Cambridge, MA: MIT Press, 2002.

Jennings, R., 'Sovereignty and International Law', in G. Kreijen *et al.* (eds), *State, Sovereignty and International Governance*, Oxford: Oxford University Press, 2002.

Jha, P., and Chaloupka, F. (eds), *Tobacco Control in Developing Countries*, Oxford: Oxford University Press, 2000.

Kawharu, A., 'Participation of Non-Governmental Organizations in Investment Arbitration as Amici Curiae', in M. Waibel *et al.* (eds), *The Backlash against Investment Arbitration: Perceptions and Reality*, The Hague: Kluwer Law International, 2010.

Kelsey, J., 'International Economic Agreements and Environmental Justice', in K. Bosselmann and B.J. Richardson (eds), *Environmental Justice and Market Mechanisms*, London: Kluwer Law International, 1999.

Kreindler, R.H., 'The Law Applicable to International Investment Disputes', in N. Horn (ed.), *Arbitrating Foreign Investment Disputes*, The Hague: Kluwer Law International, 2004.

Krommendijk, J., and Morijn, J., '"Proportional" by What Measure(s)? Balancing Investor Interests and Human Rights by Way of Applying the Proportionality Principle in Investor-State Arbitration', in P.-M. Dupuy, F. Francioni and E.U. Petersmann (eds), *Human Rights in International Investment Law and Arbitration*, Oxford: Oxford University Press, 2009.

Kuanpoth, J., 'TRIPS-Plus Rules under Free Trade Agreements: An Asian Perspective', in C. Heath and A. Kamperman Sanders (eds), *Intellectual Property and Free Trade Agreements*, Oxford and Portland: Hart Publishing, 2007.

Lauterpacht, H., *Private Law Sources and Analogies of International Law with Special Reference to International Arbitration*, London: Longmans, Green and Co., 1927.

Lauterpacht, H., *The Function of Law in the International Community*, Oxford: Clarendon Press, 1933.

Leary, V., 'Concretizing the Right to Health: Tobacco Use as a Human Right Issue', in F. Coomans, F. Grünfeld, I. Westendorp and J. Willems (eds), *Rendering Justice to the Vulnerable: Liber Amicorum in Honour of Theo van Boven*, The Hague: Kluwer Law International, 2000.

Leibniz, G., *Discourse on Metaphysics* XIV (1686) reprinted Montana: Kessinger Publishing, 2007.

Lévesque, C., 'Distinguishing Expropriation and Regulation under NAFTA Chapter 11: Making Explicit the Link to Property', in K. Kennedy (ed.), *The First Decade of NAFTA: The Future of Free Trade in North America*, New York: Transnational Publishers, 2004.

Levi, A., 'Ordine giuridico e ordine pubblico', in *Scritti minori di filosofia del diritto*, Padova: CEDAM, 1957.

Lew, J., Mistelis, L. and Kröll, S., *Comparative International Commercial Arbitration*, The Hague: Kluwer Law International, 2003.

Loughlin, M., *The Idea of Public Law*, Oxford: Oxford University Press, 2003.

Lowe, V., 'Sustainable Development and Unsustainable Arguments', in A. Boyle and D. Freestone (eds), *International Law and Sustainable Development: Past Achievements and Future Challenges*, Oxford: Oxford University Press, 1999.

Lowe, V., 'The Politics of Law Making: Are the Method and Character of Norm Creation Changing?', in M. Byers (ed.), *The Role of Law in International Politics: Essays in International Relations and International Law*, Oxford: Oxford University Press, 2000.

Lowenfeld, A., *International Economic Law*, 2nd edn., Oxford: Oxford University Press, 2002.

Mann, H., 'The Right of States to Regulate and International Investment Law: A Comment', in UNCTAD, *The Development Dimension of FDI: Policy and Rule-Making Perspectives*, New York and Geneva: UN, 2003.

Marini, L., *Il principio di precauzione nel diritto internazionale e comunitario*, Padova: CEDAM, 2004.

Maskus, K.E. and Reichman, J.H. (eds), *International Public Goods and Transfer of Technology under a Globalized Intellectual Property Regime*, Cambridge: Cambridge University Press, 2005.

Matthews, D., *Intellectual Property, Human Rights and Development*, Cheltenham: Edward Elgar, 2011.

Mavroidis, P., 'All Clear on the Investment Front: A Plea for a Restatement', in J. Alvarez and K.P. Sauvant (eds), *The Evolving International Investment Regime – Expectations, Realities and Options*, Oxford: Oxford University Press, 2011.

McCrudden, C., 'Judicial Comparativism and Human Rights', in E. Örücü and D. Nelken (eds), *Comparative Law: A Handbook*, Oxford: Hart Publishing, 2007.

McGrady, B., *Trade and Public Health: The WTO, Tobacco, Alcohol and Diet*, Cambridge: Cambridge University Press, 2007.

McIntyre, O., 'Private Investment in Water and Sanitation Services: Rights Based Approaches and International Investment Law – A Possible Way Forward', in J.R. Engel, L. Westra and K. Bosselmann (eds), *Democracy, Ecological Integrity and International Law*, Newcastle upon Tyne: Cambridge Scholars Publishing, 2010.

McLachlan, C., Shore, L. and Weiniger, M., *International Investment Arbitration*, Oxford: Oxford University Press, 2007.

Meron, T., *The Humanization of International Law*, Leiden: Martinus Nijhoff Publishers, 2006.

Meyer, P., *Droit International Privé*, Paris: Montchrestien, 1994.

Montt, S., *State Liability in Investment Treaty Arbitration – Global Constitutional and Administrative Law in the BIT Generation*, Oxford: Hart Publishing, 2009.

Muchlinski, P., 'Global Bukovina Examined: Viewing the Multinational Enterprise as a Transnational Law Making Community', in G. Teubner (ed.), *Global Law Without a State*, Dartmouth: Aldershot, 1997.

Muchlinski, P., *Multinational Enterprises and the Law*, Oxford: Oxford University Press, 2007.

Muchlinski, P., 'The Diplomatic Protection of Foreign Investors: A Tale of Judicial Caution' in C. Binder, U. Kriebaum, A. Reinisch and S. Wittich (eds), *International Investment Law for the 21st Century – Essays in Honour of Christoph Schreuer*, Oxford: Oxford University Press, 2009.

Muchlinski, P., Ortino, F. and Schreuer, C. (eds), *The Oxford Handbook of International Investment Law*, Oxford and New York: Oxford University Press, 2008.

Musungu, S.F. and Dutfield, G., 'Multilateral Agreements and a TRIPS-Plus World: The World Intellectual Property Organization', Geneva: Quacker United Nations Office, 2003.

Musungu, S.F., 'The TRIPS Agreement and Public Health', in C. Correa and A.A. Yusuf (eds), *Intellectual Property and International Trade – The TRIPS Agreement*, 2nd edn., The Hague: Kluwer, 2008.

Newcombe, A. and Paradell, L., *'Law and Practice of Investment Treaties – Standards of Treatment*, Austin/Boston: Kluwer Law International, 2009, p. 45.

Nussbaum, M., *Women and Human Development: The Capabilities Approach*, Cambridge: Cambridge University Press, 2000.

Obijiofor, A., *Global Health Governance: International Law and Public Health in a Divided World*, Toronto: University of Toronto Press Inc, 2005.

Orakhelashvili, A., *Peremptory Norms in International Law*, Oxford: Oxford University Press, 2006.

Orakhelashvili, A., *The Interpretation of Acts and Rules in Public International Law*, Oxford: Oxford University Press, 2008.

Orellana, M., 'Science, Risk and Uncertainty: Public Health Measures and Investment Disciplines', in P. Kahn and T. Wälde (eds), *New Aspects of International Investment Law*, Leiden/Boston: Martinus Nijhoff and Hague Academy of International Law, 2007.

Ortino, F., 'Non-Discriminatory Treatment in Investment Disputes', in P.-M. Dupuy, F. Francioni and E.-U. Petersmann (eds), *Human Rights in International Investment Law and Arbitration*, Oxford: Oxford University Press, 2009.

Ost, F. and M. Van de Kerchove, *De la pyramide au réseau, Pour une théorie dialectique du droit*, Bruxelles: Publication des facultés universitaires St-Louis, 2002.

Pallemaerts, M., 'Introduction: Human Rights and Environmental Protection', in M. Déjeant-Pons and M. Pallemaerts (eds), *Human Rights and the Environment*, Strasbourg: Council of Europe Publishing, 2002.

Paulsson, J., *Denial of Justice in International Law*, Cambridge: Cambridge University Press, 2005.

Paulsson, J., 'International Arbitration and the Generation of Legal Norms: Treaty Arbitration and International Law', ICCA Congress Series, The Hague: Kluwer Law, 2006.

Pauwelyn, J., *Conflict of Norms in Public International Law*, Cambridge: Cambridge University Press, 2003.

Pauwelyn, J., 'The Dog That Barked But Didn't Bite: 15 Years of Intellectual Property Disputes at the WTO', in J. de Werra (ed.), *La Resolution des Litiges de Propriété Intellectuelle*, Bruxelles: Bruylant, 2010.

Peel, J., *Science and Risk Regulation in International Law*, Cambridge: Cambridge University Press, 2010.

Peterson, L.E., *Bilateral Investment Treaties and Development Policy Making*, Winnipeg: IISD, 2004.

Peterson, L.E., *The Global Governance of Foreign Direct Investment: Madly Off in All Directions*, Geneva: Friedrich Ebert Stiftung Publisher, 2005.

Pierik, R., 'Globalization and Global Governance: A Conceptual Analysis', in W. Heere (ed.), *From Government to Governance*, The Hague: TMC Asser Press, 2004.

Pires de Carvalho, N., *The TRIPS Regime of Patent Rights*, 3rd edn., Aalphen aan den Rijn: Wolters Kluwer, 2010.

Plantey, A., *International Negotiation in the Twenty-First Century*, London: Routledge Cavendish, 2007.

Prabhu, M., 'International Health and Sustainable Development Law', in M.-C. Cordonier Segger and A. Khalfan (eds), *Sustainable Development Law – Principles, Practices and Prospects*, Oxford: Oxford University Press, 2004.

Prabhu, M. and S. Atapattu, 'The WHO Framework Convention on Tobacco Control: When the WHO Meets the WTO' in M.-C. Cordonier Segger and C.G. Weeramantry (eds), *Sustainable Justice: Reconciling Economic, Social and Environmental Law*, Leiden: Brill, 2005.

Prabhu, M. and Garforth, K., 'International Public Health and Trade Law', in M. Gehring and M.-C. Cordonier Segger (eds), *Sustainable Development in World Trade Law*, The Hague: Kluwer Law International, 2005.

Prott, L., *The Latent Power of Culture and the International Judge*, Abingdon: Professional Books, 1979.

Raes, K., 'The Philosophical Basis of Social, Economic and Cultural Rights', in P. Van der Auweraert *et al.* (eds), *Social, Economic and Cultural Rights: An Appraisal of Current European and International Developments*, Antwerp: Maklu, 2002.

Raiffa, H., *The Art and Science of Negotiation*, Cambridge, MA: Harvard University Press, 1982.

Redgwell, C., 'Life, the Universe and Everything: A Critique of Anthropocentric Rights', in A. Boyle and M. Anderson (eds), *Human Rights Approaches to Environmental Protection*, Oxford: Clarendon Press, 1996.

Ripinsky, S., *Damages in International Investment Law*, London: BIICL, 2008.

Robalino-Orellana, J. and Rodríguez-Arana Muñoz, J. (eds), *Global Administrative Law Towards a Lex Administrativa*, London: Cameron & May, 2010.

Rolin, H., 'Vers un ordre public rèellement international', in *Hommage d'une génération de juristes au Président Basdevant*, Paris: Pedone, 1960.

Romano, S., *L'ordinamento giuridico*, 2nd edn., Firenze: Sansoni, 1946.

Ronzitti, N., 'Trattati contrari a norme imperative del diritto internazionale', in *Studi in onore di Giuseppe Sperduti*, Milan: Giuffrè, 1984.

Rubino-Sammartano, M., *International Arbitration Law and Practice*, The Hague: Kluwer Law International, 2001.

Rubins, N. and Kinsella, S., *International Investment, Political Risk and Dispute Resolution*, Oxford: Oxford University Press, 2005.

Rudra, N., *Globalization and the Race to the Bottom – Who Really Gets Hurt?* Cambridge: Cambridge University Press, 2008.

Ryan, M., *Knowledge Diplomacy – Global Competition and the Politics of Intellectual Property*, Washington, D.C.: Brookings Institution Press, 1998.

Sadat-Akhavi, S.A., *Methods of Resolving Conflicts between Treaties*, Leiden: Martinus Nijhoff Publishers, 2003.

Salacuse, J., 'The Treatification of International Investment Law', in J.J. Norton and C.P. Rogers (eds), *Law, Culture, and Economic Development – Liber Amicorum for Professor Roberto McLean*, London: BIICL, 2007.

Sands, P., 'Sustainable Development: Treaty, Custom and the Cross-Fertilization of International Law', in A. Boyle and D. Freestone (eds), *International Law and Sustainable Development – Past Achievements and Future Challenges*, Oxford: Oxford University Press, 1999.

Sands, P., 'Litigating Environmental Disputes: Courts, Tribunals and the Progressive Development of International Environmental Law', in T. Ndiaye and R. Wolfrum (eds), *Law of the Sea, Environmental Law and Settlement of Disputes – Liber Amicorum Judge Thomas Mensah*, Leiden/Boston: Martinus Nijhoff Publishers, 2007.

Saulle, M.R., 'Jus Cogens and Human Rights', in *Le droit international à l'heure de sa codification*, Milan: Giuffrè, 1987.

Sauvant, K. (ed.), *Appeals Mechanism in International Investment Disputes*, Oxford: Oxford University Press, 2008.

Schill, S.W., *The Multilateralization of International Investment Law*, Cambridge: Cambridge University Press, 2009.

Schill, S.W. (ed.), *International Investment Law and Comparative Public Law*, Oxford: Oxford University Press, 2010.

Schneiderman, D., 'Constitution or Model Treaty? Struggling Over the Interpretative Authority of NAFTA', in S. Choudry (ed.), *The Migration of Constitutional Ideas*, Cambridge: Cambridge University Press, 2006.

Schneiderman, D., *Constitutionalizing Economic Globalization – Investment Rules and Democracy's Promise*, Oxford: Oxford University Press, 2008.

Schreuer, C., *The ICSID Convention: A Commentary*, Cambridge: Cambridge University Press, 2001.

Schwebel, S.M., 'The Reshaping of the International Law of Foreign Investment by Concordant Bilateral Investment Treaties', in S. Charnovitz, D.P. Steger and P. van den Bossche (eds), *Law in the Service of Human Dignity – Essays in Honour of Florentino Feliciano*, Cambridge: Cambridge University Press, 2005.

Scott, J., *The WTO Agreement on Sanitary and Phytosanitary Measures – A Commentary*, Oxford: Oxford University Press, 2007.

Sen, A., *Commodities and Capabilities*, Oxford: Oxford University Press, 1985.

Seraglini, C., *Lois de police et justice arbitrale internationale*, Paris: Dalloz, 2001.

Shan, W., Simons, P. and Singh, D. (eds), *Redefining Sovereignty in International Economic Law*, Oxford: Hart Publishing, 2008.

Shapiro, M. and Stone Sweet, A., *On Law, Politics and Judicialization: Path Dependence, Precedent and Judicial Power*, Oxford: Oxford University Press, 2002.

Shelton, D., 'Law, Non-Law and the Problem of Soft Law', in D. Shelton (ed.), *Commitment and Compliance: The Role of Non-Binding Norms in the International System*, Oxford: Oxford University Press, 2000.

Sinclair, I., *The Vienna Convention on the Law of Treaties*, Manchester: Manchester University Press, 1984.

Slaughter, A.-M., *A New World Order*, Princeton and Oxford: Princeton University Press, 2004.

Sodipo, B., *Piracy and Counterfeiting GATT, TRIPS and Developing Countries*, London: Kluwer Law International, 1997.

Sornarajah, M., *The Settlement of Foreign Investment Disputes*, The Hague: Kluwer Law International, 2000.

Sornarajah, M., 'Right to Regulate and Safeguards', in UNCTAD, *The Development Dimension of FDI: Policy and Rule Making Perspectives*, New York and Geneva: UN, 2003.

Sornarajah, M., *The International Law on Foreign Investment*, 2nd edn., Cambridge: Cambridge University Press, 2004.

Sornarajah, M., 'The Neo-Liberal Agenda in Investment Arbitration: Its Rise, Retreat and Impact on State Sovereignty', in W. Shan, P. Simons and D. Singh (eds), *Redefining Sovereignty in International Economic Law*, Oxford: Hart Publishing, 2008.

Stern, B., 'In Search of the Frontiers of Indirect Expropriation', in A. Rovine (ed.), *Contemporary Issues in International Arbitration and Mediation*, Leiden: Martinus Nijhoff Publishers, 2008.

Stiglitz, J., *Globalization and Its Discontents*, New York: W. Norton & Co., 2002.

Stone Sweet, A., *Governing with Judges*, Oxford: Oxford University Press, 2000.

Subedi, S.P., *International Investment Law – Reconciling Policy and Principle*, Oxford: Hart Publishing, 2008.

Suda, R., 'The Effect of Bilateral Investment Treaties on Human Rights Enforcement and Realization', in O. De Schutter (ed.), *Transnational Corporations and Human Rights*, Oxford: Hart Publishing, 2006.

Sztucki, J., *Jus Cogens and the Vienna Convention on the Law of Treaties*, Vienna/New York: Springer, 1974.

Taylor, A.L., 'Trade, Human Rights, and the WHO Framework Convention on Tobacco Control: Just What the Doctor Ordered?', in T. Cottier, J. Pauwelyn and E. Bürgi Bonanomi (eds), *Human Rights and International Trade*, Oxford: Oxford University Press, 2005.

Tienhaara, K., *The Expropriation of Environmental Governance*, Cambridge: Cambridge University Press, 2009.

Toebes, B., *The Right to Health as a Human Right in International Law*, Amsterdam: Intersentia, 1999.

Toebes, B., 'The Right to Health', in A. Eide, C. Krause and A. Rosas (eds), *Economic Social and Cultural Rights*, 2nd edn., The Hague: Martinus Nijhoff, 2001.

Tomuschat, C., *Human Rights: Between Idealism and Realism*, Oxford: Oxford University Press, 2003.

Trachtman, J., 'FDI and the Right to Regulate: Lessons from Trade Law', in UNCTAD, *The Development Dimension of FDI: Policy and Rule-Making Perspectives*, New York and Geneva: UN, 2003.

Tudor, I., *The Fair and Equitable Treatment Standard in the International Law of Foreign Investment*, Oxford: Oxford University Press, 2008.

Tyenhaara, K., *The Expropriation of Environmental Governance: Protecting Foreign Investors at the Expense of Public Policy*, Cambridge: Cambridge University Press, 2009.

Van Der Schyff, G., *Limitation of Rights – A Study of the European Convention and the South African Bill of Rights*, Nijmegen: Wolf Legal Publishers, 2005.

Van Harten, G., *Investment Treaty Arbitration and Public Law*, Oxford: Oxford University Press, 2007.

Verhoeven, J., *Droit International Public*, Bruxelles: Larcier, 2000.

Verweij, M. and Dawson, A., 'The Meaning of Public in Public Health', in A. Dawson and M. Verweij (eds), *Ethics, Prevention and Public Health*, Oxford: Oxford University Press, 2009.

Von Moltke, K., *Discrimination and Non-Discrimination in Foreign Direct Investment Mining Issues*, Paris: OECD, 2002.

Wälde, T., 'Sustainable Development and the 1994 Energy Charter Treaty: Between Pseudo-Action and the Management of Environmental Investment Risk', in F. Weiss, E. Denters and P. De Wart (eds), *International Economic Law With a Human Face*, The Hague: Kluwer, 1998.

Wallerstein, I., 'States? Sovereignty?', in D.A. Smith, D.J. Solinger and S.C. Topik (eds), *States and Sovereignty in the Global Economy*, London: Routledge, 1999.

Watson, A., *Legal Transplants An Approach to Comparative Law*, 2nd edn., Athens/London: University of Georgia Press, 1994.

Weiler, T., 'Good Faith and Regulatory Transparency: The Story of Metalclad v Mexico', in T. Weiler (ed.), *International Investment Law and Arbitration: Leading Cases from ICSID, NAFTA, Bilateral Treaties and Customary International Law*, London: Cameron May, 2005.

Wortley, B.A., *Expropriation in Public International Law*, Cambridge: Cambridge University Press, 1959.

Yamane, H., *Interpreting TRIPS – Globalization of Intellectual Property Rights and Access to Medicines*, Oxford: Hart Publishing, 2011.

Yannaka Small, C., (ed.), *Arbitration Under International Investment Agreements: A Guide to the Key Issues*, Oxford: Oxford University Press, 2010.

Zander, J., *The Application of the Precautionary Principle in Practice – Comparative Dimensions*, Cambridge: Cambridge University Press, 2010.

Articles

Abbott, E., 'The Police Power and the Right to Compensation' (1889) 3 *Harvard LR*, 189–205.

Abbott, F., 'WTO TRIPS Agreement and Its Implications for Access to Medicines in Developing Countries', Study Paper for the British Commission on Intellectual Property Rights, Geneva (2002) 56–7.

Abline, G., 'Les observations générales, une technique d'élargissement des droits de l'homme' (2008) *Revue trimestrielle des droits de l'homme*, 449–79.

Akinsanya, A., 'International Protection of Foreign Direct Investments in the Third World' (1987) 36 *ICLQ* 58–75.

Alemanno, A. and Bonadio, E., 'The Case of Plain Packaging of Cigarettes' (2010) *European Journal of Risk Regulation* 268–70.

Alemanno, A. and Bonadio, E., 'Do You Mind My Smoking? Plain Packaging of Cigarettes Under the TRIPS Agreement' (2011) 10 *John Marshall Review of Intellectual Property Law* 450.

Alexander, E.A., 'Taking Account of Reality: Adopting Contextual Standards for Developing Countries in International Investment Law' (2007–2008) 48 *Vanderbilt JIL* 823.

Alston, P., 'U.S. Ratification of the Covenant on Economic, Social and Cultural Rights: The Need for an Entirely New Strategy' (1990) 84 *AJIL* 365–93.

Alston, P., 'Ships Passing in the Night: The Current State of the Human Rights and Development Debate Seen Through the Lens of the Millennium Development Goals' (2005) 27 *Human Rights Quarterly* 755–829.

Altangerel, T., 'The Principle of Balance: Balancing Economic, Environmental and Social Factors in International Economic Law' (2004) 1 *Manchester JIEL* 4–19.

Appleton, B., 'Regulatory Takings: The International Law Perspective' (2003) 11 *NYU Environmental Law Journal* 35–48.

Arfazadeh, H., 'In The Shadow of the Unruly Horse: International Arbitration and The Public Policy Exception' (2002) 13 *American Review of International Arbitration* 1–10.

Balasubramanyam, V.N., Salisu, M. and Sapsford, D., 'Foreign Direct Investment and Growth: New Hypotheses and Evidence' (1999) 8 *Journal of International Trade and Economic Development* 27–40.

Baldwin, E., Kantor, M. and Nolan, M., 'Limits to Enforcement of ICSID Awards' (2006) 23 *Journal of International Arbitration* 1–24.

Barraguirre, J.A., 'Los Tratados Bilaterales de inversion (TBIs) y el Convenio CIADI – La evaporación del derecho administrativo domestico?' (2007) 3 *Res Pubblica Argentina* 107.

Baughen, S., 'Expropriation and NAFTA Environmental Regulation: The Lessons of NAFTA Chapter Eleven' (2006) *Journal of Environmental Law* 207–28.

Bénassy-Quéré, A., Coupet, M., and Mayer, T., 'Institutional Determinants of Foreign Direct Investment' (2007) 30 *World Economy* 764–82.

Benvenisti, E., 'Margin of Appreciation, Consensus and Universal Standards' (1999) 31 *NYU J of Int'l Law & Politics* 843.

Bhagwati, J., 'Why Multinationals Help Reduce Poverty' (2007) 30 *World Economy* 211–28.

Bianchi, A., 'Human Rights and the Magic of Jus Cogens' (2008) 19 *EJIL* 491–508.

Bird, R. and Cahoy, D.R., 'The Impact of Compulsory Licensing on Foreign Direct Investment: A Collective Bargaining Approach' (2008) 45 *American Business Law Journal* 306.

Bloche, M.G., 'Introduction: Health and the WTO' (2002) 5 *JIEL* 821–3.

Böckstiegel, K.-H., 'Enterprise v. State: the New David and Goliath?' (2007) 23 *Arbitration International* 93–104.

Boyle, A., 'Some Reflections on the Relationship of Treaties and Soft Law' (1999) 48 *ICLQ* 901–13.

Bradley, C.A., 'Unratified Treaties, Domestic Politics, and the US Constitution' (2007) 48 *Harvard ILJ* 307–37.

Brower, C.N., 'Fair and Equitable Treatment under NAFTA Chapter 11' (2002) 96 *ASIL Proceedings* 9.

Brower, C.N. and Schill, S.W., 'Is Arbitration a Threat or a Boon to the Legitimacy of International Investment Law?' (2008–9) *Chicago J Int'l L* 471–98.

Brower, C.H. II, 'Investor-State Disputes Under NAFTA: The Empire Strikes Back' (2001) 40 *Columbia Journal of Transnational Law* 43.

Brower, C.H. II, 'NAFTA's Investment Chapter: Initial Thoughts About Second Generation Rights' (2003) 37 *Vanderbilt Journal of Transnational Law* 1533–66.

Brown, C., 'The Use of Precedents of Other International Courts and Tribunals in Investment Treaty Arbitration' (2008) 5 *TDM* 1–4.

Brunetti, M., 'Introduction' (2003) 5 *Int'l L Forum* 150.

Burdeau, G., 'Nouvelles perspectives pour l'arbitrage dans le contentieux economique intéressant l'Etat' (1995) *Revue de l'Arbitrage* 3.

Burke White, W. and von Staden, A., 'Investment Protection in Extraordinary Times: The Interpretation and Application of Non-Precluded Measures Provisions in Bilateral Investment Treaties' (2008) 48 *Vanderbilt J. Transnational L.* 307.

Cahoy, D.R., 'Confronting Myths and Myopia on the Road from Doha' (2007–2008) *Georgia L Rev.* 131.

Cappelletti, M., 'Alternative Dispute Resolution Processes Within the Framework of the World-Wide Access to Justice Movement' (1995) *Modern Law Review* 287.

Castro Bernieri, R., 'Intellectual Property Rights in Bilateral Investment Treaties and Access to Medicines: The Case of Latin America' (2006) 9 *JWIP* 548–72.

Cavallaro, J. and Schaffer, E., 'Less As More: Rethinking Supranational Litigation of Economic and Social Rights in the Americas' (2004) 56 *Hastings L J* 217.

Chapman, A., 'Conceptualizing the Right to Health: A Violations Approach' (1998) 65 *Tennessee Law Review* 389.

Charnovitz, S., 'Environment and Health Under WTO Dispute Settlement' (1998) 32 *International Lawyer* 901.

Chayes, A., 'The Role of the Judge in Public Law Litigation' (1976) 89 *Harv L Rev* 1281.

Cheng, T.-H., 'Power, Authority and International Investment Law' (2004–2005) 20 *American University L Rev* 465.

Chinkin, C.M., 'The Challenge of Soft Law: Development and Change in International Law' (1989) 38 *ICLQ* 850.

Cho, S., 'GATT Non-Violation Issues in the WTO Framework: Are They the Achilles' Heel of the Dispute Settlement Process?' (1998) 39 *Harvard ILJ* 311.

Choudhuri, B., 'Recapturing Public Power: Is Investment Arbitration's Engagement of the Public Interest Contributing to Democratic Deficit?' (2008) 41 *Vanderbilt Journal of Transnational Law* 775–1042.

Christie, G.C., 'What Constitutes a Taking of Property Under International Law?' (1962) 33 *BYIL* 307.

Cohen Smutny, A., 'Some Observations on the Principles Relating to Compensation in the Investment Treaty Context' (2007) 22 *ICSID Review-FILJ* 1–23.

Collins, D., 'Environmental Impact Statements and Public Participation in International Investment Law' (2010) 7 *Manchester JIEL* 4.

Cordero Moss, G., 'Is The Arbitral Tribunal Bound by the Parties' Factual and Legal Pleadings?' (2006) 3 *Stockholm International Arbitration Review* 1–31.

Cornides, J., 'Human Rights and Intellectual Property, Conflict or Convergence?' (2004) 7 *JWIP* 143.

Correa, C., 'Implications of Bilateral Free Trade Agreements on Access to Medicines' (2006) 84 *Bull. WHO* 399–404.

Criddle, E.J. and Fox-Decent, E., 'A Fiduciary Theory of Jus Cogens' (2008) 34 *Yale JIL* 331.

Crook, J., 'New Investment and Dispute Settlement Provisions in U.S.–Peru Trade Agreement,' (2009) 103 *AJIL* 768.

Crow, M., 'Smokescreens and State Responsibility: Using Human Rights Strategies to Promote Global Tobacco Control' (2004) 29 *Yale J Int'l L* 209–50.

D'Amato, A., 'It's a Bird, It's a Plane, It's Jus Cogens!' (1990–1991) 6 *Conn. J. Int'l L.* 1.

Dattu, R., 'A Journey From Havana to Paris: The Fifty Year Quest for the Elusive Multilateral Agreement on Investment' (2000–2001) 24 *Fordham Int'l L J* 275–316.

Dennis, M., and Stewart, D., 'Justiciability of Economic, Social and Cultural Rights: Should There Be an International Complaints Mechanism to Adjudicate the Rights to Food, Water, Housing and Health?' (2004) 98 *AJIL* 462–515.

De Silva, R. de Alwis and Daynard, R., 'Reconceptualizing Human Rights to Challenge Tobacco' (2008–2009) 17 *Michigan State Journal of International Law* 291–376.

Devillier, N., 'La Convention cadre pur la lutte anti-tabac de l'Organisation Mondiale de la Santé' (2005) 38 *Revue Belge de Droit International* 701–28.

De Visscher, C., 'Contribution à l'étude des sources de droit international' (1933) 60 *Revue de droit international et législation comparée* 60.

Dias Varella, M., 'The WTO, Intellectual Property and AIDS – Case Studies from Brazil and South Africa' (2004) 7 *Journal of World Intellectual Property* 523–47.

Di Mascio, N., and Pauwelyn, J., 'Non-Discrimination in Trade and Investment Treaties: Worlds Apart or Two Sides of the Same Coin?' (2008) 102 *AJIL* 48–89.

Dolzer, R., 'Indirect Expropriations: New Developments?' (2003) 11 *NYU Environmental LJ* 64–93.

Dolzer, R., 'Fair and Equitable Treatment: A Key Standard in Investment Treaties' (2005) 39 *International Lawyer* 87–106.

Douglas, Z., 'The Hybrid Foundations of Investment Treaty Arbitration' (2003) 74 *BYIL* 221–2.

Dresler, C. and Marks, S., 'The Emerging Human Right to Tobacco Control' (2006) 28 *Human Rights Quarterly* 599–651.

Dupuy, P.-M., 'Some Reflections on Contemporary International Law and the Appeal to Universal Values: A Response to Martti Koskenniemi' (2005) *EJIL* 131–7.

Dupuy, P.-M., 'A Doctrinal Debate in the Globalization Era: On the "Fragmentation" of International Law' (2007) 1 *EJLS* 1.

Dupuy, P.-M., 'The Unity of Application of International Law at the Global Level and the Responsibility of Judges' (2007) *EJLS* 1–23

Eeckhout, P., 'The Scales of Trade – Reflections on the Growth and Functions of the WTO Adjudicative Branch' (2010) 13 *JIEL* 3–26.

Egger, P. and Merlo, V., 'The Impact of Bilateral Investment Treaties on FDI Dynamics' (2007) 30 *World Economy* 1536–49.

El Said, M., 'The Road From TRIPS-Minus to TRIPS, to TRIPS-Plus: Implications of IPRs for the Arab World' (2005) 8 *JWIP* 53–65.

El Said, M., 'Surpassing Checks, Overriding Balances and Diminishing Flexibilities – FTA-IPRS Plus Bilateral Trade Agreements: From Jordan to Oman' (2007) 8 *JWIT* 243–68.

Ely Yamin, A., 'Not Just a Tragedy: Access to Medications as a Right Under International Law' (2003) 21 *Boston University Int'l L J* 101–44.

Evans, D. and Padilla, A.J., 'Excessive Pricing: Using Economics To Define Administrable Legal Rules' (2005) 1 *Journal of Competition Law and Economics* 97–122.

Ewing-Chow, M., 'Thesis, Antithesis and Synthesis: Investor Protection in BITs, WTO and FTAs' (2007) 30 *UNSW L. J.* 548.

Fagerström, K.O., 'Measuring Degree of Physical Dependence to Tobacco Smoking with Reference to Individualization of Treatment' (1978) 3 *Addictive Behaviours* 235–41.

Fidler, D.P., 'Trade and Health: The Global Spread of Diseases and International Trade' (1997) 40 *GYIL* 309–54.

Fidler, D.P., 'Challenges to Humanity's Health: The Contributions of International Environmental Law to National and Global Public Health' (2001) 31 *Environmental Law Reporter* 10048–78.

Fidler, D.P., 'A Globalized Theory of Public Health Law' (2002) 30 *Journal of Law, Medicine & Ethics* 150–61.

Fidler, D.P., 'From International Sanitary Conventions to Global Health Security: The New International Health Regulations' (2005) 4 *Chinese Journal of International Law* 325–92.

Fong, G., Hammond, D. and Hitchman, S.C., 'The Impact of Pictures on the Effectiveness of Tobacco Smoking' (2009) 87 *Bull. WHO* 640–3.

Fortier, L.Y., 'Caveat Investor: The Meaning of "Expropriation" and the Protection Afforded Investors under NAFTA' (2003) 20 *News From ICSID* 1.

Fortier, L.Y. and S.L. Drymer, 'Indirect Expropriation in the Law of International Investment: I Know When I See It, or *Caveat Investor*' (2004) 19 *ICSID Review-FILJ* 293–327.

Foster Halabi, S., 'The World Health Organization's Framework Convention on Tobacco Control: An Analysis of Guidelines Adopted by the Conference of the Parties' (2010) 39 *Ga. J. International Law and Comparative Law* 1.

Francioni, F., 'Compensation for Nationalization of Foreign Property. The Borderland between Law and Equity' (1975) *ICLQ* 255–83.

Francioni, F., 'Access to Justice, Denial of Justice and International Investment Law' (2009) 20 *EJIL* 729–47.

Franck, S., 'Development and Outcomes of Investment Treaty Arbitration' (2009) 50 *Harv. Int'l L.J.* 435.

Frati, P., 'Quarantine, Trade and Health Policies in Ragusa-Dubrovnik until the Age of Armmenius Baglivi' (2000) 12 *Medicina nei secoli* 103–27.

Freeman, B., Chapman, S. and Rimmer, M., 'The Case for Plain Packaging of Tobacco Products' (2008) 103 *Addiction* 580–90.

Freeman, E., 'Regulatory Expropriation under NAFTA Chapter 11: Some Lessons from the European Court of Human Rights' (2003–2004) 42 *Columbia Journal of Transnational Law* 177–215.

Friedrichs, J., 'The Meaning of New Medievalism' (2001) 7 *European Journal of International Relations* 475–502.

Friedrichs, J., 'What's New About the New Middle Ages' (2003) 16 *Leiden J Int'l L* 649–53.

Gal-Or, N., 'The Investor and Civil Society as Twin Global Citizens: Proposing a New Interpretation in the Legitimacy Debate' (2008–2009) 32 *Suffolk Transnational Law Review* 271.

Galva, J.E., Atchison, C. and Levey, S., 'Public Health Strategy and the Police Powers of the State' (2005) 120 (suppl. 1) *Public Health Reports* 20–7.

Ganguly, S., 'The Investor-State Dispute Mechanism (ISDM) and a Sovereign's Power to Protect Public Health' (1999–2000) 38 *Columbia J Transnational L* 113.

Geiger, C., '"Constitutionalising" Intellectual Property Law? The Influence of Fundamental Rights on Intellectual Property in the European Union' (2006) 37 *Jot' Rev Intellectual Property and Competition L* 351.

Ghanotakis, E., 'How the US Interpretation of Flexibilities Inherent in TRIPS Affects Access to Medicines for Developing Countries' (2004) 7 *JWIP* 563–91.

Giardina, A., 'International Investment Arbitration: Recent Developments as to the Applicable Law and Unilateral Recourse' (2007) 5 *Law and Practice of International Courts and Tribunals* 29–39.

Gibson, C., 'A Look at the Compulsory License in Investment Arbitration: The Case of Indirect Expropriation' (2009) 6 *TDM* 1–54.

Gibson, C., 'A Look at the Compulsory License in Investment Arbitration: The Case of Indirect Expropriation', Am. U. Int'l L. Rev. 25, 2010, p. 393.

Gilmore, A., Collin, J. and McKee, M., 'British American Tobacco's Erosion of Health Legislation in Uzbekistan' (2006) 332 *BMJ* 355–8.

Giovannini, T., 'The Making and Enforcement of the Arbitral Award: What Are the Grounds On Which Awards Are Most Often Set Aside?' (2001) 1 *Business Lawyer International* 115–27.

Goldberg, D.S., 'Against the Very Idea of the Politicization of Public Health Policy' (2012) 102 *American J of Public Health* 44–9.

Gonzales Rojas, F., 'The Notion of Discrimination in Article 1102 NAFTA' (2005) *Jean Monnet Working Paper 05/05*.

Gordon, K., and Pohl, J., 'Environmental Concerns in International Investment Agreements: The "New Era" Has Commenced, But Harmonization Remains Far Off' 44 *Columbia FDI Perspectives*, 15 August 2011.

Gostin, L.O., and Taylor, A.L., 'Global Health Law: A Definition and Grand Challenges' (2008) 1 *Public Health Ethics* 53–63.

Gross, S., 'Inordinate Chill: BITs, Non-NAFTA MITs and Host-State Regulatory Freedom – An Indonesian Case Study' (2002–2003) 24 *Michigan J Int'l L* 893.

Guzman, A., 'Explaining the Popularity of Bilateral Investment Treaties: Why LDCs Sign Treaties that Hurt Them' (1997) 38 *Vanderbilt Journal of Transnational Law* 667.

Haffajee, R. and Bloche, G., 'The FCTC and the Psychology of Tobacco Control' (2010) 5 *Asian J. WTO & Int'l Health L. & Pol'y* 87.

Hallward-Driemeier, M., 'Do Bilateral Investment Treaties Attract Foreign Direct Investment? Only a Bit . . . And They Could Bite' (2003) *World Bank Policy Research Working Paper No 3121*.

Hamida, W.B., 'La prise en compte de l'intérêt général et des impératifs de développement dans le droit des investissements' (2008) *Revue trimestrielle de droits de l'homme* 999–1033.

Haugen, H.M., 'Patents Rights and Human Rights: Exploring their Relationship' (2007) 10 *JWIP* 97–124.

Helfer, L.R., 'Towards a Human Rights Framework for Intellectual Property' (2006–2007) 40 *UC Davis L Rev* 971–1020.

Helfer, L.R., 'The New Innovation Frontier? Intellectual Property and the European Court of Human Rights' (2008) *Harvard ILJ* 1–52.

Hertz, A.Z., 'Shaping the Trident: Intellectual Property under NAFTA, Investment Protection Agreements and at the World Trade Organization' (1997) 23 *Can.-U.S. L. J.* 261.

Herz, J.H., 'Expropriation of Foreign Property' (1941) 35 *AJIL* 243.

Higgins, R., 'Conceptual Thinking About the Individual in International Law' (1978–1979) 24 *New York Law School L. Rev* 11.

Higgins, R., 'The Taking of Property by the State: Recent Developments in International Law' (1982) 176 *Rec des Cours* 276–7.

Higgins, R., 'Ethics and International Law' (2010) 23 *Leiden J. Int'l L.* 277–89.

Hirsch, M., 'Interactions between Investment and Non-Investment Obligations in International Investment Law' (2006) 3 *TDM* 5.

Hirsch, R., 'The Question of Case Selection in Comparative Constitutional Law' (2005) 53 *American Journal of Comparative Law* 125.

Hunter, M. and Conde e Silva, G., 'Transnational Public Policy and its Application in Investment Arbitrations' (2003) 4 *JWIT* 367–78.

Janis, M.W., 'The Nature of Jus Cogens' (1987–1988) 3 *Connecticut J Int'l L.* 359–63.

Janis, M.W., 'Jus Cogens: An Artful Not a Scientific Reality' (1987–1988) 3 *Conn. J. Int'l L.* 370.

Jenks, C.W., 'The Conflict of Law-Making Treaties' (1953) 30 *BYIL* 401.

Jones, R., 'NAFTA Chapter 11 Investor-to-State Dispute Resolution: A Shield to Be Embraced or a Sword to be Feared?' (2002) *BYUL Review* 527.

Kennedy, D., 'New Approaches to Comparative Law: Comparativism and International Governance' (1997) *Utah Law Review* 545.

Kingsbury, B., Krisch, N. and Stewart, R.B., 'The Emergence of Global Administrative Law' (2005) 68 *Law & Contemporary Problems* 15.

Kinney, E.D., 'The International Human Right to Health: What Does this Mean for Our Nation and the World?' (2001) 34 *Indiana L Rev* 1457.

Kinney, E.D. and Clark, B., 'Provisions for Health and Health Care in the Constitutions of the Countries of the World' (2004) 37 *Cornell Int L J* 285–355.

Koplan, J.P. *et al.*, 'Towards a Common Definition of Global Health', 373 *The Lancet*, 6 June 2009, 1993.

Koskenniemi, M., 'Study on the Function and Scope of the *Lex Specialis* Rule and the Question of Self-Contained Regimes' (ILC(LVI)/SG/FIL/CRD.1 and Add 1).

Koskenniemi, M., 'International Law in Europe: Between Tradition and Renewal' (2005) 16 *EJIL* 113–25.

Kreindler, R.H., 'Approaches to the Application of Transnational Public Policy by Arbitrators' (2003) 4 *JWIT* 239.

Kreindler, R.H., 'Fair and Equitable Treatment – A Comparative International Law Approach' (2006) 3 *TDM* 3.

Kurtz, J., 'A General Investment Agreement in the WTO? Lessons from Chapter 11 of NAFTA and the OECD Multilateral Agreement on Investment' (2003) 23 *University of Pennsylvania JIEL*, 713–89.

Kurtz, J., 'The MFN Standard and Foreign Investment – An Uneasy Fit?' (2004) 5 *JWIT* 861–86.

Lalive, P., 'Ordre public transnational (ou réellement international) et arbitrage international' (1986) *Revue de l'Arbitrage* 329–73.

Lamb, S. and Garcia, A., 'Arbitration of Intellectual Property Disputes' (2008) *European and Middle Eastern Arbitration Review*, Section 3.

Lamm, R.D., 'The Culture of Growth and the Culture of Limits' (1999) 9 *The Social Contract TSC Journal*.

Leal Arcas, R., 'Towards the Multilateralization of International Investment Law' (2009) 10 *JWIT* 865–919.

Lemley, M., 'The Modern Lanham Act and the Death of Common Sense' (1999) *Yale L.J.* 1687.

Lévesque, C., 'Les Fondements de la distinction entre l'expropriation et la réglementation en droit international' (2003) 33 *R.G.D.* 39.

Lin, T.-Y., 'Addressing the Issue of Trade in Services and Public Health in the Case of Tobacco' (2006) 7 *JWIT* 561.

Lo, C.-F., 'A Comparison of BIT and the Investment Chapter of Free Trade Agreements from Policy Perspective' (2008) 3 *Asian J of WTO & Int'l Health L* 147.

Lowe, V., 'Regulation or Expropriation?' (2002) 55 *Current Legal Problems* 447.

Lowe, V., 'Corporations as International Actors and International Law Makers' (2004) 14 *IYIL* 30.

Lowenfeld, A.F., 'Investment Agreements and International Law' (2003–2004) 42 *Columbia Journal of Transnational Law* 123–30.

Lowenfeld, A.F., 'The Party-Appointed Arbitrator in International Controversies: Some Reflections' (1995) *Texas Int'l L J* 59–72.

MacDonald, K., 'A Right to a Healthful Environment – Humans and Habitats: Re-thinking Rights in an Age of Climate Change' (2008) *European Energy and Environmental L Rev* 213–26.

Mann, H. and Soloway, J., 'Untangling the Expropriation and Regulation Relationship: Is There a Way Forward?' Report to the Ad Hoc Expert Group on Investment Rules and the Department of Foreign Affairs and International Trade, Canada (2002).

Mann, H. and Von Moltke, K., 'Protecting Investor Rights and the Public Good: Assessing NAFTA's Chapter 11' (2003) report, *available at* http://www.iisd.org/trade/ILSDWorkshop/pdf/background_en.pdf.

Marceau, G., 'A Call for Coherence in International Law – Praises for the Prohibition Against Clinical Isolation in WTO Dispute Settlement' (1999) 33 *JWT* 87.

Mason Meier, B., 'Breathing Life into the Framework Convention on Tobacco Control: Smoking Cessation and the Right to Health' (2005) 5 *Yale Journal of Health Policy & Ethics* 137–88.

Mavroidis, P., 'No Outsourcing of Law? WTO Law as Practised by WTO Courts' (2008) *AJIL* 421.

McIntyre, O. and Mosedale, T., 'The Precautionary Principle as a Norm of Customary International Law' (1997) 9 *Journal of Environmental Law* 221.

McLachlan, C., 'The Principle of Systemic Integration and Article 31(3)(c) of the Vienna Convention', 2005, *ICLQ* 54, 279–319.

Melish, T., 'Rethinking the "Less as More" Thesis: Supranational Litigation of the Economic, Social and Cultural Rights in the Americas' (2006) 39 *NYU Journal of International Law & Policy* 171.

Michelman, F.I., 'Property, Utility, and Fairness: Comments on the Ethical Foundations of "Just Compensation" Law' (1967) *Harvard L Rev* 1165.

Miller, T.S. and Smith-Savage, R., 'Medieval Leprosy Reconsidered' (2006) 81 *International Social Science Review* 16–28.

Moloo, R. and Jacinto, J., 'Environmental and Health Regulation: Assessing Liability Under Investment Treaties' (2011) 29 *Berkeley Journal of International Law* 101.

Moore, J.B., 'Brazilian Watermelons' (1894) 6 *Digest of International Law* 751.

Mostafa, B., 'The Sole Effects Doctrine, Police Powers and Indirect Expropriation Under International Law' (2008) *Australian ILJ*.

Mountfield, H., 'Regulatory Expropriations in Europe: The Approach of the European Court of Human Rights' (2002–2003) *NYU Environmental L J* 136–47.

Muchlinski, P., '"Caveat Investor?" The Relevance of the Conduct of the Investor Under the Fair and Equitable Treatment Standard' (2006) 55 *ICLQ* 527–58.

Munro, M.A., 'Expropriating Expropriation Law: The Implications of the Metalclad Decision on Canadian Expropriation Law and Environmental Land Use Regulation' (2005) 5 *Asper Rev Int'l Bus. & Trade Law* 75.

Newcombe, A., 'The Boundaries of Regulatory Expropriation in International Law' (2005) 20 *ICSID Review-FILJ* 1–57.

Nouvel, Y., 'Les Measures équivalent à une expropriation dans la pratique récente des tribunaux arbitraux' (2002) 106 *RGDIP* 79.

Okediji, R., 'Back to Bilateralism? Pendulum Swings in International Intellectual Property Protection' (2003) 1 *U Ott Law & Tech J* 125.

Oppenheim, L., 'The Science of International Law: Its Tasks and Methods' (1908) 2 *AJIL* 313–56.

Orellana, M., 'The Role of Science in Investment Arbitrations Concerning Public Health and the Environment' (2006) 17 *YIEL* 48–72.

Ortino, F., 'External Transparency of Investment Awards', *SIEL Working Paper No. 49/08* (2008).

Outterson, K., 'Pharmaceutical Arbitrage: Balancing Access and Innovation in International Prescription Drug Markets' (2004) *Yale Journal of Health Policy, Law & Ethics* 193–286.

Park, W., 'Private Disputes and the Public Good: Explaining Arbitration Law' (2004–2005) 20 *Am. U. Int'l L. Rev.* 903.

Paulsson, J., 'Arbitration without Privity' (1995) 10 *ICSID rev-FILJ* 232.

Pauwelyn, J., 'The Role of Public International Law in the WTO: How Far Can We Go?' (2001) 95 *AJIL* 535.

Pauwelyn, J., 'Bridging Fragmentation and Unity, International Law as a Universe of Inter-Connected Islands' (2004) 25 *Michigan J Int'l Law* 903.

Pfaff, C., 'Alternative Approaches to Foreign Investment Protection' (2006) 3 *TDM* 1–16.

Picciotto, S., 'Linkages in International Investment Regulation: The Antinomies of the Draft Multilateral Agreement on Investment' (1998) 19 *University of Pennsylvania JIEL* 123.

Ratner, S., 'Regulatory Takings in Institutional Context: Beyond the Fear of Fragmented International Law' (2008) 102 *AJIL* 475–528.

Rau, A.S., 'Integrity in Private Judging' (1997) 38 *S Texas L R* 485–539.

Raustiala, K., 'Rethinking the Sovereignty Debate in International Economic Law' (2003) 6 *JIEL* 841–78.

Reisman, W.M., 'Why Regime Change is (Almost Always) a Bad Idea' (2004) 98 *AJIL* 516.

Reynolds, G., and Kopel, D., 'The Evolving Police Power: Some Observations for a New Century' (2000) *Hastings Constitutional Law Quarterly* 511–37.

Roach, K., 'The Uses and Audiences of Preambles in Legislation' (2001) 47 *McGill L J* 129–60.

Rogers, D., 'The TRIPS Regime of Trademarks and Designs' (2007) *European Intellectual Property Review* 76–8.

Rose-Ackerman, S. and Rossi, J., 'Disentangling Deregulatory Takings' (2000) 86 *Virginia L Rev* 1435.

Rothstein, M., 'Rethinking the Nature of Public Health' (2002) 30 *J.L. Med. & Ethics* 144–149.

Rothstein, M., 'The Limits of Public Health: A Response' (2009) 2 *Public Health Ethics* 84–8.

Ruiz-Fabri, H., 'The Approach Taken by the European Court of Human Rights to the Assessment of Compensation for "Regulatory Expropriations" of the Property of Foreign Investors' (2002–2003) 11 *NYU Environmental L J* 148–74.

Salacuse, J. and Sullivan, N., 'Do BITs Really Work? An Evaluation of Bilateral Investment Treaties and Their Grand Bargain' (2005) 46 *Harvard ILJ* 67–115.

Salazar, A.R., 'NAFTA Chapter 11, Regulatory Expropriation, and Domestic Counter-Advertising Law' (2010) 27 *Ariz. J. Int'l & Comp. L.* 31.

Samet, J., Wipfli, H., Perez-Padilla, R., Yach, D., 'Mexico and the Tobacco Industry: Doing the Wrong Thing for the Right Reason?' (2006) 332 *BMJ* 353–4.

Sands, P., 'International Law in the Field of Sustainable Development' (1994) 65 *BYIL* 303.

Sands, P., 'Searching for Balance: Concluding Remarks' (2002) 11 *NYU Environmental LJ* 198.

Sanwal, M., 'Trends in Environmental Governance: The Emergence of a Mutual Supportiveness Approach to Achieve Sustainable Development' (2004) 4 *Global Environmental Politics* 16–22.

Sauvé, P., 'Multilateral Rules on Investment: Is Forward Movement Possible?' (2006) 9 *JIEL* 325–55.

Sax, J.L., 'Takings and the Police Power' (1964–1965) 74 *Yale LJ* 36.

Schachter, O., 'The Decline of the Nation-State and Its Implications for International Law' (1998) 36 *Columbia Journal of Transnational Law* 7.

Schill, S.W., 'Fair and Equitable Treatment Under Investment Treaties as an Embodiment of the Rule of Law' *NYU Int'l Law & Justice Working Papers No 6/2006*.

Schill, S.W., 'Crafting the International Economic Order: The Public Function of Investment Treaty Arbitration and its Significance for the Role of the Arbitrator' (2010) 23 *Leiden J. Int'l L.* 401–30.

Schreuer, C.H., 'The Concept of Expropriation under the ETC and other Investment Protection Treaties' (2005) 2 *TDM* 1–39.

Schreuer, C.H., 'Fair and Equitable Treatment in Arbitral Practice' (2005) 6 *JWIT* 357–86.

Schreuer, C.H., 'Conversations Across Cases – Is There a Doctrine of Precedent in Investment Arbitration?' (2008) 5 *TDM*.

Schwarzenberger, G., 'International *Jus Cogens?*' (1964–1965) 43 *Tex. L. Rev.* 455–78.

Schwarzenberger, G., 'The Problem of International Public Policy' (1965) 18 *Current Legal Problems* 191–214.

Scott, C., 'The Interdependence and Permeability of Human Rights Norms: Towards a Partial Fusion of the International Covenants on Human Rights' (1989) 46 *Osgoode Hall L. J.* 769.

Sebrié, E., Barnoya, J., Pérez-Stable, E.J. and Glantz, S.A., 'Tobacco Industry Successfully Prevented Tobacco Control Legislation in Argentina' (2005) 14 *Tobacco Control* 2.

Sebrié, E. and Glantz, S.A., 'The Tobacco Industry in Developing Countries has Forestalled Legislation on Tobacco Control' (2006) 332 *BMJ* 313–14.

Sedlak, D., 'ICSID's Resurgence in International Investment Arbitration: Can the Momentum Hold? (2004) 23 *Penn St Int'l L Rev* 147.

Setear, J.K., 'An Iterative Perspective on Treaties: A Synthesis of International Relations Theory and International Law' (1996) 37 *Harvard ILJ* 139–229.

Shany, Y., 'Towards a General Margin of Appreciation Doctrine in International Law?' (2005) 16 *EJIL* 907.

Sheppard, A., 'Public Policy and the Enforcement of Arbitral Awards: Should There Be a Global Standard? (2004) 1 *TDM* 1.

Shibuya, K. *et al.*, 'WHO Framework Convention on Tobacco Control: Development of an Evidence Based Global Health Treaty' (2003) 327 *BMJ* 154–7.

Simma, B., 'Self-Contained Regimes' (1985) *Netherlands YIL* 111–36.

Simma, B. and Pulkowski, D., 'Of Planets and the Universe: Self-Contained Regimes in International Law' (2006) 17 European Journal of International Law p. 483.

Singer, J.W., 'The Ownership Society and Takings of Property: Castles, Investments and Just Obligations' (2006) 30 *Harvard Environmental Law Review* 309.

Slaughter, A.-M., 'Judicial Globalization' (1999–2000) 40 *Virginia J Int'l L* 1103–24.

Slaughter, A.-M., 'A Global Community of Courts' (2003) 44 *Harvard J Int'l L* 191–219.

Smith, R.D., 'Foreign Direct Investment and Trade in Health Services: A Review of the Literature' (2004) *Social Science & Medicine* 2313–23.

Smith, S., 'Ecologically Sustainable Development: Integrating Economics, Ecology and Law' (1995) 31 *Willamette Law Review* 263.

Smyth, S.W., Kerr, A. and Phillips, P.W.B., 'Recent Trends in the Scientific Basis of Sanitary and Phytosanitary Trade Rules and Their Potential Impact on Investment' (2011) 12 *JWIT* 5–26.

Sornarajah, M., 'The Clash of Globalizations and the International Law on Foreign Investment' (2003) 12 *Canadian Foreign Policy* 2–10.

Starner, G., 'Taking a Constitutional Look: NAFTA Chapter 11 as an Extension of Member States' Constitutional Protection of Property' (2002) 33 *Law and Pol'y Int'l Bus* 405.

Steger, D., 'The Culture of the WTO: Why it Needs to Change' (2007) 10 *JIEL* 483–95.

Suda, R., 'The Effect of Bilateral Investment Treaties on Human Rights Enforcement and Realization' (2005) *NYU School of Law Global Law Working Paper no 01/05*.

Taubman, A., 'Rethinking TRIPS: "Adequate Remuneration" for Non-Voluntary Patent Licensing' (2008) 11 *JIEL* 927–70.

Taylor, A., 'Global Health Governance and International Law' (2003) 25 *Whittier Law Review* 253–72.

Taylor, A. and Bettcher, D.W., 'International Law and Public Health' (2002) 80 *Bull. WHO* 823.

Tobin, J. and Rose-Ackerman, S., 'Foreign Direct Investment and the Business Environment in Developing Countries: The Impact of Bilateral Investment Treaties' (2005) *Yale Law and Economics Research Paper No. 293/2005*.

Vadi, V., 'Towards Arbitral Path Coherence and Judicial Borrowing: Persuasive Precedent in Investment Arbitration' (2008) 5 *TDM* 1–16.

Vadi, V., 'Mapping Uncharted Waters: Intellectual Property Disputes with Public Health Elements in Investor-State Arbitration' (2009) *TDM* 1–22.

Vadi, V., 'Trademark Protection, Public Health and International Investment Law: Strains and Paradoxes' (2009) *EJIL*, 773–803.

Vadi, V., 'Critical Comparisons: The Role of Comparative Law in Investor State Arbitration' (2010) *Denver Journal of International Law & Policy* 67–100.

Vadi, V., 'Environmental Impact Assessment in Investment Disputes' (2010) 30 *Polish YIL* 169–205.

Valcke, C., 'Comparative Law as Comparative Jurisprudence – The Comparability of Legal Systems' (2004) 52 *American Journal of Comparative Law* 713.

Van Harten, G. and Loughlin, M., 'Investment Treaty Arbitration as a Species of Global Administrative Law' (2006) 17 *EJIL* 121–50.

Van Harten, G., 'The Public-Private Distinction in the International Arbitration of Individual Claims Against the State' (2007) 56 *ICLQ* 371–94.

Van Harten, G., 'Five Justifications for Investment Treaties: A Critical Discussion' (2010) 2 *Trade Law and Development*.

Vaver, D., 'Does the Public Understand Intellectual Property? Do Lawyers?', *Oxford Legal Studies Research Paper No. 23* (2006).

Verdross, A., 'Forbidden Treaties in International Law' (1937) 31 *AJIL* 571.

Verdross, A., 'Jus Dispositivum and Jus Cogens in International Law' (1966) 60 *AJIL* 55–63.

Verhoosel, G., 'The Use of Investor-State Arbitration under Bilateral Investment Treaties to Seek Relief for Breaches of WTO Law (2003) 6 JIEL 495.

Virally, M., 'Réflexions sur le "jus cogens"' (1966) *Annuaire Français de droit international* 5–29.

Von Schirnding, Y., Onzivv, W. and Adede, A.O., 'International Environmental Law and Global Public Health' (2002) 80 *Bull. WHO* 970.

Voon, T. and Mitchell, A., 'Implications of International Investment Law for Tobacco Flavouring Regulation' (2011) 12 *JWIT* 12.

Vranes, E., 'The Definition of Norm Conflict in International Law and Legal Theory' (2006) 17 *EJIL* 395–418.

Wälde, T., 'The Umbrella Clause in Investment Arbitration: A Comment on Original Intentions and Recent Cases' (2005) 6 *JWIT* 183.

Wälde, T. and Kolo, A., 'Environmental Regulation, Investment Protection and "Regulatory Taking" in International Law' (2001) *ICLQ* 811–48.

Walker, H. Jr., 'Modern Treaties of Friendship, Commerce, and Navigation' (1957) 42 *Minn. L. Rev.* 805.

Wang, V.H.W., 'Investor Protection or Environmental Protection? "Green Development" Under CAFTA' (2007) 32 *Colum. J. Envtl. L.* 251.

Watal, J., 'Pharmaceutical Patents, Prices and Welfare Losses: Policy Options for India Under the WTO TRIPS Agreement' (2002) 23 *World Economy* 733.

Weale, A., 'Invisible Hand or Fatherly Hand? Problems of Paternalism in the New Perspective on Health' (1983) 7 *Journal of Health Politics, Policy and Law* 784–807.

Weiler, T., 'The Treatment of SPS Measures Under NAFTA Chapter 11: Preliminary Answers to an Open-Ended Question' (2003) 26 *Boston College International and Comparative Law Review* 229.

Weiler, T., 'Balancing Human Rights and Investor Protection: A New Approach for a Different Legal Order' (2004) 1 *TDM* 1–15.

Weiler, T., 'Philip Morris v. Uruguay – An Analysis of Tobacco Control Measures in the Context of International Investment Law', Report for Physicians for a Smoke Free Canada, 28 July 2010.

Weston, B.H., '"Constructive Takings" Under International Law: A Modest Foray Into the Problem of Creeping Expropriation' (1975) 16 *Vanderbilt J. Int'l L.* 103.

Wiles, E., 'Aspirational Principles or Enforceable Rights? The Future for Socio-Economic Rights in National Law' (2006–2007) 22 *American University ILR* 35–64.

Wirth, D.A., 'The Role of Science in the Uruguay Round and NAFTA Trade Disciplines' (1994) 27 *Cornell Int'l L. J.* 817.

Young, K., 'The Minimum Core of Economic and Social Rights: A Concept in Search of Content' (2008) 33 *Yale J Int'l L* 113.

Newspaper articles

'US and Bayer Settle Anthrax Row', *BBC News*, 24 October 2001.

'Thailand: Latest Talks with Patent Owners of Cancer Drugs Show Positive Results', *IP Watch*, 5 November 2007.

'Fat Taxes Could Save Thousands', *BBC News*, 11 July 2007.

'Australia to Ban Cigarette Logos', *BBC News*, 29 April 2009.

'Uruguay to Relax Tobacco Laws to Combat Philip Morris Claim', *Global Arbitration Review Briefing*, 28 July 2010.

'Julia Gillard Stands Firm on Cigarette Plain Packaging', *Herald-Sun*, 27 June 2011.

'Philip Morris Launches Legal Battle Over Australian Cigarette Packaging' 15 *Bridges Weekly Trade News Digest* 4, 29 June 2011, p. 6.

'Canada and Dow Chemical Settle Claim over Pesticide Ban', *ITN*, 12 July 2011.

'Denmark Introduces the World's First Food Fat Tax', *BBC News*, 1 October 2011.

'UK Could Introduce "Fat Tax", Says David Cameron', *Guardian*, 4 October 2011.

Benzie, R., 'Cement Company Seeks $275M in Compensation over Scuttled Quarry', *The Star*, 10 August 2011.

Cabrera Diaz, F., 'Spanish Firms Launch ICSID Dispute Against Mexico Over Stalled Toxic Waste Disposal Project', *ITN*, 12 January 2010.

Gentleman, A., 'Setback for Novartis in India Over Drug Patent', *New York Times*, 7 August 2007.

Gerhardsen, T., 'Brazil Takes Steps To Import Cheaper AIDS Drugs Under Trade Law', *IP Watch*, 7 May 2007.

Kenny, C., 'Big Tobacco Ignites Legal War', *The Australian*, 27 June 2011.

Peterson, L.E., 'Canadian Pharmaceutical Maker Files Notice of Arbitration against the United States', *IAR*, 5 January 2009.

Peterson, L.E., 'France's Second Largest Pharmaceutical Company Quietly Pursues Arbitration Against Republic of Poland', *IAR*, 18 August 2011.

Peterson, L.E., 'Investor Withdraws Stay Request, and Plans to Proceed with Two NAFTA Arbitration Claims', *IAR*, 13 January 2011, pp. 9–10.

Peterson, L.E., 'Plain Packaging of Tobacco Products Decried as Expropriation, Contrary to Treaties; Long-Running Debate Rejoined', *IAR*, 9 February 2010.

Peterson, L.E., 'Philip Morris Files First-Known Investment Treaty Claim against Tobacco Regulations', *IAR*, 3 March 2010.

Peterson, L.E., 'Canada Prevails in NAFTA Arbitration Over Thwarted Garbage Disposal Project', *IAR*, 27 September 2011.

Porterfield, M.C. and Byrnes, C.R., 'Philip Morris v. Uruguay: Will Investor-state Arbitration Send Restrictions On Tobacco Marketing Up In Smoke?' *ITN*, July 2011, p. 3.

'Roxon Introduces Plain Packaging Bill', *ABC News*, 6 July 2011.

Vincenzi, M., 'L'emergenza mucca pazza, oggi muore la fiorentina', *La Repubblica*, 31 March 2001.

Wilson, D., 'Coded to Obey Law, Lights Become Marlboro Gold', *New York Times*, 19 February 2010.

Wilson, D., 'Bloomberg Backs Uruguay's Anti-smoking Laws', *New York Times*, 15 November 2010.

Documents of international organizations

ILC, *ILC Draft Articles on Diplomatic Protection*, Official Records of the General Assembly, Sixty First Session, Supplement No. 10 (A/61/10), 2006.

NAFTA Free Trade Commission, Notes of Interpretation of Certain Chapter 11 Provisions, 31 July 2001, available at http://www.dfait-maeci.gc.ca/tna-nac/NAFTA_interpr-en.asp.

NAFTA Free Trade Commission, *Statement of the Free Trade Commission on Non-Disputing Party Participation*, 7 October 2003, 16 W.T.A.M. (2004).

OECD, *OECD Guidelines for Multinational Enterprises*, Paris: OECD, 2000 available at http://www.oecd.org.

OECD Multilateral Agreement on Investment, Consolidated Text and Commentary, Draft DAFFE/MAI/NM (97) 2.

OECD, *The MAI Negotiation Text*, Paris: OECD, 1998.

OECD, 'Indirect Expropriation and the Right to Regulate in International Investment Law', Working Paper on International Investment No 4 (2004).

OECD, *The OECD*, Paris: OECD, 2008.

UNCTAD, *Bilateral Investment Treaties: 1959–1999*, Geneva: UNCTAD, 2000.

UNCTAD, *Investor-State Disputes Arising From Investment Treaties: A Review*, New York and Geneva: UN, 2005.

UNCTAD, *WIR 1996 – Investment Trade and International Policy Agreements*, New York and Geneva: UNCTAD, 1996.

UNCTAD, *WIR 1999 – Foreign Direct Investment and the Challenge of Development*, Geneva: UN, 1999.

UNCTAD, *WIR 2003 – FDI Policies for Development: National and International Perspectives*, Geneva: UN, 2003.

UNCTAD, *WIR 2006 – FDI from Developing and Transition Economies: Implications for Development*, Geneva: UN, 2006.

UNCTAD, *WIR 2007 – Transnational Corporations, Extractive Industries and Development*, New York: UNCTAD, 2007.

UN Commission on Human Rights Resolution 2003/29, *Access to Essential Medicines in the Context of Pandemics such as HIV/AIDS, Tuberculosis and Malaria*, (E/CN.4/2003/L.11/Add. 3), adopted on 22 April 2003.

United Nations Commission on International Trade Law (UNCITRAL) Model Law on International Commercial Arbitration, UN documents A/40/17 Annex 1 and A/61/17, Annex I, adopted on 21 June 1985 and amended on 7 July 2006.

UN Committee on Economic, Social and Cultural Rights, *General Comment No. 19, The Right to Social Security*, 4 February 2008, E/C.12/GC/19.

UN Committee on Economic, Social and Cultural Rights, *General Comment No. 14, The Right to the Highest Attainable Standard of Health*, adopted at the Committee's twenty-second session, 25 April–25 May 2000 (E/C.12/2000/4).

UN Committee on Economic, Social and Cultural Rights, *General Comment No. 17, The Right of Everyone to Benefit from the Protection of the Moral and Material Interests Resulting from Any Scientific, Literary or Artistic Production of Which He Is the Author (Art. 15(1)(c))*, UN Doc. E/C.12/GC/17, 12 January 2006.

UN Committee on Economic, Social and Cultural Rights, *General Comment No. 6, Right to Life*, adopted 30 April 1982, UN Doc. HRI/GEN/1/Rev.1.

UN Conference on Environment and Development (UNCED) *Agenda 21*, Report, Rio de Janeiro, 3–14 June 1992, I (1992) UN Doc. A/CONF.151/26/Rev. 1, (1992) 31 ILM 874.

UN Global Compact, available at http://www.globalcompact.org.

UN Human Rights Council, *Protect, Respect and Remedy: A Framework for Business and Human Rights* – Report of the Special Representative of the Secretary General John Ruggie, on the issue of human rights and trans-national corporations and other business enterprises to the Human Rights Council, 7 April 2008 A/HRC/8/5.

UN, International Law Commission 'Fragmentation of International Law: Difficulties arising from the Diversification and Expansion of International Law, Report of the Study Group on the International Law Finalized by Martti Koskenniemi' UN Doc A/CN.4/L. 682, 13 April 2006, at ¶ 35.

World Bank, *Curbing the Epidemic: Governments and the Economics of Tobacco Control*, Washington, DC: WB, 2000.

World Bank, *Tobacco Control Policy: Strategies, Successes and Setbacks*, Washington, DC: WB, 2003.

World Commission on Environment and Development, *Our Common Future*, (*Brundtland Report*), 4 August 1987, UN GA Res A/42/427 (1987).

WHO, *Health and the Millennium Development Goals*, Geneva: WHO, 2005.

WHO, *Macroeconomics and Health: Investing in Health for Economic Development*, Geneva: WHO, 2001.

WHO, *Medicines Strategy: Countries at the Core 2004–2007*, Geneva: WHO, 2004.

WHO, *Nutrition, Physical Activity and the Prevention of Obesity: Policy Developments in the WHO European Region*, Copenhagen: WHO Regional Office for Europe, 2007.

WHO, *Working for Health – An Introduction to the World Health Organization*, Geneva: WHO, 2007.

WHO/World Trade Organization Secretariat, *WTO Agreements and Public Health*, Geneva, 2002.

WTO, General Council, Decision on Implementation of Paragraph 6 of the Doha Declaration on the TRIPS Agreement and Public Health, 30 August 2003 (document WT/L/540) at http://www.wto.org.

WTO General Council, Amendment of the TRIPS Agreement, Decision of the 6th December 2005, (document WT/L/641) at http://www.wto.org.

WTO Ministerial Conference, Doha Declaration on the TRIPS Agreement and Public Health, Doha, WT/MIN(01)/DEC/W/2, 20 November 2001.

Index

643Edict of Rothari 26